Managing Service Companies

Strategies for Success

The EIU Series

This innovative series of books is the result of a publishing collaboration between Addison-Wesley and the Economist Intelligence Unit. Our authors draw on the results of original research by the EIU's skilled research and editorial staff to provide a range of topical, information-rich and incisive business titles. They are specifically tailored to the needs of international executives and business education worldwide.

Titles in the Series

Managing Service Companies

Strategies for Success

Ken Irons

E·I·U
The Economist
Intelligence Unit

ADDISON-WESLEY PUBLISHING COMPANY

Wokingham, England • Reading, Massachusetts • Menlo Park, California • New York
Don Mills, Ontario • Amsterdam • Bonn • Sydney • Singapore
Tokyo • Madrid • San Juan • Milan • Paris • Mexico City • Seoul • Taipei

© 1994 KIA Ltd

This book uses material drawn from the report, *Managing Services Companies: Strategies for Success,* first published by the Economist Intelligence Unit.

Many of the designations used by manufacturers and sellers to distinguish their products are claimed as trademarks. Addison-Wesley has made every attempt to supply trademark information about manufacturers and their products mentioned in this book.

Cover designed by Pencil Box Ltd, Marlow, Buckinghamshire
incorporating photograph by Kerry Lawrence
and printed by The Riverside Printing Co. (Reading) Ltd.
Text designed by Valerie O'Donnell.
Line diagrams drawn by Margaret Macknelly Design, Tadley.
Typeset by Meridian Phototypesetting Limited, Pangbourne.
Printed in Great Britain at the University Press, Cambridge.

First printed 1993. Reprinted 1995.

ISBN   0-201-62426-5

British Library Cataloguing in Publication Data
A catalogue record for this book is available from the British Library.

Library of Congress Cataloging in Publication Data applied for

To Kathy, Jo and Dominic,
who know only too well that the practice does not always live
up to the theory, my thanks for their patience over the years.

Preface

Service businesses now account for some 60% of the world's economic activity, and finding a formula for managing them successfully, for profit, has become akin to the quest for the holy grail. This book does not set out to provide yet another summary of management ideas on the subject, but to show in depth how a number of major European companies have achieved service success and to explore the fundamental issues which underpin this. In this, the book is neither purely a report nor a textbook, since it goes beyond simple reportage of 'what was done' and the key results to exploring and explaining the underlying concepts. It is, therefore, of practical value to the manager who wants to understand 'how' he can apply the thinking.

The book is primarily based on an original research programme, carried out in 1990-91 and funded by the Economist Intelligence Unit and KIA Management Consultants, which comprised:

- In-depth discussions with the management and staff of eight service companies located in Denmark, France, Sweden and the UK – five of these had already achieved long-run success, the other three had embarked on major change in recent years.
- Ad hoc discussions with another ten or so companies in these countries and in Germany, Holland and Switzerland.
- 2700 questionnaires sent to the staff of 24 companies (the eight core companies plus 16 others) probing their understanding of their organization's objectives, the way they did their work and what they thought of their customers. These questionnaires, processed and analysed by a leading market research company, give a unique insight into what makes some businesses succeed where others fail.

Further work was then carried out in 1993, both updating the research with existing contributors and creating further in-depth discussion with three UK companies.

Success in any business comes from strategies that ensure that an organization has a purpose, and that resources are used to achieve this aim effectively and consistently over time. Service organizations can only do this through people, both staff and customers. Staff not only execute the plans but are, in virtually every aspect, the focus of activity if service is to be delivered consistently; customers then help shape and form this delivery.

Success using such strategies cannot be measured in the short term since external variables or luck may play a much bigger role; it must, therefore, be measured over the long term. The core organizations in our study had all either demonstrated such success over 20 years or more or, in going through a process of change in recent years, demonstrated that they were taking a fundamental – and long-term – view. Their results, both in financial terms and with their markets supported this.

This book shows the key factors that make for this long-term success as well as providing a framework for debating and judging service initiatives.

Acknowledgements

It would be impossible to acknowledge everyone who gave so much help, but particular thanks are due to those 12 companies – and their executives and staff – who gave so willingly of their time, knowledge and experience, to the further 16 who participated in the quantitative research and to the many people in other companies who provided advice, reviewed research, read texts and added helpful comments so generously.

In particular, thanks are due to Anne-Grethe Blush, Tisbeth Tayler and Ann Smith for their help with the typing – and retyping – of the script and to Anne-Grethe, too, for her patient help with the illustrations.

Ken Irons
London
September 1993

Research respondents

Twelve companies gave particular help with the preparation of this book, and the earlier report, and have provided many of the quotes and case studies, or illustrative cameos. For ease of reference, these companies are called throughout the text by the shortened name given in brackets below.

BP Oil International plc, London (BP)

BPOI is the downstream arm of the BP Group, which is the third largest international oil company, operating across six continents and employing about 100,000 people. In 1992 Group operating profits were £1.9 billion on a turnover of £33 billion.

BPOI represents about one third of the Group's capital employed. It is responsible for the Group's activities in trading, shipping, refining, distributing and marketing crude oil and petroleum products. This encompasses:

- interests in 14 major refineries
- 17,900 service stations
- 48,900 employees
- five regional centres.

BP is a major brand in 70 countries, with a prominent position in many markets in Europe, the USA and Australia and also in parts of SE Asia and Africa.

Falck Redningskorps A/S, Copenhagen (Falck)

Founded in 1906, Falck is the major supplier of fire and ambulance services in Denmark. It occupies a unique position as a private enterprise organization, in a country of strong social democratic traditions.

Falck provides fire services to 167 local municipalities out of a total of 275, and ambulance services to 90% of the Danish population. Falck also provides road breakdown and rescue, a central emergency and alarm control, security alarm, environmental protection and international rescue and ambulance services. The company is the best known in Denmark, and also the most well regarded, 98% in a recent survey saying they knew of Falck and 83% expressing positive feelings towards them.

Until 1985 Falck was owned by the original family Falck, but in that year it was acquired by the major Danish financial group, Baltica Holding A/S. In 1990, Baltica sold a majority of its shares to 17 other insurance companies in Denmark, so restoring Falck's independence. In 1992 turnover was Dkr 1.9 billion and profit Dkr 34 million. This represents an increase of Dkr 20 million over 1991.

Lyonnaise des Eaux-Dumez SA, Paris (Lyonnaise des Eaux)

Lyonnaise des Eaux was founded in 1880 as a utility to provide water to the city of Cannes (and to meet the needs of the then demanding English). The company has always stayed close to its basis of municipal 'partnerships', but has expanded into areas such as waste management, water treatment, health services, heat and energy services, communications and funeral services.

The merger of Lyonnaise des Eaux and Dumez, a major construction company, was only completed in 1990. *Management Today* described it as, '[possibly] the very model of the post-1990s' post-privatization firm'. The group has laid considerable stress on ethics in business. In the mid and long term, the Group is confident of the demand for its unique grouping of complementary, customer-focused skills.

It is a large company, having a turnover of Fr 90.4 billion (about £10.8 billion) in 1992 and 124,000 employees worldwide. It is also financially strong with Fr 5.2 billion in cash flows in both 1991 and 1992, since good performances by the Group's services and environment-related sectors more than offset any losses caused by the Europe-wide stagnation of the property market and construction industries.

Royal Albert Hall, London

The Royal Albert Hall was completed in 1871 and is one of many monuments in London to the vigour and vision of 19th century Britain. However, unlike many such monuments it continues to function in the highly competitive world of venues, with regular events as varied as classical and pop concerts, ballet, fund-raising spectaculars, corporate balls, banquets and conferences, boxing and tennis.

The story of how the Hall turned itself from a slumbering giant into one of the big success stories amongst venues is part of the book, so will not be repeated here; however, the key financial performance indicators given in the table show something of the success the Hall has had.

Year ended 31 Dec.	Total Income £'000	Surplus from operations £'000	Total investment in improvements to Hall £'000
1988	2462	283	503
1989	2837	357	1085
1990	3550	580	1123
1991	4253	1010	1449
1992	4414	1056	1274

In addition to the expenditure on improvements (final column), the Hall has been able to add £550,000 to reserves in the past two years for future developments. Future plans envisage further growth in income and investment in the building of £1¾ million in 1993 and about £2 million a year in succeeding years.

Saga Group Ltd, Folkestone (Saga)

Founded in 1951 by Sydney De Haan, Saga has grown to be Britain's best-known company providing services for people in or approaching retirement. Initially, Sydney De Haan started the business as a way of filling empty capacity during the winter months in his Folkestone hotel, subsequently extending this first to other hotels in Folkestone, then across Britain and finally abroad. More importantly, he realized long before 'direct marketing' became fashionable – and computers made it relatively easy – that building relationships with his customers was going to be crucial, and right from the start he built an information base that would be the envy of many companies even today.

Today Saga has thriving subsidiaries in the USA and Australia and has developed well beyond travel into many types of service for its target market. It has been outstandingly successful and in 1992, another terrible year for many companies heavily involved in travel, Saga achieved a 17% increase in turnover, and record pre-tax profits, up 36% on the previous year.

Awareness of Saga amongst the older market has risen significantly since 1989, as they have developed their diversification strategy. Most importantly, awareness of Saga has now reached 85% of all those aged 60-79 in the ABC1 (the higher) socio-economic groups – Saga's core target market – and Saga succeeded in communicating with 45% of these people. Since there are about 3.3

million people aged 60-79 in these socio-economic groups, 2.8 million of them know Saga, and Saga succeeded in communicating at least once with 1.5 million of them. Time and again, independent studies and internal customer research shows that not only do Saga achieve a high level of satisfaction, meeting and exceeding expectations, but that the Company has a special position of trust within its target market.

J Sainsbury plc, London (Sainsburys)

Founded in 1869, Sainsburys is arguably the most successful retailer in the Western world with turnover of £10.2 billion and profits of £733 million in 1992-93, up nearly 17% over 1991-92 in a difficult economic year.

Although a public company with a widespread shareholding, Sainsburys is still very much a family company with David Sainsbury as Chairman and Chief Executive. Since 1979 the company has had a non-family member as Managing Director or Joint Managing Director. A third of the staff are shareholders, mostly acquired through profit-sharing and share-option schemes.

The supermarket business is very large:

- 329 stores in the UK with 8.3 million square feet (769,000 square metres) of sales area
- over 15,000 lines stocked
- over 100,000 staff
- 21 dedicated distribution centres.

In a recent Consumers' Association Survey (*Which?* magazine, January 1992) Sainsburys was voted overall best of the nine leading British supermarket chains.

In addition Sainsburys has, in the UK, Homebase – a 70 strong chain of DIY and garden centre stores – and Savacentre, which operates nine hypermarkets selling Sainsbury foods and a wide range of textiles, household and leisure goods. In the US, Sainsburys also owns the New England food retailer, Shaw's.

Svenska Handelsbanken, Stockholm (Handelsbanken)

Founded in 1871, Svenska Handelsbanken (which translates as the 'Swedish Bank of Commerce') is one of the four major retail banks in Sweden.

Handelsbanken has had an excellent profit record, being 'above the average profitability for all Swedish banks' (its objective) for the last 19 years. For 1992, the Bank has announced a continuing substantial increase in operating profit before loan losses, from Skr 5965 million in 1991 to Skr 7159 million, but for the first time in living memory has reported an overall operating loss of Skr 840 million, against a high in profitability in 1990 of Skr 4558 million

(1991, Skr 2777 million). Nevertheless, in the truly terrible context of Swedish banking in the 1990s, this is a highly creditable result and it is the only major Swedish bank that expects to survive the bank crisis without seeking financial support from the Government. First quarter results for 1993 would support this view with an overall operating profit of Skr 351 million. In the last four annual surveys of customer satisfaction, Handelsbanken has been placed first for service to both personal and corporate customers.

The bank attributes this success to its 'close to the customer' approach to business and its ability to concentrate on profitable business cost effectively. In 1970 the bank was in deep trouble and it was the adoption of a radically decentralized approach then which changed its fortunes. It still permeates every aspect of Handelsbanken today and in a feature which the new Chief Executive, Arne Mårtensson, appointed in 1991, is keen to continue. Tom Hedelius, former Chief Executive, and an important contributor to our research, is now Chairman of the Board.

Swedish Telecom Group, Stockholm (Televerket, its common operating name in Sweden up until 1 July 1993, when it was renamed TELIA)

Televerket was the only nationally owned organization of our eight but, like Wessex Water, it has been working toward being a market-based organization, capable of privatization, for some 10 years. During 1990 the question of privatization finally reached the political agenda and this is now being debated in the Riksdag, the Swedish Parliament.

Televerket has already made substantial changes in its approach, pressurized by the many Swedish multinational organizations which had exposure to telecommunications organizations in many other parts of the world. Telecoms are a business where international comparisons are both possible and meaningful and on this basis Televerket, along with a few other major national suppliers such as British Telecom, France Telecom and the Danish Telecoms, has shown massive improvements in productivity, reliability and equipment provision.

However, what most affected our choice of Televerket for this study was its genuine attempts to become truly market orientated and its readiness to discuss the problems – and false starts – encountered along the way.

In terms of profitability, Televerket has been very successful, with a return on capital invested of 11.9% for a number of years and rising toward their target of $12\frac{1}{2}$%. Given the dramatic increase in competition, this is a highly credible result.

Like most telecom organizations, Televerket has had to reduce staff, in fact 10,000 out of a total 32,000 in just two years. In particular, 3000 of these have been forced redundancies, a substantial shock within the Swedish environment. However, after some initial difficulties this has settled down well and service levels have been maintained. Indeed, consumer research shows Televerket now ranks alongside SAS (Scandinavian Airlines System, a long-time leader in service delivery) in terms of service levels.

Virgin Atlantic Airways Ltd, London (Virgin Atlantic)

Virgin Atlantic was formed in 1984 by the British entrepreneur Richard Branson. A larger-than-life figure, Richard had made a considerable fortune from his earlier activities in the music industry and many predicted his sudden foray into running an airline would end in disaster, citing, amongst other indicators, the demise of the apparently more experienced Freddie Laker, just a few years before. But Richard Branson – and Virgin Atlantic – have confounded them all and have gone from strength to strength.

They now operate on six routes out of London and plan a few more in the next two years. Despite the difficult years for airlines, passenger numbers have continued to grow, up in 1992 to over a million, more than a 12% increase on 1991. Customer satisfaction is high and Virgin Atlantic have now won the coveted 'Best Airline of the Year Award' three years in succession – the first airline ever to do so!

The success of Virgin Atlantic is primarily due to its willingness to be different, to strike a new course and to be 'itself' – to a great extent an extension of the style of Richard Branson and his colleagues. But it is no typically autocratic business, driven by someone who has little time for others' views. Indeed, it has a sense of genuine involvement and fulfilment for employees. As such, it is something of a model for the service company, providing some neat similarities and contrasts to our other 'model', Handelsbanken.

Wessex Water plc, Bristol (Wessex Water, or simply Wessex)

Choosing a privatized utility was not easy, but Wessex Water stood out as having already established a high level of customer awareness. Almost alone amongst English water authorities it has never had to impose restrictions on water usage, having built sufficient water reserves. In addition it had been seriously involved in altering the focus of the business for some years before privatization in 1989.

That early investment, and ongoing programme of major capital works, seems to be paying off with some of the best results of any of the 10 privatized water companies of England and Wales. In the year to 31 March 1993 pre-tax profits were up 12% compared with an industry average of 5%. For the second year in succession, Wessex was the only water company to show no increase in operational costs.

Wessex Water has also shown its abilities in more than profit making, having been ranked top of the Water Section in the Economist 1992 survey,

'Britain's Most Admired Companies', with top ranking on five of the nine factors, including quality of management, quality of marketing and financial soundness. It is also recognized as having the highest standards of quality and service in the UK water industry, having achieved 100% compliance with the industry's customer charter.

Although the supply of water for 1.4 million people for commercial and domestic use in a 10,000 square kilometre area of the West country stretching from north of Bristol to Salisbury and the Dorset coast is the most obvious of its responsibilities, it also collects, treats and safely disposes the waste water from 2.5 million domestic and commercial users. It also has a joint venture, Wessex Waste Management, one of the largest waste management concerns in the UK.

Woolworths plc, London (Woolworths)

Probably the most widely familiar of all of the names in our twelve, Woolworths was founded in the UK in 1909. In 1982, the UK company was sold by the American parent to a British financial consortium, which subsequently formed Kingfisher plc. Together with B&Q, Comet and Superdrug, Woolworths remains a substantial player in the Kingfisher group.

Since 1982, the business has been severely rationalized with a focus on key sites and a reduction in store numbers. However, there are still 796 stores in total and 27,000 full- and part-time staff, so Woolworths remains one of the major retailers in the UK. Profits in the last years have risen by 11% a year on average and in the last year to January 1993 were £77.8 million, an increase of 9%.

However, the management's main task was to revitalize a store which had both an enormous asset – a household name – but also a reputation for being old fashioned and a past legacy of neglect. That they have succeeded to a great extent is shown by the profit increases, but the interest for us was that Woolworths was still in a state of transition on culture and values. Its willingness to discuss this openly is one indication of the fact that it is on the right route and the results two years on are a testimony to Management's skill in pursuing this.

Externally, Woolworths has still much to do to achieve its aim but, again, the openness of its approach and willingness to honestly admit the task ahead suggests a confidence which will lead to even greater success. So, for example, in response to our request for 'external image' data, they wrote:

- 'Woolworths' customer image improved significantly on many store image criteria over the late 1980s. Quality and range were the two main areas which improved as the Focus strategy was implemented.
- This improvement has continued into the early 1990s although it has become slower. Since doing the In-Home Diary in February 1991, we have seen the following examples.

	Feb/Mar '91	*Feb/Mar '93*
Have a good selection of merchandise to choose from	72%	79%
I can normally be confident of getting what I want	50%	54%
Are stores which I enjoy visiting	43%	46%
Stock good quality merchandise	44%	46%
Have modern and up to date stores	41%	43%

- Whilst some of these improvements are marginal, they are consistent with trends over the intervening months. In addition, we have seen no significant declines in any of our image criteria.
- However, we still lag behind the competition on many of these criteria, hence there is still much work to be done.'

Yorkshire Bank plc, Leeds (Yorkshire Bank)

Founded in 1859 as the Yorkshire Penny Bank, the bank has remained close to its roots in Yorkshire where it has 124 of its total 270 branches. Expansion has been cautious and mainly concentrated on industrial towns with a similar environment.

In 1911 the bank was 'rescued' by 11 'joint stock banks' and remained a consortium until 1989. Its four remaining shareholders then sold it to National Australia Bank, which already owned three other regional banks, the (Scottish) Clydesdale Bank, Northern Bank in Northern Ireland and the National Irish Bank in the Republic of Ireland. Yorkshire Bank has retained its existing positioning, building on its traditional strengths in England.

Profitability has been consistent up to and including 1990, but in common with all UK banks Yorkshire have felt the problems of the recession. Nevertheless, like Handelsbanken in Sweden, operating income and profit in the last full year, to 30 September 1992, would have continued to rise (by 8.2% over 1991) but for the impact of doubtful debts. Half-year results suggest that this is now fully under control, with an operating profit before tax of £60 million.

Consumer research has shown that the Bank is very much appreciated by its customers. Of particular significance, in a 1992 survey 90% of customers felt the willingness of the Bank to help customers with financial difficulties exceeded or at least met with expectations. Given the generally low esteem of banks in this respect, this result is a clear reflection of the closer relationships existing between Yorkshire and its customers.

Other contributors

In addition, thanks are due to the following companies, which helped with the original report by providing material or by participating in the quantitative research – both the 1990–91 study and the preliminary studies in 1988–89.

Air UK; Banco Popular Español; Bank of Scotland; British Gas; Club Mediterranée; Comet Group; Cornhill Insurance; FMM Group; HFC Bank; J Walter Thompson; Mastercare; National Westminster Bank; P&O European Ferries; Ramada Inns; Royal Bank of Scotland; Sally Lines; Stena Sealink; Swiss Reinsurance UK; Thomas Howell Group; WH Smith.

Contents

Executive summary

The success rate of service improvement initiatives, such as Total Quality Management (TQM) or 'customer care' is stunningly low, with at best a satisfactory success rate of one in three and some observers suggesting none! Yet the costs of mounting such initiatives can be enormous in direct costs, let alone effort diverted from other priorities. The causes lie directly in our attitudes toward management and, particularly amongst top management, a failure to see that, in a service, the implementation is inseparable from the strategy, because the final process can only happen at implementation and can never be fully planned. In such situations, delegation most often becomes abdication.

Still, despite this low rate of success, the belief that it is necessary to achieve service success is deeply held; seemingly everyone wants to emphasize service to the customer, no matter whether they are a traditional service business, a public service – a civil service department or health authority for example – or a manufacturing company, delivering 'just in time'. This is because the balance of power has shifted to the market – to the consumer and, maybe even more importantly in immediate terms, the distributor – and is unlikely to shift back in the foreseeable future. But as the research that underlies this book shows, achieving this end is not simply a matter of deciding it's 'a good thing'.

Successful management teams have realized that to achieve their success, they have to create organic change, developing a service culture of which they are an integral part, not simply the 'order givers'. Further, that such a culture requires:

- More than a series of initiatives such as 'Total Quality' or 'Process Re-engineering' but rather an holistic, cross-functional approach to service based on a deeply held but simply expressed set of objectives and values: not one organization in the research has achieved long-term success – defined, say, over 10 years or more – without this.
- Seeing such objectives as strategic, and so making a consistent effort towards their achievement even when times are tough.

- That this 'service' be seen as integral to what they are doing or selling – that is central to the business issues and not an add-on or afterthought. For customers, satisfaction with a service comes from consistent delivery across a wide range of contacts or interactions which meets or exceeds their expectations: rarely from the core product.
- A willingness to see the customer as somebody more than just a target for sales: for services are relationships; good services are good relationships.
- Not only a much deeper involvement of top management in implementation than is usually the case, but often a shift in emphasis and behaviour on their part, which is rarely even considered let alone thought through.
- A consistency in the values and management behaviours which underpin daily work – which not only creates the confidence necessary for service delivery each and every day, but will withstand the scrutiny of a demanding consumer, a less deferential employee and a growingly intrusive media.

This in turn raises questions of ethics, not necessarily in terms of 'doing good', which is how most managers appear to interpret the term when rejecting it, but in its real sense of living by a set of values which are clear, known and declared and, in turn, influence all behaviour and actions.

The importance of strong cultures

Indeed, it would appear that the key ingredients of long-term success in a service, measured both in terms of profit over 10 years or more and also a stable secure base of truly satisfied customers, are:

- A strong and pervasive customer focus
- A strong and cohesive culture.

In this, it matters less what culture you have than that it is consistent and clear and related to an equally clear market need. So, for example, a well-run 'bureaucracy' – like Swiss Railways or McDonalds – may succeed simply because everyone knows the part they must play to ensure a good outcome and the customer can feel secure in the consistency of the delivery.

However, because so much of the attention paid to culture is internal, indulgent even, it is often seen as too soft an issue to weigh in the balance of business decision making; it is not a matter for 'real' managers! Yet as this book shows it is critically important; you can externalize it and avoid looking inwards; and you can measure 'who you are' and where you should be, in a tangible and practical way.

What to do?

For the manager concerned to make service a critical part of long-term success, there are a number of key areas of concern:

Strategic management not planning

To achieve long-term service success top management must first recognize that strategy, to quote Clausewitz, 'must go with the army into the field'. In a service, strategy cannot be defined and laid down in minute terms but must be a guide which not only governs every action but is, in turn, influenced by those actions – which by definition cannot all be pre-planned. In this situation, of strategic management rather than strategic planning, top management's role continues beyond originating strategy to guiding its implementation, and learning from this and setting the example.

Such strategy cannot be simply a reaction to market demand but must be based on a deep understanding of the theory of a service – so different from manufacturing – and of the currents of social change that make it a compelling commercial advantage in today's – and even more tomorrow's – markets.

Living with the customers

Because the customer participates in – and indeed helps shape – the service delivery, they will influence how your business is run and managed. In a service, you live with your customers! Those whose job it is to create customer satisfaction in this situation must have both authority and confidence to do this. This in turn calls for skills of leadership – coaching, listening, setting an example – rather than simply control. Middle management and supervisors are key in this and to succeed they need a new relationship of influence with top management to replace the (middle managers') traditional power base of 'do as I say!'

Such a customer focus produces results. Significantly, the most successful service organizations are 'low cost' relative to the customers' perceived value, because they don't waste money on things – especially technology – that the customer does not value. Instead, they concentrate expenditure against those key interactions that do create value in a service by meeting and exceeding expectations.

Create a vision

For strategy to percolate down and influence such day-to-day implementation it needs to be distilled into a simply expressed vision – a sense of mission, which is not only shared by all but stems from their own beliefs. The evidence is overwhelming that employees give of their best in situations where they feel that their work has real worth to others – not just profit to their employers – and where this is a close correlation between their values and those of the organization.

Get individual commitment

Services are delivered to individuals by individuals and customer perceptions of good service are directly related to a recognition – however mild – of their personal individuality. That's why individualism is essential in today's world.

So to succeed you must have individual commitment, not simply acquiescence. Don't strive so much for happy employees as employees who are dissatisfied enough to fight for and create change where it matters – with the customer. Be consistent – and ethical – in responding to this and in giving recognition to that commitment and response.

Tend the orchard

Concentrate more on getting the design of the business as a whole right, and converting others to the ideals, than on sorting the good from the bad, or developing rules. However good their intentions, rules rapidly become part of a defensive mechanism which destroys spontaneity (a key ingredient of good relationships because it recognizes the individual) and legitimizes error (an equally key destroyer of these relationships).

1

What is a service?

- Service is a strategic concern.
- The service revolution is part of a much bigger transformation of society and, in turn, business.
- Technology is only really successful where it plays a part in this revolution, bridging the gap between organization and customer and helping to build relationships.
- Customers increasingly seek 'seamless' solutions where their needs and not technical considerations are supreme.
- Services are distinctive and can give distinction.
- Making service successful involves everyone in the organization and the customer!
- Service ideals and the development of a culture can be profitable.

The demands of service

In virtually every area of activity today delivery has become the key factor for success. So, for example, 'just in time' production methods mean that even the best components are only as good as their availability and regularity when required. Customers demand they be treated not as targets but as individuals; perceptions of 'the treatment I receive' are as important as 'the goods I buy'.

1

This principle does not apply only to the purchase of goods; for example 'hospital care' can be as important for many patients as 'hospital cure'. So, the key decisions faced by organizations today – whether they are profit-making or not – are linked to the consequent demands for better service.

As we can see, this affects not only organizations which currently see themselves as a 'service' but virtually every type of enterprise, for the service revolution puts increasing pressure on even manufacturing organizations to see future development in terms of service. This is a great opportunity for business, but only if it can provide such services in a straightforward way without bureaucracy.

However, our research would suggest that the critical barrier to achieving such service success on any long-term stable basis, is not that of simply identifying the need to respond to customers (eventually that becomes obvious), or even necessarily of developing the strategy required to meet this (that requires objectivity, but you can hire such skills), but of swinging staff behind the tasks necessary to achieve the new objectives and, above all, developing an approach to management which permits this. Indeed, this is probably the greatest challenge faced by business today, because what is needed is radically different from traditional management styles, with a greater consistency of both internal and external relationships.

The research for this book, and the base work which preceded it, shows not only that it is possible to achieve such changes, but that they can be planned. It is possible to identify the patterns of structure, management and organizational development that are needed to achieve service objectives and, further, to identify where you are now, where you are going and what needs to be done to bridge the gap. However, it requires an overall approach, for the solutions are not necessarily those of marketing or Information Technology (IT) or human resource management – or any other individual discipline or function – but involve finding a way to integrate these into a coherent customer focus. Further, top management must be persuaded that *they* are a part, and maybe the most decisive part, of the changes which must take place.

These are strategic concerns and are the basis of both the research and the book – how to meet consumer demands for service, control the structure and remain viable as an enterprise.

The service revolution

Services are fast becoming not simply a tertiary industry but an integral and vital part of all activity. Research and development, maintenance, distribution are all typical of the activities which were once seen as ancillary to manufacturing and agriculture but are now often greater users of economic resources than the core manufacturing processes themselves. The trend is also toward subcontracting of those services which can be dealt with more advantageously by others. This occurs when subcontractors either have specific expertise or can do the job more economically. Sometimes it is simply because the mainstream organization does not have the management time to give sufficient attention to the project. Indeed, David Quarmby, joint managing director at Sainsburys, sees such subcontracting as one of the key developments of the past few years, since it not only makes organizations more effective, but allows management to concentrate on what they do best.

Although official statistics show that over 60% of the European Community workforce is engaged in service (up 25% over the past 20 years) and the official figure for the USA in 1992 is 76% and still rising, such figures understate the real position. At a conservative estimate 90% of all employees in the European Community are engaged in service and this is probably reflective of the West as a whole. Indeed, a recent article in *The Economist* suggested a figure for the USA of close to 98%! But the service revolution goes deeper, in terms of both consumer demand and industry structure. Some of these underlying reasons for the changes in consumer demand are summarized in Box 1.1.

Box 1.1 Services and post-industrial society

The service revolution and the emergence of the post-industrial society are both inextricably linked to the shifts in demand which shape consumer reactions and priorities.

Economics

Regardless of future economic growth, which may well be more limited than in the past, we have already seen a steady transformation of society which harder times show few signs of diminishing. Rather they have emphasized careful purchasing more than trading down, for the enormous wealth creation has spread across the population in a way which has produced a qualitative and not simply quantitative change in society. It is not only that there is greater buying power but discrimination in buying, formerly the prerogative of a few, is now an increasing trend.

As John Maynard Keynes so rightly forecast in 1928, '...for the first time since his creation, man will be faced with his real, his permanent problem – how to use his freedom from pressing economic causes, how to occupy the leisure which science and compound interest will have won for him, to live agreeably and wisely and well.' [1]

continues

continued

Whilst this wealth creation has by no means been the sole source of change it has helped to nurture and accelerate those agents of change which already characterize modern society and will continue to set the pace for expectations and behaviour in the post-industrial societies of the years ahead.

Individualism

The value placed on individualism is, perhaps, the most striking change, and a dominant social trend in all societies. In advanced societies, most people feel that their needs for physiological satisfaction and financial security are met and they become more concerned in seeking a greater sense of self-expression and self-fulfilment, in being less deferential to authority, self-indulgent, even. But they also seek a feeling of belonging through deeper relationships.

Such relationships provide 'shelter' from an environment which is increasingly perceived as hostile or even violent. Within these relationships people feel that they have more significance as an individual, their views reflected (and magnified?) by others. So at the micro end we see, for example, that growth in publishing is increasingly in specialized titles for specific, often quite small, groups and that growth in travel is toward the customized and away from the package. At the macro end, we see regionalization as a key, perhaps *the* key, factor in politics and also, less happily, the increasing attraction of extremist groups.

Feminism

Research has long shown that a further key determinant of social change is the balance between what psychologists would call 'masculine' and 'feminine' values (see Table 1.1). Such values should not be equated specifically on the basis of masculine values to men and feminine values to women since considerable research has shown that each man and woman has a different combination of these, inherited and then modified by life experience and the national and other cultures to which each person is exposed. These combinations are generally grouped in up to 15 shades of masculinity/femininity, with the majority occupying the central groupings.

Christopher Lorenz wrote in the *Financial Times*, 'In some American organizations the "near masculine" category has proved to be peopled largely by women, with many men in the middle "androgynous" group (regardless of sexual proclivity)' [2].

Whilst this may merely confirm some European male prejudices about American women, nevertheless, increasingly across all countries, feminine values are no longer seen as second class or optional but as having equal, and sometimes superior, validity to masculine values. Such a change has a profound impact on all spheres of activity and, in particular, underlies such initiatives as the Citizens' Charter in the UK.

continues

continued

Table 1.1   The connotations of the masculinity-femininity dimension.

Low MAS (High femininity) People orientation	High MAS (Low femininity) Money and things orientation
Quality of life and environment	Performance and growth are important
Work to live	Live to work
Service ideal	Achievement ideal
Interdependence ideal	Independence ideal
Intuition	Decisiveness
Sympathy for the unfortunate	Sympathy for the successful achiever
Levelling: don't try to be better than others	Excelling: try to be the best
Small and slow are beautiful	Big and fast are beautiful
Men need not be assertive, and can also assume nurturing roles	Men should behave assertively, and women should be nurturing
Sex roles in society should be fluid	Sex roles in society should be clearly differentiated
Differences in sex roles should not mean differences in power	Men should dominate in all settings
Unisex and androgyny ideal	Machismo (ostentatious manliness ideal)

Source: Geert Hofstede (1980) *Culture's Consequences.* Beverly Hills CA: Sage Publications, Figure 6.6; quoted with permission.

Ageing

The predominance of older people in the population will increase in the future. Today populations not only have an older profile but are increasingly wealthy, bringing a much greater life experience to bear on choice and exhibiting a greater reluctance to take risks or cut corners. Indeed, for the first time in history, we see a shift in the cultural and commercial centres of gravity towards a dominance, in most western countries, of the middle-aged, with an overwhelming potential buying power within this age group.

The counter trend

Alongside these main trends there is a contrary trend of a smaller disadvantaged group in society – commonly between 10% and 20% – who are not sharing the economic benefits to the same extent. Nevertheless, they are open to widespread media messages and feel resentful of the mass. Of even greater concern, they see little in modern society to satisfy them.

A ready pool of entrants to this group exists amongst the rising numbers of the unemployed. Indeed, some observers[3] see this growth as reaching 25% of the working population in Western Europe within the next ten years or so. These global trends are not absolutes, and individually may be disputed, but together they represent a real shift in social values which businesses, and especially service businesses, ignore at their peril. Looked at positively, they in fact offer new opportunities such as:

- Meeting environmental concerns
- Providing leisure activities
- Finding 'seamless' solutions to multi-layer consumer problems.

As a result of these changes we are seeing the emergence of the 'Discriminating Aware Customer'. Such people are more experienced, more demanding, more inclined to seek value and more in need of an opportunity to identify with a supplier – to have a relationship. At the same time, in terms of industry structure, there is a greater emphasis on providing service and a greater willingness to identify service as commercially important. We even see manufacturers of products redefining their business as a service. This is partly because, in a world where there is a growing similarity in manufactured products, it is service which can differentiate between them.

Service is also a way of making individual what is otherwise a mass produced item, of responding to individual needs. So motor manufacturers and business equipment manufacturers, even oil companies and brewers, are becoming increasingly involved in service. For Televerket, the Swedish telecom organization and one of our 'core companies', 'installing and maintaining a [telecommunications] network used to be the task; now it is worthless. Our focus must be the customers and the service we provide them.'

This view is confirmed as a general trend in a recent study which showed that in the EC, the USA and Japan managers saw 'service as a differentiator' as being the most important reason for emphasizing service issues in future[4]. The full results are shown in Table 1.2 and you can see that the top three reasons are clearly interrelated.

Service may also be the only way a manufacturer can make money in the long term. For example, a car manufacturer may sell a car for £10,000 but, because of competitive pressures, this may be close to the cost of making it and the manufacturer therefore makes little or no profit. But if the consumer spends an average of £3000 on 'service' over the first three years' life of the vehicle, this may be a source of £300 or more profit. Little wonder that car

Table 1.2   External pressures for service.

Compelling reasons for improving customer service	Average mean scores			
	Europe	USA	Japan	UK
Service is more important as a differentiator	4.3	4.4	4.6	4.4
Competition is fiercer	4.1	4.3	4.6	4.2
Customers are more demanding	3.9	4.0	4.5	4.1
Development of advanced information technology	3.2	3.3	4.2	3.2
Shortening life cycle of products and services	2.7	2.7	3.7	2.7

How important have the following external pressures been in compelling companies to give more attention to customer service?

Responses are based on a 5 to 0 scale (5 = very important, 0 = least important)

Source: Service, The New Competitive Edge, a survey of executive opinion in the United Kingdom, Digital Equipment Company in association with John Humble and the Management Centre of Europe.

manufacturers increasingly talk of 'controlling the cash flow over the life of the vehicle' and see an increasing need to reposition themselves as service businesses. These structural changes are affecting all commercial activity and we may note the following trends:

- Those businesses with control of the 'delivery' are becoming increasingly dominant;
- Consumers are seeking to be more involved, less passive;
- Marketing – even mass marketing – is more directed at the particular, at identified groups and even at individuals;
- Advertising is becoming more dialogue, less monologue.

The value of technology

In all this, technology has particular significance since it can shape and expand consumer demands, allowing them to achieve the unexpected or the previously unthinkable. We have only to think of the impact of telephones earlier this century, air travel in the past few decades or fax today, to understand this. Much of the upheaval in financial services, for example, is due to technology making obsolete old practices and lowering the barriers of entry to those who are more prepared to listen to the consumer.

However, technology can be an expensive distraction. Two of the leading Swedish banks, Handelsbanken (much quoted in this book) and SE Banken, illustrate this. Handelsbanken has seen people and not technology as preeminent: SE Banken has embraced technology and technological answers to problems with enthusiasm. Yet it is Handelsbanken which has been the most consistently successful, with a lower cost base and, on average, better profitability for over 20 years. As SE Banken has, on occasions, found, technology can alienate customers and staff. Indeed, in any enterprise, technology can only be really successful where it helps to bridge the gap between organization and customer; where it consolidates and deepens the relationship.

A further example of technology relative to service development is that of Televerket (see Case 1.1). Televerket has been through a change which is reflected in the experience of many other organizations with a predominantly technical base – from computers through to insurance – and shows how easy it is to become trapped in innovation for its own sake, whilst seemingly being 'external'.

Case 1.1   Technology as a barrier

Like all suppliers of telephone equipment, Televerket has been caught up in the race for technological advancement and excellence, but personal customers had not been impressed. Now Televerket has seen that technology has to be tamed to meet the real needs of the consumer, and that not all consumers are alike.

As Morgan Svensson, deputy director of Televerket, relates, the original problem lay in their very skill: 'Technically, Televerket were excellent and our contact with the many Swedish multinational companies accentuated this. It meant that we had access to the best international practice. As a result we became very sophisticated but our industrial customers were better considered than our personal. At first, our traditional culture of proud engineers and technicians failed to learn from this market'.

Bertil Thorngren, corporate planning director, takes up the story: 'Our personal customers have been confused and alienated by our technical excellence. They are worried by having masses of features on a 'phone for example, which they don't understand and never use. We saw it as a competitive advantage; they saw it as confusing, and as a barrier to use.

Now we have seen the need to develop equipment in which the features a customer wants can be 'programmed in' personally; probably no more than six and capable of variation to suit changes in personal circumstance.

That way the customer is back in control. We have to develop such customer-oriented 'soft key' approaches throughout the business rather than our traditional and technical 'hard key' approach, if we are to be successful in the future'.

It is of particular importance to bear these points in mind in considering the impact of IT-based mass-marketing techniques. Underpinning the latest thinking on mass marketing is a need for systems to play a part in the relationship-creating process, as the American business writer Regis McKenna has stated '[to create] an approach that stresses the building of relationships rather than the promotion of products; these relationships are more important than low prices, flashy promotions or advanced technology. Changes in the marketplace can alter prices and technology but close relationships can last a lifetime – if not longer!' [5]

It is vital, therefore, that technology be seen as a part of the service, as a method of 'delivery', rather than as a method of administration if it is not to be a barrier between the business and the customer. For all service businesses, from supermarkets to airlines, the challenge is to create a service environment in which technology is servant, not master.

The strategic issue

In short, the impact of service is to be felt way beyond the confines of 'customer care' or other such tactical considerations. In true service companies, customer expectations are the basis for strategic management; customer experiences the judgement of success or failure.

These criteria strike at the very root of the approach to, and the management of, the business. Good service requires a high degree of operational efficiency across many areas of activity and competence. But, unless it has a strategic context, such efficiency will never become effective at the only point where it really matters – with the customer. It is here that satisfaction and profit are generated, and to achieve these ends a dialogue, or 'relationship', is necessary.

This need for concentration on the customer's experience is a parallel to the growing demand for 'seamless' solutions – total solutions to specific, identified user or consumer problems. For example, the installation and maintenance of office equipment becomes integral to the original decision to buy or lease a particular system; advising on effective saving or investment may be more important than selling any particular form of the same such as life assurance; older people may feel that their needs cross the traditional 'barriers' set up by suppliers and be attracted to companies like Saga, who are perceived as 'understanding them and their problems'.

Such seamless solutions cannot be provided simply through adding 'service' to products. This approach is likely simply to add to costs without appreciably creating greater customer satisfaction. Rather, the total business activity has to be developed as a cohesive process, with the supplier assuming full responsibility for satisfying all needs in a particular area.

This failure to see service as a process is a key reason for the poor results of programmes to improve customer service or promote quality. In one study, a firm of US consultants found that, although 75% of their respondents had instituted such programmes, 'few tangible results ensued; only a third found significant improvements in market share or profitability'. [6] More recently, a British study has suggested that the figure for success is more like 20%.[7]

What characterizes a service?

Until the 1970s it was the generally accepted belief that all businesses were fundamentally similar; that the same management and marketing theory could be applied to all; that, whatever your business, in the end you were selling

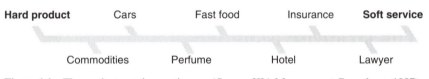

Figure 1.1   The product–service continuum. (*Source*: KIA Management Consultants 1987)

something to make a profit or achieve some other aim, such as more efficient telecommunications, faster trains or more patients cured. Today services are more readily seen as different from manufacturing industries, but it is still comparatively rare for evidence to be produced to show in what respects they are 'different'. For example, do different management and marketing theories apply? If so, how can you use them?

All of us will have an instinctive feel for what is or is not a service. It is easily illustrated by thinking about two typical decisions, say the choice of a car or whom to consult as a professional, say a lawyer. In both cases there will be uncertainties and doubts. In turn, these will be overlaid with personal feelings and views. But in the one case there will be specific and concrete criteria one can turn to – the car which can be seen, touched, heard and even smelled. In the other case, the lawyer is clearly providing a service which, if the opinions are simply verbal, may be seen only in the person of the lawyer, probably may not be touched, hopefully can be heard but probably not smelled, and (an important point in a service) may be open to being talked to and so influenced by the customer concerning his or her views and delivery.

Obviously, though, defining service is not quite as simplistic as this. The car will be sold by a dealer – who is a service. The lawyer may provide his opinion in a written document – which is a product, though a one-off. In fact, it may be best to see services and manufacturing as two ends of a continuum with, in the majority of situations, a mixture of the two, as illustrated by Figure 1.1.

There can be no hard-and-fast rules in this. The balance of the factors present in each of the examples given in Figure 1.1 can cause substantial variation. For instance, you would have to vary the position of insurance on the continuum for different types of insurance for different situations; maybe even to take account of claims frequency. Earth-moving equipment, a major capital item and on the face of it a 'hard' product, is quite likely to be chosen on a basis of service, especially if it is to be used in an out-of-the-way place.

In a commercial sense, you will need to consider if it is the service which gives distinction or a significant competitive advantage, rather than simply the values of the core product. On this basis, the definition of a service business could be one, 'where service is a significant part of the expenditure, perceptions or reason for choice on the part of customers'.

Pure services are intangible. Although they may make available a tangible product (for example retailing) or they may add value to a tangible product (for example contract maintenance), the service itself does not result in the transfer of ownership of anything and may leave only memories or promises. Nor can market contact be limited to a dedicated group of consumer-oriented specialists, such as a salesforce. Research shows that, whilst only 10% of the staff of the average manufacturing company directly influence the consumer, the comparable figure in a service company is 90% – and not uncommonly 100%.

Each service will present its own mix and emphasis. You may even shift the balance, or introduce 'hard' (tangible) elements to reduce the transiency of the service or strengthen the memory, as for example an airline might give passengers a gift or a restaurant might give customers a copy of the menu. But the essentially 'soft' nature of a service remains – and for the management of services it is these seven aspects which are crucial.

Box 1.2   Distinguishing services

In summary, seven elements distinguish services:[8]

(1)   Services are transient – they are 'consumed' then and there. They have no lasting material being and may leave only memories or promises.

(2)   Services are mainly represented by people – they cannot be separated from the person of the provider, whose personal characteristics and self-perceptions are 'on show' to the consumer and indeed form an important part of consumer perception.

(3)   Services are only finally selected face to face with the consumer and at the time of consumption. They are perishable – generally you cannot have a production run and store services against future demand.

(4)   Services are, therefore, essentially a series of 'one-off' production runs. It is difficult to achieve standardization or exercise the same controls over production as you would with a product, for example through quality controls.

(5)   This production/consumption process goes on, for the most part, unsupervised and depends on the individual reactions of the operator for success.

(6)   The process is also open to influence from the consumer, not just in some indirect way, as through research or even the exercise of choice, but directly since they participate in and help make the final product. Indeed, in some cases – as, for example, a restaurant or a bar – the customers may actually be the key ingredient in success; it is they, rather than the food or drink, who are the attraction to others.

(7)   As a result of the previous six points, it is the culture in which these acts are performed which mostly conditions perceptions of service and this culture is internal *and* external. It is about the way we work and the way we manage.

The basis of service

In a very real sense, therefore, service is the business of everyone, but if we are not to lose the significance of this – and its value as a business concept – it is necessary to be firmer in definition. Service is seen by the consumer not as what is done, in terms of time to achieve a task or delivery of an item, but in qualitative terms, how it is done.

In most cases, and for most buyers, one service offer seems much like another until they have sampled it. Expectation will be based on the clues provided, but because the core products – that is, the 'plane seat, the telephone call, the meal, the insurance policy – are difficult to differentiate, putting the emphasis on them is self-defeating and can only lead to price competition, because the necessary ability to be distinctive has been lost. It is more likely that expectations will be taken from other elements, in particular the image conveyed.

Once sampled, perceptions, and therefore experiences, of service are most often taken from the delivery of the service, both at the time of sale and after the sale, that is at all of the often transient points of contact during the 'relationship', rather than from anything to do with the core product itself.

For this is what any service company is selling: not 'plane seats, or meals or insurance policies, but millions and millions of contacts, every year, even every day. These are the 'moments of truth' when ideas and plans are bought or rejected. This will include many aspects normally beyond marketing control, such as, in the case of an airline, travel to and from the airport and the experiences at the airport itself as well as the culture within which these events happen.

As a result, each member of the management team of a service enterprise is faced with a fundamentally different task from their counterpart in manufacturing. None of those in operational roles (and not just sales) is able to organize their tasks free of customer interference; those in personnel and marketing find that their roles overlap and may even conflict; finance managers find costing more subject to variables and with a higher percentage of people costs which are difficult to allocate; general managers find that control through simple functional splits is difficult and may even be impossible or counterproductive.

The role of the other party involved in the formation of the service, the consumer, is also very different, and more difficult. In fact, the intangibility, the transience, the variability and the personal involvement make it almost impossible to make clear distinctions. Instead of rating the intrinsic merits of the offer, consumers either consciously or subconsciously individualize the situation, 'What can they do for me? How well do they understand me and my problems?'

So, expectations and experiences mingle, and consumers draw much of their final belief from the personality and behaviour of the person they meet, because he or she provides more clues as to the personal suitability of the solution offered than does the core product itself, thus emphasising the old cliché that services are about people, though it would be better to rephrase it as services are people! This decision-making process on the part of the consumer is critical in managing a service.

Services as a triangular relationship

The service organization has lost the direct simplicity of the market perception that exists in manufacturing. To take an example, if you say Ford or Cadbury to a group of people they will usually have an immediate and firm image of a car or a chocolate bar. It may even be of a particular model or brand, perhaps one they have just bought. But say Avis or Prudential and their view is less clear. Where they do have a firm view it will almost certainly be from direct contact with the organization, and influenced by their experience with the people employed by it.

In fact it may be seen that services are relationships and that successful services are successful relationships. Building a relationship with a chosen market, whether that relationship is transient (a one-time visit to a restaurant) or long term (as with a bank or professional adviser) is the essence of building a belief in yourself.

Such a relationship will be based on a series of contacts or interactions. It is from these interactions with the organization that consumers form their perceptions of the individual rightness of a solution whether it be to assess value, decide to buy, repeat purchase or recommend to others. In turn, these interactions are repeated in the internal relationships within the organization, which can be seen as a triangle, as in Figure 1.2. For this to be in balance it is necessary for the culture on the base axis to relate to that on the other axes.

Whereas the traditional manufacturing company operates only along the right-hand axis, the service business operates along all three, with those inter-actions that are so vital to customers' perceptions – and where on average 90% of the staff will be involved – being along the base axis. The service triangle has a number of fundamental strategic implications for both the structure and management of a service organization.

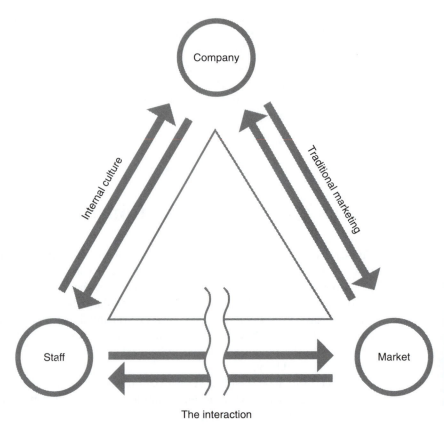

The interaction

Figure 1.2   The service triangle. *(Source*: KIA Management Consultants 1982)

What it means

(1) *You cannot dissociate the internal culture from the external culture.* What happens internally is directly linked to what happens externally. We will examine the basis for this critical aspect in great depth in the next two chapters, but it means that the culture of an organization is a critical part of its external presence. Not unreasonably, the creation of relationships involves your culture.

(2) *Power must be devolved.* Those whose task it is to set up, maintain and develop the relationship must have not only the skills but also the knowledge and authority to do this effectively and to the customer's satisfaction.

(3) *The values of the organization are critical.* Given that by definition these interactions are not only decentralised but are happening largely without

immediate supervision and possibly with strong external influences, the values of the organization need to be simple, clear and understood and shared by everyone. These values must be the priorities that govern action at this key point of achievement.

(4) *Management must lead.* Empowering people to be responsive to external pressures – both external to the organization and external to their immediate task – means that management cannot just 'control' in the traditional authoritarian sense. Instead of managers seeing themselves with a job to do and with a number of people to help them to achieve it, managers and supervisors will need to see that they have a number of people with jobs to do and that it is their task to help them to achieve their objectives. This calls for an emphasis on leadership more than simply control.

(5) *Customer focus, not function, is the key.* Bringing the competence of the organization to bear on the interaction will be confused, even confounded, if customers are divided up by various functions. The product – the relationship – will be seamed rather than seamless. Consumers will be unsure and the attempt to make them the focus will merely produce aimlessness and even chaos.

Is culture profitable?

If culture and the establishment of service ideals are so important, can a direct linkage between a particular culture and profit be established? As we will go on to see, there is no right culture but more a need for cohesive cultures that consistently match expectations and experiences through delivery.

However, the research evidence of the value of investing in service ideals and creating strong, harmonious cultures is compelling if not conclusive. So, for example, the Bain & Co report mentioned earlier [6], calculated the impact on profits with three examples from improved market relationships – specified as a five per cent improvement in retention – as follows:

- For a credit card issuer, an increase of 125%
- For an insurance broker, an increase of 50%
- For a software company, an increase of 35%.

In another survey the CEOs of 500 top European companies calculated that an increase in quality could increase the gross margin on sales by an average 17%. [9]

Our research substantiates this, particularly with the experiences of Handelsbanken. For the 20 years until 1990, it might be said that their persistently good performance was simply luck allied to the generally favourable Swedish market conditions, though such consistency seems, of itself, to be compelling. But in the two years since then, it is unquestionably the strength of their relationships, their close-to-the market stance, which has produced results so much better than the market as a whole.

But it has to be emphasized that the benefits are long term and a number of reasons rooted in cultural values account for this:

(1) Cultures are rooted in the people that make up an organization. The values of a culture usually take time to develop or decay and, in a large organization particularly, will vary in both timescale and effect. Except in unusual circumstances, or with very small organizations, cultural development will, therefore, be difficult to relate directly to performance on any short timescale.

(2) It is in the very nature of a culture that its true impact is only evident in the long term. It is a strategic issue and, as with safety, cultural development can actually impair short-run performance. Like all strategies, it may mean forgoing early wins for ultimate victory. Many of the managers interviewed in the research resisted the idea that there could be such a conflict, but the evidence is strong.

It is important to bear this in mind, because attention to service cultures is likely to need consistent long-term pressure and an unswerving belief in some higher goals than immediate profit.

Falck, Lyonnaise des Eaux, Sainsburys, Saga and Yorkshire Bank, as well as Handelsbanken highlight this. Each has had long-term success and each has developed a consistent set of values. All are cost conscious but relative to a vision; all are highly profitable or have fared substantially better than their competitors in markets which have ruined others.

In the case of Sainsburys, the culture has grown with the family and is rooted in the values the family believed in. In the words of David Quarmby, joint managing director, 'We don't talk about it because we know it's there…it oozes from the walls'. The culture is clear, and the recognition that success flows from this is equally clear.

However, Handelsbanken illustrates that it is not necessary to wait to imbue family values over the decades. It instituted major changes to its structure in 1970 and managers estimate it took six or seven years to become really effective, although by 1973 it was achieving its objectives in terms of profit and cost. What it does share with Sainsburys is a belief in firm values and the need, to quote David Quarmby again, to be, 'seriously hard working at what we believe in, some might even say obsessively so'. Or, as Handelsbanken express it, 'We are almost religious about our beliefs'. The need for such consistent development and implementation of values was best expressed by a former executive vice president with Handelsbanken who had lived through the change at the top, 'Our management were consistent. They and the bank stuck to their strategic views. As a result we all had the confidence to work together.'

In conclusion

Services have qualities that separate them from conventional approaches to management and marketing, because people – both customers and staff – impact directly on each other and form an integral part of the perceived product and of satisfaction/dissatisfaction. Further, the internal culture of an organization is a part of the external culture: the two cannot be separated. In the next chapter we will look at the impact of this on the service culture and the creation of distinctiveness.

References

1. Keynes J.M. (1928). In the valedictory article by Norman McRae, in *The Economist*. 12 August 1989
2. Lorenz C. (1991). In *Financial Times*. 30 January
3. Barnevik P. (1993). In *Financial Times*. 4 January
4. Digital Equipment Co. Ltd (1991). Survey, *Service, The New Competitive Edge*
5. McKenna R. (1989). *Who's Afraid of Big Blue?* Reading MA: Addison-Wesley
6. Bain & Co. (1990). In *Financial Times*. 16 July
7. A.T. Kearney & Co (1992). In *Financial Times*. 14 February
8. Based on the work of Professor Christian Grönroos, Svenska Handelshögskolan, Helsinki
9. McKinsey & Co. (1989). In *Management Europe*. January 1990

2

Living with the customer

- A focus on customers is a key ingredient of service success.
- Organizations with harmonious cultures experience less role conflicts in dealing with customers.
- Such cultures are often a balance of conflicting forces, for example between bureaucracy and enthusiasm.
- The strength of a well-balanced culture shows through to customers, who 'buy-in' to this and, in turn, themselves form a part of the culture.
- Management is the key factor in creating such harmony but a great deal of self-knowledge about yourself and the organization is required.
- Successful services have close value patterns. Everyone shares these values and has a clear view of what the organization is trying to achieve, and how.

Focus on customers

If the distinctiveness of a service business is that people – both customers and staff – have a direct impact on each other and form an integral part of the product, then the research and work on which this book is based would suggest that the overwhelming element of such distinction and success is a strong market focus. Indeed, the research indicated that a positive attitude toward the market, and specifically customers, was a marked characteristic of service companies, with over 73% of all management and staff in the survey being aware of the impact of their job on the customer. Further, amongst those companies who also collaborated in the in-depth qualitative research, and had been chosen for their track record of success, this focus was particularly marked:

- Customers were integral to their thinking, a part of the process of creating value and not simply a target. In planning and in execution these companies *brought the customer into their business*.
- They showed a clear difference from the average of all service companies surveyed in seeing satisfied customers as the cornerstone of success, not just at management level but across all levels of personnel.

Table 2.1 shows an extract from this research. Line 1 shows the percentage of management and staff who believed that the single most important priority in achieving success should be customer satisfaction. Line 2 shows what they believed to be the actual priority adopted in their business. Not only are the successful group higher on all scores, particularly management, but the level of fall-off between their personal beliefs and what they perceive as the actuality is lower too – only 29% against 39%. Even more telling are the shifts with supervisors and staff, of 38% to 24% and 42% to 31% respectively. Clearly, in these organizations there is less ambiguity, and the instinctive belief in customers as individuals receives more support.

This greater consistency between own beliefs and the perceived actual situation highlights another key factor proved in the research to support sustained success – an harmonious or cohesive internal culture with low levels of conflict over objectives.

So, seeing customers as a part of commercial success and having close cultural values, is critical in creating a relationship with the market and building long-term success, not simply short-term advantage. Service organizations differ sharply from manufacturing in the respect that, in this relationship, both

Table 2.1   Priorities for service company success.

Percentage selecting customer satisfaction as top priority				
	Total	*Management*	*Supervisors*	*Staff*
All respondents:				
1. Own opinion of priority	57	48	61	64
2. Perceived actual priority	35	31	38	37
% change	39	35	38	42
Core respondents:				
1. Own opinion of priority	62	61	62	65
2. Perceived actual priority	44	41	47	45
% change	29	33	24	31

Source: KIA/EIU research (1991) questions B1.1 and B1.2.

employees and customers have to 'live' with each other. So the internal values of the organization are on show to the world.

A recent newspaper article[1], on the problems of providing customer service, highlighted this issue with various quotes from service employees who were clearly unhappy with the customer. 'When you take a job dealing with the public, there's a hell of a lot of things you have to swallow', said one, whilst another said, 'They don't even give you common courtesy. They don't smile or say hello.' The article seemed to conclude that the only way forward was to educate the customer. Obviously, this would be a valuable step because there is no doubt that customers could get more from a service by being better at the task, but this is unlikely to help any individual business or give rise to gaining a competitive advantage – nor is it likely to happen on any significant scale, even though it is a viable course of action in some specific areas.

So, the manager concerned to develop a distinctiveness for his or her service has to operate within this imperfect world, recognizing that it is this interplay between 'our world' (that is our business) and 'their world' (that is the customer's expectations and experiences) which is paramount.

The customer in the organization

Some important earlier research in the United States also demonstrated clearly the importance of an organization's culture for the competitiveness of service organizations.[2] In this earlier American work, the researchers took the view that all service organizations are a balance between bureaucracy and enthusiasm for the customer (because without some bureaucracy things don't happen, but equally service organizations also depend on customers and so try to please them, to be enthusiastic). An example of the bureaucratic extreme is provided by Professor Charles Handy, who tells the story of asking why there was no station clock at Bonn, and being told by the railwayman, 'We don't need it; we can tell the time by the trains'.[3] However, no competitive organization could live for long at either extreme. Being totally enthusiastic never gets anything done, despite exciting promises; being totally bureaucratic would have the doors closed to customers, because they hinder the efficiency of the system!

The American research took the form of a survey of attitudes toward enthusiasm and bureaucracy amongst the staff and the customers of each of 23 branches of an American bank. There were, therefore, 23 separate models. No one was asked whether they were bureaucratic or enthusiastic; they were asked instead to respond to questions which established their attitudes towards these two emphases.

The results showed that:

- Employees perceived themselves to be more enthusiastic but their management thought them more bureaucratic in service orientation. This suggested a gap between the goals of employees vis-à-vis service and the management goals as perceived by the employees.
- Employees who worked in settings that were more in harmony with their own service orientation experienced less role ambiguity and role conflict and, as a result, were generally more satisfied.
- Even though they viewed service from different perspectives, employee and customer perceptions of organizational effectiveness were positively related. Support for this assumption was quite strong; when employees reported that their branch emphasised service by word and deed, customers reported superior experiences.

This study also showed that:

(1) Employees were strongly orientated toward giving service but felt frustrated that the system prevented them.
(2) The organization cannot be hidden from those who are served: the internal culture in service organizations is clearly evident to the buyer.

Later work in the UK [4], and a preliminary to the original research which underpins this book, not only confirmed the general correctness of the 'bureaucracy v. enthusiasm' model suggested by this earlier American research but also indicated that:

- Not only did staff see the system as frustrating their efforts, but they saw management behaviour, too, as creating barriers, to an extent that they could, on occasions, question managements' sincerity on the issue;
- Management, in turn, felt frustrated by the system, but also felt that staff behaviour put in question the sincerity of the staff;
- This gap between management and staff values was smaller where there was evidence of long-term customer satisfaction and commercial success. That is, a cohesive organization was more likely to be successful;
- Systems of themselves were not necessarily wrong; it was those systems which functioned badly or, seemingly, purely for the benefit of 'good order' without regard to their effect on the customer which were the problem.

There are many lessons to be learned from all of this earlier research:

(1) *There is always a gap.* The perfect situation, where there are no conflicts, can never be achieved in practice. As we have already seen, dealing with individual consumers and meeting their needs is always going to be at variance, to some extent, with achieving internally focused results, particularly those of a short-term nature such as sales and given that 'their world' is different from 'our world'.

In pursuing one aspect, quality, Saga almost succeeded in widening this gap, despite their customer focus (see Case 9.1).

(2) *Good service is not just a function of enthusiasm.* It is tempting to think of enthusiasm as being the key to service success. However, on its own – that is lacking some measure of bureaucracy – it will quickly fade. Moreover, you can be as successful by being systematic and making the system work well – some prime examples exist, such as fast food outlets.

Two of the organizations involved in the research for this study, Sainsburys and Handelsbanken, could easily be seen as representing, if not extremes, then an emphatic reflection of this aspect, though it is certain they would prefer the labels 'routine' and 'flexible' used in our research. Case 2.1: 'A tale of two cultures', highlights the contrast between these two very different organizations.

(3) *The internal culture 'gets through to' the customers.* In fact, you could say that customers effectively buy into the internal culture because it is this that conditions the crucial interactions between company and customers, between 'our world' and 'their world'. For Virgin Atlantic, this has been a key part of the development of their business – developing those values internally which customers respond to and see as distinctive.

(4) *An important part of marketing as a service is knowing enough about yourself, about 'our world'.* Only then are you able to be true to your own strengths and to achieve success through exploiting them. In a service, that means having a firm set of values, which everyone knows and understands and which are in harmony, not in conflict, with market objectives, what Woolworths describe as 'two sides of the same coin'. It is not enough to have brilliant core products and great advertising, or even a fine salesforce; all of the elements of the business have to be kept in a balanced relationship.

A framework for culture

As already stressed, services are relationships, and good services are good relationships. These relationships are created from the perceptions of daily practice and reward shared between the three parties involved in the triangle (namely management, staff and customers). However, what the original research for this book has shown is that the simple 'bureaucratic v. enthusiastic' analysis, quoted earlier, merely highlights the problem, though it is a highly graphic description of the balance you have to achieve. In fact, our research suggests there are four dimensions which are critical (see Box 2.1 for a more

Case 2.1   A tale of two cultures

Sainsburys and Handelsbanken both have unquestioned claims to success, and both recognize that their culture has been a significant element in this achievement. Each has a profoundly different culture, which cannot be solely attributed to their specific type of business.

Sainsburys

'Retail is detail' is almost the company motto and it manifests itself at every level of operation. David Quarmby, joint managing director, is quite clear about the significance of this culture to its success. He described this as follows:

- Setting and aspiring to achieve high standards in what we do and how we do things
- Being hands on in terms of management style
- Being committed to doing things properly and doing things well
- Being customer sensitive and market aware
- Being very IT driven, probably more than any other retailer
- Being information hungry
- Being seriously hard working at it.

Cecil Roberts, buying director, continues this theme: '[Success] is centralized buying done centrally. The development of IT imposes its own discipline, in a centralized way. Therefore an operational style has to be efficient, though we have to allow creativity to come through. So we are stern, even uncompromising, on logistics but make sure the creativity is there, in the development of the product.'

Jeremy Grindle, director of branch services, supports this: 'Our success? It's attention to detail. Very close to detail, obsessively close which has its own merits. Some meetings go on endlessly, grinding things excessively small, but it means everyone is aware of the significance of, say, a change of pack size. Letters regarding quality of service have always been dealt with individually and signed by a Director. Now, because of the size of the business, they are signed by Area Directors. It hurts...and it's meant to!'

And this is echoed at store level. Quotes from our interviews included the following:

- 'We have an obsessional interest in detail.'
- 'We are a strongly directed bureaucracy.'
- 'You certainly know when the Chairman has been. His attention to detail is astounding.'
- 'Being a Sainsburys' person means being obsessive about detail.'

continues

continued

Svenska Handelsbanken

Tom Hedelius, former Chief Executive, and now Chairman, is equally clear and describes their culture as: 'Totally decentralized in terms of decision making but with a centralized control system, and the products are secondary. In fact, decentralized is the key word and we see other organizations only have a problem with this when they fail to implement customer focus completely. The customer is our focus, not the product. We refer all business to the branch even from the biggest customers. We see the Chief Executive's main task as talking to people and he should contact any manager direct if he wants to query any action, but he should never override! Decentralization is not a 'for once' activity. We constantly have to work at it.'

Again, our interviews showed that this theme is echoed throughout the bank:

- 'We don't have cost controls. We are just cost aware.'
- 'It's an informal organization. There isn't an organizational plan, just a telephone book.'
- 'We do not produce budgets for business since we assume everyone is doing his best.'
- 'Our culture? Oh, quick decisions, personal responsibility, informality, having fun if you do a good job.'
- 'It is easier to sell Handelsbanken because we are decentralized.'

Two contrasting styles, both outstandingly successful. More significantly, what Sainsburys and Handelsbanken share is:

- A close understanding of the way they do business at all levels and right across each company – to the extent that if the researcher forgot to record the position or location of the person talked to, the quotations could easily be interchanged between speakers within the organization.
- A firm grasp of costs and an attention to cost consciousness which could be obsessional.
- A spontaneous focus on the customer, for example:
  - 'The customer comes first. They don't realize how important they are to us.' (Sainsburys)
  - 'The customer is first; everything is secondary to our meetings with the customer.' (Handelsbanken)

detailed explanation of the research and Appendix B for an explanation of methodology). Additionally, in order to understand why certain results on these dimensions are achieved, you need to know the similarity, or disparity, of views on the key objectives and the key values of the organization between the various 'players' involved.

Box 2.1   Service strategies research

During the latter part of 1990 and January 1991, KIA, in conjunction with the EIU, carried out some research into service cultures and their relationship to strategy and success. Success in this context was based on long-term success rather than simply success over a limited period. Subsequently, the research has been used extensively in in-company projects.

The research was based on the initial codification of KIA's experience in 15 countries as a specialist consultancy in the field of service businesses and through preliminary research in 1988/90. The KIA/EIU research comprised:

(1) Qualitative research with the management and staff of eight successful service organizations, none of whom were KIA clients. Four of these were in the UK, one in Sweden, one in Denmark and one in France, though some companies took samples in more than one country. Further, in 1993 we had in-depth discussions with most of these original eight respondents and with two more UK organizations.

(2) Quantitative research using a specially constructed questionnaire (see Appendix A) with the original 8 companies and 16 others.

In addition, since that specially commissioned research, the work has been used on an in-company project basis in Denmark, Holland and Switzerland and with one (British) company on a worldwide basis, but primarily in the UK and USA. This has doubled the base size and introduced professional services and insurance as further categories. For this in-company work the questionnaire has been modified to fit the needs of the individual company, though Part C remains unchanged throughout, to provide a central basis of inter-company and inter-sector comparison.

Table 2.2 Organizations participating in KIA research.

Industry sector	Denmark	France	Great Britain	Spain	Sweden
Banking	–	–	6	1	1
Hotels	–	2*	2*	–	1*
Retailing	–	–	4	–	–
Travel operators	–	–	5	–	–
Utilities	1	1	2	–	1

* one group represented in all three countries, the other in Britain and France.

continues

continued

The structured questionnaire had three parts:

Part A established background information on job level (three categories: senior or middle management; supervisory; staff), whether the respondent dealt directly with the customer or not, length of service with the company and their perceptions of how recently their organization had undergone major change. In-company work since then has been on a more complex basis, reflecting the specific needs of the client involved and, in particular, allowing for a fourth level of Board or top management.

Whilst responses were strongly affected by job level, they appeared less affected by the other factors. In fact the only other factor which appeared to have any consistent effect was length of service, which, in turn, was related to the industry sector: banks have proportionately many more long-service people; travel and retail many more short-service people. The commentary on results has therefore been limited to industry sector and job level.

Part B sought specific information on respondents' beliefs and perceptions of:

- The factors that would determine the success of their organization – in this, respondents rated both what *they thought were the key objectives* and what they perceived as *the organization's objectives*;
- The factors that would best provide the basis for the achievement of these key objectives – the support objectives or values of the business. Again, respondents were asked to rate both *their own beliefs* and what *they perceived as those of the organization*:
- The consistency of the approach taken by the organization;
- The training they had received in the past year;
- The value of this training in helping them to achieve.

The first two sets of questions in effect tested respondents' perception of and reaction to the objectives and values of the organization. Direct questioning would have been unlikely to have uncovered this or have been able to measure the 'gaps'. The responses to these questions were then mathematically converted to give scores out of five and then plotted to give:

- A direct comparison between '*my belief*' and '*my perception*'.
- The relationship between the results for the various levels of management/staff.

These are plotted into matrices as in Figures 2.1 and 2.2. These show:

- Those results for 'my view' along the bottom, or horizontal, axis.
- Those results for 'perception of company view' along the side, or vertical, axis.
- As a result, those objectives/values where there is a high rating, one way or the other, are either to the right (mine) or towards the top (theirs).

continues

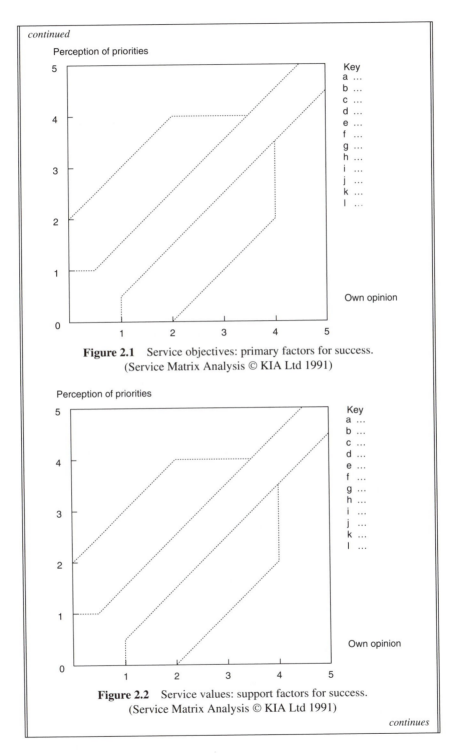

continued

Figure 2.1 Service objectives: primary factors for success.
(Service Matrix Analysis © KIA Ltd 1991)

Figure 2.2 Service values: support factors for success.
(Service Matrix Analysis © KIA Ltd 1991)

continues

continued

- Those objectives/values where there is a consensus are in the middle diagonal band, with high scoring *and* consensus towards the top right.
- Whereas those with an imbalance are spread to the right or left. A secondary boundary line on the chart indicates the division between those results where the imbalance is normal and those where the imbalance is a real concern. The shape of the area of imbalance is determined by the fact that the more strongly a view is held, the more easy it is to create such imbalance or dissatisfaction, a reflection of role conflict, touched on earlier. Conflicts arise over uncertainties about objectives and the methods to achieve those objectives (values). In particular, there will be a high degree of conflict where personal beliefs are not reconciled with the beliefs of the business.

Examples of results are to be found later in this chapter, in Figures 2.11–2.14.

Part C asked a series of questions on perceptions of the culture and style of the company. These covered perceptions of procedures and dealing with customers, their feelings of involvement, the way the organization was managed and the importance of quality. Of these answers, those on quality will be dealt with separately in Chapter 9. The other answers were analysed in depth and then plotted to create 'comparative maps' onto two charts, on structure and style in matrix form. In Figure 2.3, the responses to the balance of structure (questions C1, C3) are plotted on two axes:

(1)   Horizontal, that is left to right: the degree of routine necessary to run that particular business. This is more an outcome of the type of business than anything else, so travel operators are to the left, since they have to work to rigid timetables. However, to an extent, it is possible for an organization to liberate itself from rigid constraints. This information is based on the responses to statements under C3.

(2)   Vertical, that is top to bottom: the way in which this degree of routine is handled. This measure of responsiveness to situations is based on the responses to the statements under C1.

This set of answers has been referred to as service structure, and examples are to be found in Figures 2.7 and 2.8.

In Figure 2.4, the responses to style (questions C2, C4) are also plotted on two axes:

(1)   Horizontal, that is left to right: the degree of involvement felt by management and staff. This information is based on opinions about the statements under C2.

(2)   Vertical, that is top to bottom: the balance toward a control style of management or toward a leadership style. This information is based on the responses to questions under C4.

continues

continued

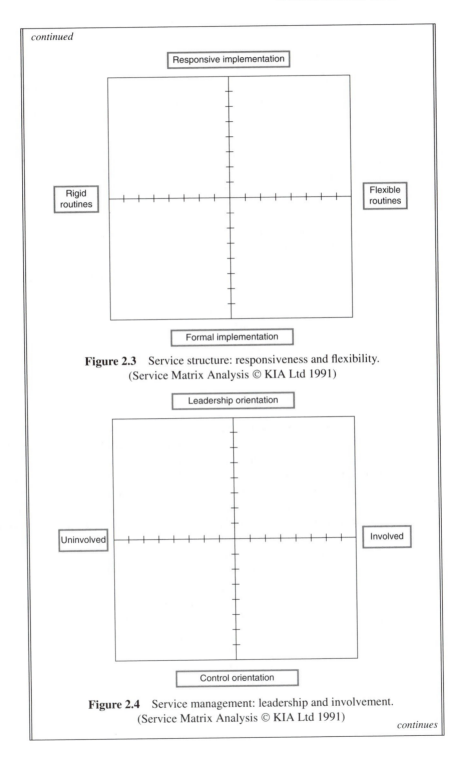

Figure 2.3 Service structure: responsiveness and flexibility.
(Service Matrix Analysis © KIA Ltd 1991)

Figure 2.4 Service management: leadership and involvement.
(Service Matrix Analysis © KIA Ltd 1991)

continues

continued

In this context, control may be seen as 'taking charge of', 'exercising control', 'gaining one's ends'; leadership may be seen as 'going in front', 'encouraging others', 'influencing'. Management involves both, but the correct balance is critical for the development of any particular service strategy. There are also strong links to the 'masculinity-femininity' dimension shown in Table 1.1, and so important implications in terms of social change amongst customers and staff.

This set of answers has been referred to as service management, and examples of results are to be found in Figures 2.9 and 2.10.

Service structure and service management are linked to the question of role ambiguity which arises where the basic structure and systems of the organization are unclear or unbalanced relative to the market task. So, a market aim to be flexible and responsive towards customers would create ambiguity where methods were inflexible or management unwilling to give authority.

For a more detailed outline of the research methodology see Appendix B.

The balance between bureaucracy and enthusiasm has two dimensions. All organizations need basic systems, or routines, which can vary between the rigid and flexible. For some, the very nature of the business imposes rigid restrictions, which may in fact be critical to their success. So, for example, an airline or ferry operator must not only meet exacting time deadlines but may be seen positively as 'good' because timekeeping is important to the customer, too. On the other hand, the implementation of routines involves a balance between formality (an unbending application) and responsiveness (being sensitive to external pressures and immediate issues).

These two dimensions, which together have been titled service structure, can be illustrated by showing the average positioning for all respondents in two of the industry sectors where the research has been conducted to date. This is shown in Figure 2.5. Travel operators are fairly rigid, as we would expect, but are more balanced toward responsiveness. On the other hand, banks do not have such rigid routines, but overall are much less responsive. This would reflect most people's experience and illustrates some of those sector cultural characteristics which are difficult to overcome. Whilst both industry averages group toward the centre, which is a 'true centre' being the average for all results not an arbitrary selection, the results for individual organizations would be seen to vary widely. An illustration of these is shown in Figure 2.6, where the

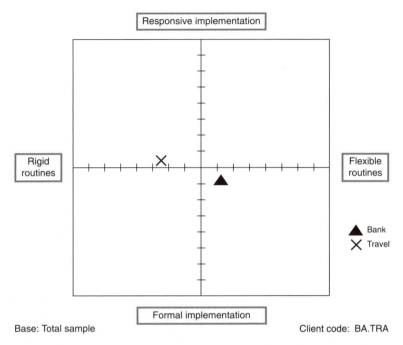

Figure 2.5   Service structure: responsiveness and flexibility. (Service Matrix Analysis © KIA Ltd 1991)

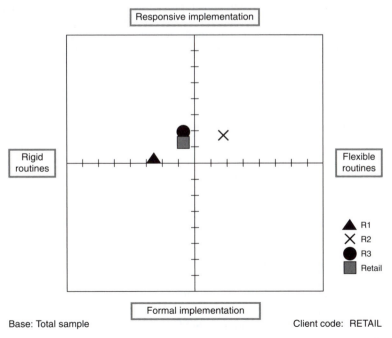

Figure 2.6   Service structure: responsiveness and flexibility. (Service Matrix Analysis © KIA Ltd 1991)

average positioning for retailing is compared with the individual results for three retailers.

In addition, there is the question of the management style. The way in which the business is managed also has two key dimensions in this context. All management needs to be a balance between the demands for control and leadership, although social change is increasingly putting an emphasis on leadership. In a service industry this is of particular significance, as demands to exercise authority at a lower level, close to the customer inevitably conflict with old-style, authoritarian and power-based control management. However, aspiring to leadership for its own sake will not produce results, since creating an ability to act at lower levels also requires involvement.

This set of dimensions has been entitled service management. Unlike service structure there do not appear to be clear industry patterns. All of the previous work had suggested that management cohesiveness was the key to success, and that one should expect to see close-knit patterns of shared values in the answers to our questionnaire. This is largely true, and the research showed successful organizations to have:

- A closer correlation than the average between the answers to the own opinion and perceived actual priorities questions (B1 and B2);
- Less variation in response between different levels of management and staff;
- A much closer grouping of results at all levels in respect of the questions about systems and their implementation (that is service structure).

With service management, however, two patterns were associated with success. Both showed that consistency in perceptions of involvement was important, but:

- In one pattern there was the expected close grouping on both dimensions, producing a cluster;
- In the other, senior management apparently exercised control but staff had the feeling of being led, producing not a cluster but a line, from south to north on the chart. Subsequent work has shown this to be a critical factor and we will discuss this further in the next section.

An example of research

Figures 2.7 to 2.14 inclusive give the results for two organizations using this research, which has been called Culture, Values and Objectives (CVO) Research. Organization 908(M) is a utility; organization 908(V) a retailer.

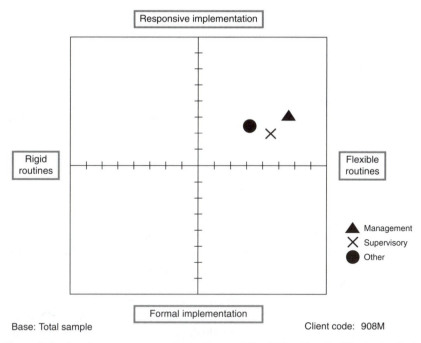

Figure 2.7 Service structure: responsiveness and flexibility. (Service Matrix Analysis © KIA Ltd 1991)

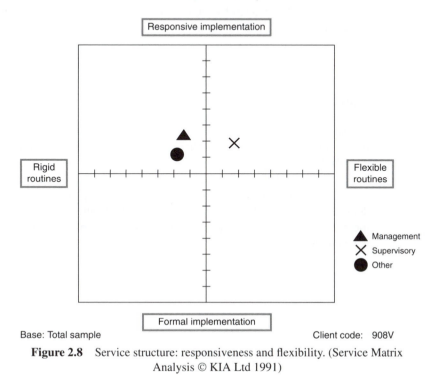

Figure 2.8 Service structure: responsiveness and flexibility. (Service Matrix Analysis © KIA Ltd 1991)

Both have gone through a great deal of change in the past few years and have achieved a high measure of success in this. However, at the time of the research, M's success had been financially consistent and had generated increasing customer satisfaction year-on-year, with a sound attention to building the people within the business as integral to delivery of satisfaction. V, on the other hand, had at the time of research been somewhat ragged with less consistent results, and an ambivalence towards people and cultural issues.

Service structure

Both of these patterns are close or harmonious, that for 908(M) (Figure 2.7) particularly so. Organization V (Figure 2.8) is very close to the average for all retail results (see also Figure 2.6, where V is R3) but M has achieved a very high degree of flexibility in routines, relative to utilities in general. This is no accident. Management identified that the provision of utility services, whether water, gas or telecoms, is largely routine by definition and, therefore, there is a need to demonstrate individuality in dealings with customers through other interactions – dealing with invoicing, complaints, queries and the like. No doubt management will be disappointed by the relative lack of responsiveness but this may be explained by the failure, to date, of getting a clear value basis installed, which we will come to later.

Service management

Again, we see close patterns (Figures 2.9, 2.10) which would suggest, taking into account structure also, that there is a low degree of role ambiguity in both organizations.

This means that there is a great deal of agreement about the match between market aims and reality; the way the business is set-up is seen as matching the demands of delivery. For organization V, despite the high level of involvement, there must be some concern that the organization is so control oriented in this day and age.

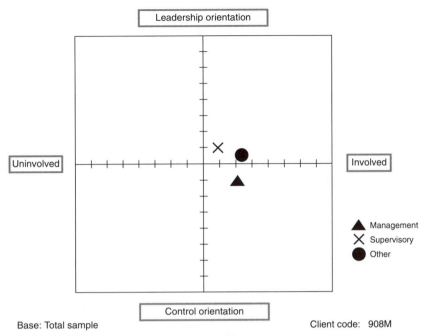

Figure 2.9 Service management: leadership and involvement. (Service Matrix Analysis © KIA Ltd 1991)

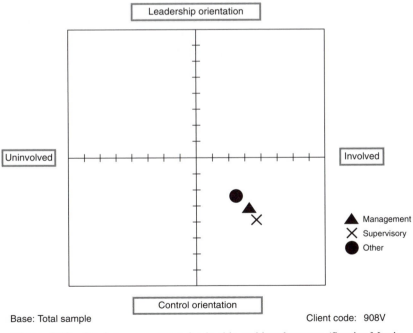

Figure 2.10 Service management: leadership and involvement. (Service Matrix Analysis © KIA Ltd 1991)

Moving to an analysis of the B questions (that is those that seek opinions about objectives and values) we can see clues to this in Figures 2.11–2.14.

Service objectives

In Figure 2.11, organization M has a fairly strong consensus both as regards the balance between own view and perception and between the various levels of respondents, as you can visually judge from the grouping of (a) and (b) etc. In particular, there is a clear belief in satisfied customers, though staff may have some uncertainty. The positioning of responses to keen workforce (f) is not untypical of an organization in change, and whilst a warning signal of possible concerns, is not into any danger zone. The biggest concern would be the spread of responses, with few clear winners but overall there are few role conflicts; that is there is a good balance of personal beliefs with organizational beliefs. (Note that for clarity, in all 'objectives' and 'values' charts, results which would appear in the bottom left-hand corner, have been suppressed.)

In Figure 2.12 by contrast, organization 908(V) has a tendency to polarize between 'my' priorities and 'their' priorities, creating role conflicts, with almost no results falling into the centre channel, though again nothing is in the danger zones. In particular, note the discrepancy in (a) and (c) scores – profits and customers – and especially the positioning of management relative to all other employees. Nevertheless, the *relativity between levels* is quite strong, reflecting the already noted close patterns of structure and management.

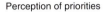

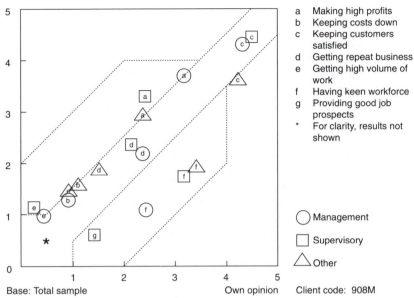

Figure 2.11   Service objectives: primary factors for success. (Service Matrix Analysis © KIA Ltd 1991)

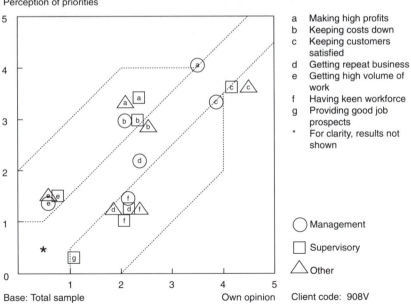

Figure 2.12   Service objectives: primary factors for success. (Service Matrix Analysis © KIA Ltd 1991)

Service values

In Figure 2.13, we can see that organization M has, as yet, failed to establish a clear value base, though there is an overwhelming support for high quality of service. However, such a value – and one which is very general – is insufficient on its own and we can see some signs of cultural stress with sales (b) and staff motivation (f). Getting a clear and accepted basis for values and then living them is going to be a key concern for management, if success is to be sustained.

In Figure 2.14, organization V has an obvious uncertainty about the emphasis on sales – seen even by management as a company preoccupation. As with M, it is difficult to see clearly what is a value in this company. But that is of less importance than the low scoring for so many factors; there is a wide spread of belief and not one generally held belief. Organization V has (or had at that time) yet to come to terms with the role of people within a service and without substantial change would be unlikely to build a strong culture. (This conflict is further illustrated by the quotes at the top of Chapter 3, which are also organization V.)

In summary

Overall, we may see that these two organizations have a well-integrated basis for going forward, with low levels of ambiguity about the match of structure, systems and style relative to the tasks in hand. However, there are potential conflicts – especially for organization V – in terms of their failure to establish sufficiently robust objective and value systems. Left unchecked this would result in a serious erosion of the plans. The players would simply be unable to perform to full effectiveness because beliefs – what 'I think' is important – have not been reconciled. Interestingly, the higher the calibre of staff, the more this becomes a concern, as we shall see in Case 3.1: The PSVR case.

Perception of priorities

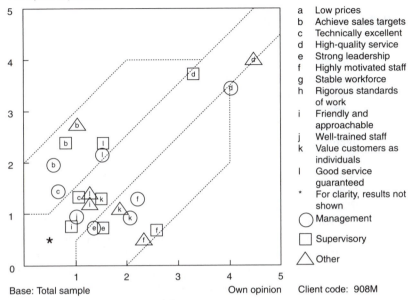

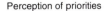

Figure 2.13   Service values: support factors for success. (Service Matrix Analysis
© KIA Ltd 1991)

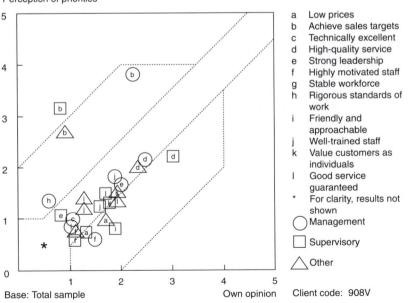

Figure 2.14   Service values: support factors for success. (Service Matrix Analysis
© KIA Ltd 1991)

Management as leaders

The position on the service management matrix has proved to be of substantial significance. As described earlier, unlike all the other measures, whilst close clusters are still a favourable sign, they are not the only pattern of results which accompany success. They can also be in a line from south to north *but management must be to the south*. Even in a cluster result this is still true. If management are at the bottom, that is, more toward control, then all is well. If they are on top, that is, more toward leadership, then the research would suggest this signifies a problem. A typical reason for this may be that, despite what they say, many managers are too involved in 'hands on' aspects of the business, rather than leadership

Although this result at first seemed surprising, in fact it can be seen to make sense. After all, the point of leadership has to be that staff feel led, not that management feel themselves to be leaders. In fact, there appears to be a close correlation between the distance northwards from others and poor cultural health. We have called this result a virtuous link and it will be developed in Chapter 8 on leadership, as well as further illustrated in the next chapter.

This result is also of outstanding significance because it indicates that in a successful service organization:

● It is possible to develop successful management styles where senior management remain in control;
● Yet, at the same time, develop high levels of feelings of leadership with those in the 'front line' – at the point of interaction with the customer.

This has important implications for the future direction of development, especially where there is a need to break away from an authoritarian style while continuing to exercise a large measure of control.

Critical ingredients of this appear to be:

● A very high measure of decentralization;
● Strong central controls;
● A feeling on the part of supervisors and staff that they have some freedom in interpretation, such as for example to make mistakes.

Figures 2.15 and 2.16 illustrate this further. Organizations 908(H) and 908(J) are both banks.

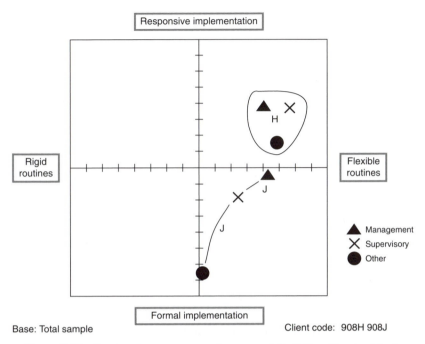

Figure 2.15   Service structure: responsiveness and flexibility. (Service Matrix Analysis © KIA Ltd 1991)

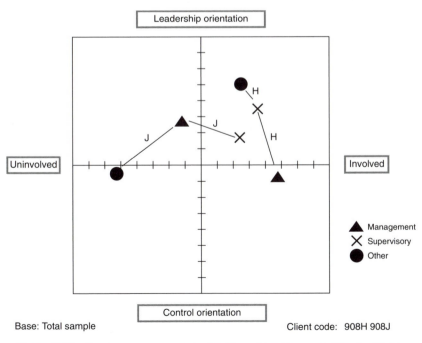

Figure 2.16   Service management: leadership and involvement. (Service Matrix Analysis © KIA Ltd 1991)

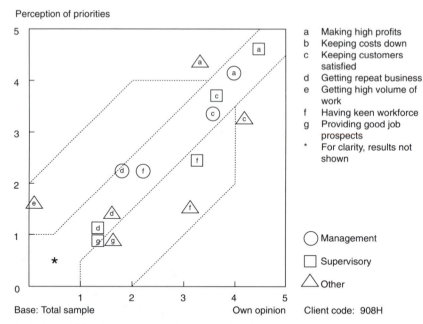

Figure 2.17 Service objectives: primary factors for success. (Service Matrix Analysis © KIA Ltd 1991)

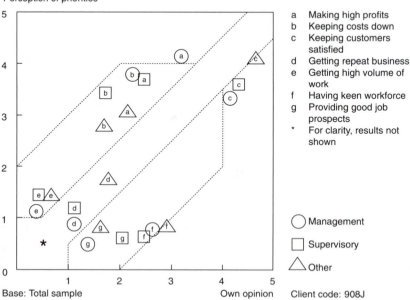

Figure 2.18 Service objectives: primary factors for success. (Service Matrix Analysis © KIA Ltd 1991)

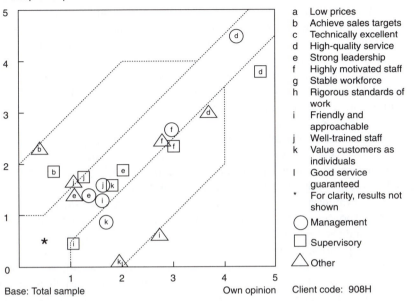

Figure 2.19 Service values: support factors for success. (Service Matrix Analysis
© KIA Ltd 1991)

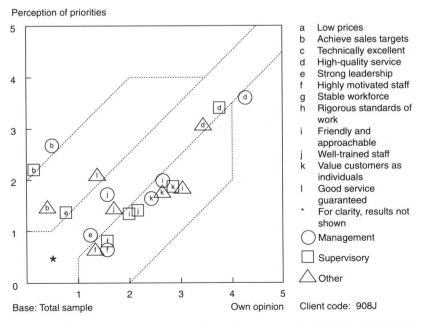

Figure 2. 20 Service values: support factors for success. (Service Matrix Analysis
© KIA Ltd 1991)

Organization H, a consistently successful bank, is an excellent example of the virtuous link. The close cohesion of service structure (Figure 2.15) is matched not by a close cohesion of service management but by a control-led leadership (Figure 2.16) – and indeed the organization concerned has strong central controls allied to a remarkable degree of decentralization.

Organization J, on the other hand, has not yet been able to sustain any marked degree of success; the financial results have been variable, its market position ambiguous. The profiles in Figures 2.15 and 2.16 reflect this lack of cohesion on almost every point.

The same variance between these two organizations may also be seen in the objectives and values in Figures 2.17-2.20. Almost without exception there is consensus within organization H about objectives and, largely, about values too. By contrast, organization J has a much wider spread of results.

It is of importance to note that at an in-company review, the positioning of staff responses within organization H would give rise to some concern. It would indicate, at the least, a need to review current staff perceptions of the bank's position. It must be stressed, however, that the objective of the original KIA/EIU research was to plot broad patterns of culture relative to results, rather than micro cultures within organizations. Such in-depth organizational studies have been completed since and form a large part of the next chapter.

In conclusion

Recognizing that our staff 'live' with our customers is crucial because then the importance of building bridges between 'our world' and 'theirs' becomes not only apparent but also worth the effort. This is not something for a dedicated group of people but for everyone in the organization, not least top management. The less there is role ambiguity and role conflict within the organization, the less conflict there will be between that organization and the customer, and the more the customer is likely to be satisfied.

This customer focus is itself a part of the creation of an harmonious or strong culture and in the next chapter we will look in more depth at what makes a culture.

References

1. Fielding H. (1993). In *The Independent on Sunday*. 7 February
2. Schneider B. and Bowen D.E. (1983). *Employee and customer perceptions of service in banks: replication and extension.* University of Maryland
3. Handy C. (1990). *Inside Organisations.* London: BBC Books
4. KIA Management Consultants, confidential client work (1984–8) and pilot work for the KIA/EIU report (1988–90).

3

Service cultures

'I see culture as very important. It is the indication of why we exist and how we are different. This is important because we do not serve as obvious a [customer] need as some of our competitors.'

'I'm not sure I go along with culture. I'm not sure it's important.'[†]

- Cultures are critical because in a service it is a strong culture which most often gives you a competitive edge – and, in the long run, success.

- The failure of top management to see themselves as the crucial part of this culture – and of any change required – is a key cause of failure.

- The close value patterns of strong or harmonious cultures must also extend to sharing values on managements' roles. Clear views on responsibilities, authorities and management priorities engender confidence towards the customer.

- In fact, cultures are like personalities. The successful ones are those which know enough to be able to build on their strengths and compensate for their weaknesses; strong cultures, like strong personalities, are most likely to succeed.

- Cultural values vary from country to country and even from region to region.

[†] These quotes, taken from the original research for this book, are from two directors of the same company. Not surprisingly, the researcher involved prefaced her report, 'I am finding it difficult to understand or write about this company.'

Why culture?

The overwhelming evidence of our research, both that originated specifically for this book and company-specific work for commercial assignments, shows that the culture of a service organization – that is the way it is organized and thinks and behaves – is critical to its success. Yet most managers are reluctant to accept such evidence – even sometimes in organizations where culture and success are clearly linked. Even where we do see culture being accepted as important – and a recent British Institute of Management (BIM) report [1] showed that respondent managers saw their main role in the future as changing the culture – we still find that top management see themselves as somehow outside of the culture and of the need for change.

Our research – and that of many others – would suggest quite the opposite. *The culture of top management is the critical part of organizational culture and their failure to recognize this is most often the barrier to successful change.*

Culture exists, whether you acknowledge its existence or not. All organizations possess a culture, this being the set of beliefs about the purpose of the organization, the values by which it executes that purpose and the structures and style which have evolved or have been developed to control the organization. Without such a framework it would be difficult, if not impossible, for people to collaborate; with it, it is possible to give direction, at least to some extent, towards common goals.

The need to ensure that culture is orientated externally is particularly severe in a service organization because distinctiveness, a competitive edge, is largely – and in some cases entirely – a reflection of culture. In other words, the external impact of your internal values is critical. Take a simple example. In a manufacturing company, the career ambitions of the majority of staff will never have a direct impact on the customer. The production line worker may have ambitions to be supervisor, managing director, entrepreneur or politician and this may well affect his or her work, but it is unlikely ever directly to affect a buyer. A worker in a service organization – behind a counter, on the 'phone or in your home – will be unable to stop such personal influences coming through. You may not know the reason, but his or her whole way of working will be influenced, for good or bad, by these ambitions.

This influence at individual level is paralleled at organizational level. The culture of the factory floor may affect quality, but the buyers' perceptions will be related to the performance, design and economy of the product. On the other hand, the culture of the airline, the bank, the shop, the hotel – or even more the restaurant, bar or pub – may be precisely what is bought, the reason for choice or satisfaction, even though this may not be explicitly recognized by the customer. However, the quotes at the beginning of this chapter are by no means an uncommon example, if stark in their contradictions.

One of the reasons for such conflicting views is that many managers have viewed talk about culture as indulgent, encouraging introspection and having little, if indeed anything, to do with the real objectives of the business (making a profit, or achieving high levels of care or service) let alone keeping costs under control. This can hardly be surprising. Much attention has been paid to management cultures in the past few years, and most of it is indulgent and introspective, concerned solely with the internal objectives and with the way people interact with each other as members of the team, not with the market. It has done little to show how culture, or its development, can be of value in achieving objectives in the world outside where it matters; how it can provide a bridge between 'our world' and 'their world'.

Even where there has been an attempt to give culture a commercial value, it has all too often failed to maintain this connection. A recent report on company cultures, which emphasized the importance of culture relative to competitiveness, summarized 'why' in 11 points – but never once mentioned the customer![2] Pressures on costs, simplistic analysis, division of responsibility for the customer, the tendency to see cultural issues as soft and without tangible value, have all contributed to this.

A second reason is that top managers feel altogether too threatened if the process of change actually involves them. Typically, they will adopt defensive routines and seek to control the situation by eliminating paradox or possible contradiction. Table 3.1 illustrates this. Taken from the book *Strategy, Change and Defensive Routines* by the American author Chris Argyris (James Bryant Conant Professor of Education and Organizational Behaviour at Harvard University) it represents his Model 1 Theory of reaction, which he goes on to describe as, 'self reinforcing and [so] not particularly good at self-correcting. [It] is so pervasive, it must be taught early in life'.[3] It is also illustrated in Case 3.1, in which the CVO research, described in the previous chapter, was used to help locate, understand, and so breakdown, such barriers.[4]

Table 3.1   Model 1 Theory in use.

Governing values	*Action strategies*	*Consequences*
Control the purpose of the meeting or encounter	Advocate your position in order to be in control and win	Miscommunication
Maximize winning and minimize losing		Mistrust
		Protectiveness
	Unilaterally save face – own and others	Self-fulfilling prophecies
Minimize negative feelings		Seal-sealing processes
Maximize rationality		Escalating error

Source: Chris Argyris, *'Strategy, Change and Defensive Routines'*, Pitman Publishing Inc., 1989.

Case 3.1   The PSVR case

Paul Smidt, van Rijn bv (PSVR) (not its real name) is a successful firm of marine insurers based in Rotterdam. Of the 220 staff, 18 form a top management group, with six of these being 'Executive' members, with general as well as specific responsibilities, whilst the remaining 12 are heads of departments and regional managers. Mainly through acquisition, turnover has doubled over the past three years and staff numbers have increased by over 50%. However, most of the top management group are drawn from the original PSVR team – and this includes all six Executives – or have joined from outside, mainly since the mergers. Despite extremely adverse market conditions losses have been contained to two per cent of the total premium plus linked investment, against an overall market loss percentage substantially in excess of this. Current (1992) results look good.

However, the Chief Executive, Kees Langman, was concerned that the business lacked a clear direction, and that morale was not as good as he would have expected given the high calibre of staff generally and of the new recruits particularly. This was worrying, because a year before PSVR had gone through the process of producing a mission statement and had involved all of the top team – yet it was many of these who appeared to be least supportive.

Paul Smidt, van Rijn bv

Mission statement

PSVR is a worldwide marine insurer working for its customers and providing a guaranteed

- *security*
- *professionalism*
- *quality*
- *personal service*

We seek profitability from long-term partnerships with our clients.

Kees Langman invited a firm of management consultants to look at this problem and their preliminary report confirmed that there were problems.

Paul Smidt, van Rijn bv

Extract from preliminary report by consultants

Summary of impressions:

(1) The overall standard of staff is high, with an impressive enthusiasm, particularly amongst the many younger people in

continues

continued

>   *lower/middle management. They appear constructive and seem to be genuinely concerned to see PSVR succeed.*
>
> *(2)   The Company seems very hierarchical with not only numerous layers of management but a rather formal, unbending attitude towards business and, particularly, new ideas. Cross-departmental communication is poor and frequently routed through top management. For a small company, in particular, this must be of concern.*
>
> *(3)   There is a great deal of frustration with younger managers, many of whom were attracted to PSVR because of the smallness and ability to exercise initiative.*
>
> *(4)   The top management group are frequently described as remote, even 'invisible'.*
>
> *(5)   Empowerment exists but is inconsistent, mainly being 'taken' by a few strong managers – or those with long-term personal contacts with top management. There is insufficient trust and coaching to allow true delegation.*
>
> *(6)   As a result, customer focus is a somewhat haphazard affair. It all depends on 'who' and chance.*
>
> *(7)   The mission statement is not 'owned' below top management. The reasoning and purpose are not understood. What it means to the individual – other than the expectation of him or her saying 'yes' – is unclear. Nor is there any clear link between this statement and the 'way we work'.*
>
> *We strongly recommend a more thorough analysis to identify the precise weak spots and to provide sufficient detail to design a route forward, which will reflect the Company's undoubted strengths.*
>
> *Finally, it must be clearly stated that the cause of most – if not all – of the concerns is the very high degree of motivation to be found in PSVR. They are judging the Company – and its management – from a point of high expectations. Given a correction to these points, the future should be excellent.*

This report was accepted and the core part of the further work undertaken was the usage of the CVO research. This consisted of a specially structured questionnaire, based on that used in the KIA/EIU research (see Chapter 2). The C questions remained unchanged – to provide international and inter-company comparisons – but the B questions were modified to reflect the company's situation. (See charts in Figures 3.1 etc. for criteria.)

In this case, given the small numbers involved, all employees were invited to participate and the 95% uptake confirms the substantial degree of involvement in the concern for the company. The headline results are shown in Figures 3.1–3.4 and give considerable insight into the situation in PSVR.

continues

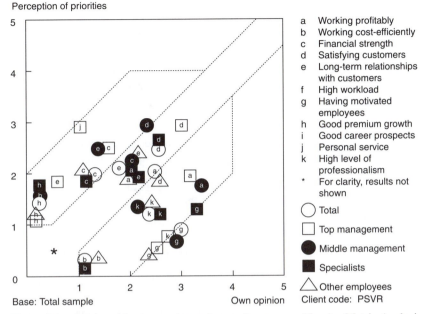

Figure 3.1   Service objectives: primary factors for success. (Service Matrix Analysis © KIA Ltd 1991)

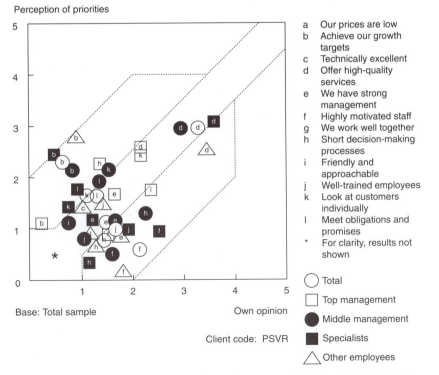

Figure 3.2   Service values: support factors for success. (Service Matrix Analysis © KIA Ltd 1991)

continued

Service objectives (Figure 3.1)

There are no clear, shared objectives. The spread across the bottom left triangle, which is below an imaginary line between the two 5s, suggests that management has not conveyed precisely what the key objectives are.

Grouping of the different levels is no more than average for such an exercise, and management (the top 18, 16 of whom responded) is markedly different.

There are, however, no results in the danger zones (top left/bottom right) but experience would suggest that the positioning of (g), along the edge of this zone, is indicative of an incipient morale problem.

The positioning of (a), (d) and (e) must also give rise to some concern, given the stated objectives of PSVR.

Service values (Figure 3.2)

Again, a wide spread of results. The organizational imperatives, which should govern behaviour toward achievement of objective, are not at all clear.

Grouping is still only average, or a little above, with management again the obviously different group.

For the size/nature of the company, the positioning of (d) is surprisingly low. The positioning of (g) and (h) must be seen as of concern, given the objectives of PSVR.

Service structure (Figure 3.3)

The positioning on the horizontal (routines) is typical of the industry, but that on the vertical (implementation) is below average, except for management, which is average.

The causes of this difference are:

- Management feel less hindered by procedures
- similarly, management feel more able to make mistakes.

Service management (Figure 3.4)

The positioning on the horizontal axis (involvement) is below average for the industry, that on the vertical axis (style) is confused.

Based on other interview work within PSVR, we incline to the belief that the low horizontal (involvement) scores are more due to a lack of under-standing than a lack of knowledge. The position of management north of everyone else , on the vertical, suggests a typical change drift, with failure to carry others and incipient, if not real, isolation. It may also be a reflection of a 'hands-on' tendency, either from a lack in trust in others or lack of self-confidence.

Overall, the positioning of management must give rise to concern. They are different, or have different perceptions, on almost every score, on all charts.

continues

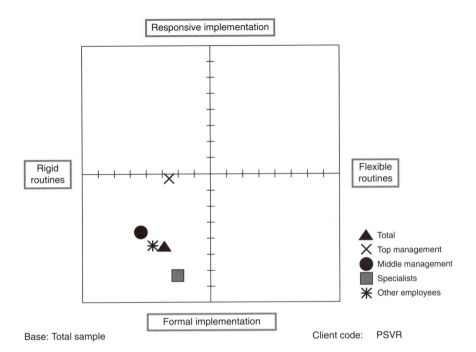

Figure 3.3 Service structure: responsiveness and flexibility. (Service Matrix Analysis © KIA Ltd 1991)

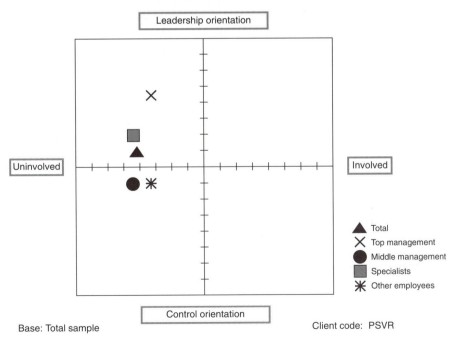

Figure 3.4 Service management: leadership and involvement. (Service Matrix Analysis © KIA Ltd 1991)

continued

Further action

The overwhelming evidence of the CVO research (linked to the previous observations) convinced top management – after a number of extremely fraught meetings – that they were the barrier to success. They not only needed a personal commitment to change, but had to carry it through and be seen to do so. This would require considerable personal training and input, on their part. Further, it was necessary to produce a fresh mission statement, which set out the purpose and beliefs of PSVR more clearly and could be employed as an active guide. (This is shown in Chapter 6 on strategy.) This was produced by a much wider group and subsequently introduced at a series of meetings which involved all staff, allowing – indeed encouraging – debate.

The realization of this key management problem – and the catharsis that accompanied it – released an enormous flood of energy and a detailed programme of information, questioning, involvement and development. This included:

- An introductory series of discussion groups on the mission statement, what it meant and the action to be taken. These meetings involved all middle managers and supervisors and subsequently, on a section-by-section basis, all staff.
- A reorganization of activities, based on customer groups, rather than function.
- A re-appraisal of marketing effort and a segmentation of customers by agreed criteria of 'relationships'.
- Increased expenditure on non-technical development and training.
- A strategic initiative to identify long-term developments and their implications for an organization of the size and culture of PSVR.

Perhaps the most important benefit has been the understanding of the fact that good plans were not enough; that the organization not only had to want to achieve them but had to be able to do so through its culture – that set of beliefs about the purpose, the values by which that purpose is executed and the structure and style of the organization. Top management forms the critical factor in this. As Kees Langman said, 'Without the CVO research, we would have had difficulty in accepting the real problem. With it, we could not avoid it. In fact, it has helped us to completely change the focus of what we do, away from our products, to our people. It will take time to realize the full investment but already (two months later) we can feel the benefit'.

The importance of culture

As Case 3.1 shows, the culture of an organization plays a significant part in its success or lack of it. The real importance of the research undertaken for this book is that it is at last possible to take culture out of the realms of purely internal, often indulgent, activities and see and treat it as part of the strategic assessment of market positioning and commercial advantage. This involves paying attention to the following:

(1) Making an assessment of where an organization is now, and 'designing' a way forward to where it needs to be; understanding its strengths and weaknesses, not in some abstract way but with direct reference to the needs for external achievement.
(2) Being sharply aware of the potential dangers attaching to a particular course of action in terms of change. In terms of service structure this may seem simple – 'routines' are less critical than being 'responsive' in implementation. But this is deceptive. Such responsiveness requires some fundamental considerations of management. Either it is necessary to achieve a cohesion of style, with a broad acceptance of the values among all of the players, or it is necessary to create a 'virtuous link', building strong central controls together with significant decentralization.

   The dangers of an unplanned approach to change are illustrated in Figure 3.5, which identifies the values that attach to the extremes of different styles of service management. With too little understanding of the current management

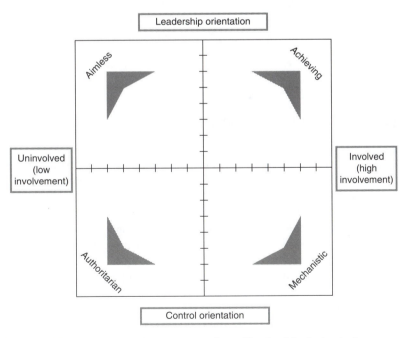

Figure 3.5   Service management: extreme values. (Service Matrix Analysis
© KIA Ltd 1991)

position and too little concern for the destination, a move to create greater responsiveness to external issues (one which calls for an emphasis on leadership rather than control) will be more likely to achieve aimlessness than focused activity, because the leadership, the inspiration, is creating no sense of direction. Everyone is excited at the prospects but they don't quite know what these are or where they are going!

This may seem an unusual situation but it is, in fact, quite common; without clear objectives for change and control the whole process rapidly starts to 'drift'. Indeed, it is a critical part of the problem for PSVR in Case 3.1. As a further example, analysis of the strategic implementation assignments of a service consultancy shows that fully three-quarters of them fall into a category of 'rescuing' such situations. Evidence of failure of this kind to this degree is supported by the reports quoted in Chapter 1, which suggest that the overwhelming majority of service improvement initiatives fail to achieve success.

It is also possible to see that the pursuit of involvement without leadership may simply create a mechanistic situation where staff know what they have to do but take little pleasure in doing it and do not display much creativity. In such situations it will be difficult to achieve sustained responsiveness because there will be little of the sense of personal responsibility necessary to create individuality at the interaction. There may well be enthusiasm, but customers will tend to be targets – 'punters' even, to quote a term which almost always seems to indicate lack of concern for the customer – rather than partners in a relationship. In fact, 'punters' is precisely how management and staff often referred to customers in organization V, quoted in Chapter 2.

Change through people

The root of the problem is that in a service business creating change in cultures can only be achieved through people. But is such an emphasis on people simply a passing fashion? This seems unlikely, given that the service revolution is, in fact, allied closely to the shifts occasioned in society as a whole. (See Chapter 1.) These changes are real and deep and may be seen more realistically as a series of steps forward in a society which – increasingly educated, increasingly wealthy, increasingly seeking fulfilment through something more than simply working (or even pleasure) – is moving away from accepting authoritarian roles and toward the desire to be treated more as individuals.

This shift has profound consequences for any service business. That customers want to be treated as individuals provides an opportunity to create a commercial advantage from service; but the corollary of this is that the very people who have to perform the service also want to be treated as individuals. Unless this is clearly understood, then the seeds of destruction of change are sown at the same time as the seeds of creation.

Box 3.1   The role of the individual

The role of the individual in a service organization assumes such importance because:

(1) It is only at the interaction points between the organization and its customers that the 'product' is finally made.
(2) In these 'moments of truth' it is the ability of the individual involved to meet and cope successfully with these necessarily unstructured, or at best semi-structured, interactions which decides the outcome – customer satisfaction or dissatisfaction.

The term 'moments of truth' is an allusion to the final moment in a bull-fight when the matador is alone and was first developed by the Swedish consultant Richard Normann [5].

Further, and in general terms, the higher the desired value added to a basic core concept or idea – the 'plane seat, the insurance policy, the hotel bed – the greater the element of variability in the interaction.

But in every case that final interaction will be individual. This is because:

(1) Customers themselves are involved in the formation of the final interaction. They can be the disruptive element in your plans, just like the opposing team in a game. This is true even where the interaction is with a machine – a cash machine, a ticket machine or a computer terminal.
(2) Each interaction between the organization and the customer is being individualized by the customer. Customers find it difficult to distinguish between one service and another in the same field. Customers finally make their decision not by considering the intrinsic values of the service offering itself (they rarely have the knowledge or even information to make such a judgement) but by transference of the 'offering' – including particularly their perceptions of this – to themselves: 'Does this organization, does this person, understand me and my problem? Will they help me solve it?'

This is the critical area of managing a service: the need to translate the, necessarily, average plans of the service organization into individual – and successful – interactions. These interactions are both the final production process and the point of consumption, involving both the organization and the customer. The degree of structure in this is linked to the value added to the

continues

continued

basic core idea or product, but in all cases it will be individual to those involved since it is through transference to the individual situations that decisions are made or perceptions formed.

There is ample proof for this. For example, a recent piece of research showed that the primary factor in customers' perceptions of service was the ability and willingness of staff to be non-routine, to bend the rules to meet individual need, even if it was just to deal with an enquiry in the customer's order of concern and not in some pre-planned sequence.

Turning the final moment of truth – the key experiences of the customer – into success thus depends crucially on the development of individual responsibility. But this individual responsibility must also be developed as a part of a team, where interpersonal competence is part of the way in which the individual responds to the formal organization.

What is meant by interpersonal competence? Most writers suggest that it comprises five major elements:

(1)   The capacity to receive and send information and feelings reliably.
(2)   The capacity to evoke the expression of feelings in others.
(3)   The capacity to process information and feelings reliably.
(4)   The capacity to take action based on accurate perceptions.
(5)   The capacity to learn from one's experience of oneself.

Listening as a critical skill

Listening is the critical skill in this – not simply hearing, but listening, one definition of which is: 'The integrated usage of the five senses on the part of both sender and receiver, leading to effective perception of the spoken and unspoken communications between people.'

Listening is the critical skill because research and experience show that:

- Customers 'individualize' among service offerings through a belief that their choice is most likely to solve their problem – and they reach this decision through a perception of having been listened to.
- This is also true of the ongoing relationship, particularly at points of discontinuity, as for example at a time of complaint, renewal or change in personal circumstances.
- Such behaviour at the staff/customer interaction works successfully only when the climate of the organization – its culture, its reward systems – reflects the same values; that is, listening is valued and seen to be valued within the organization and role conflict is reduced to a minimum.

Listening and communication

Listening, as we define it, is about completing the cycle of communication by ensuring understanding of what has been said (or written or implied). It emphasizes that what is important in this is not 'what I say' but 'what people hear and understand' – for it is on this basis that they will act. Sometimes there is a complete match between these two. More often, though, there is a substantial difference, and for good reasons:

continues

continued

- People's thought processes – the way in which they relate to each other and assimilate information – vary from individual to individual;
- As part of this, we usually adopt a filtering process, based on preconceptions, which can give pre-set values to what people say – or what we think we hear;
- We can think, on average, four times faster than we talk, so we have plenty of time to develop our thoughts between the words, and this may be directed toward the subject in hand or to other non-related subjects;
- This ability is severely affected by disturbance to the system – emotion, other distractions, tiredness and so on;
- We can retain only a proportion of what we hear – typically we retain at most 50% for a few hours, and no more than 20/25% 48 hours later.

Individual responsibility

To summarize, the individual's ability and willingness to accept personal responsibility is the key. Willingness though, is more than personal willingness, in the sense of wanting; it is also being prepared to participate, to listen, and knowing that it is this behaviour which is the organizational imperative, which management want and will reward.

Change highlights values

Many of the organizations in this project had experienced, or were going through, a period of major change. For almost everyone involved this had highlighted the significance of the values involved in the way the organization worked or the way in which it now had to work. Lars Nørby (Chief Executive of Falck, and previously a key executive with the largest Danish insurance company, Baltica) has stated, 'The values here are quite different. In Baltica everybody was very willing but the aim was to be correct, to do it right and be fair. Here, the only judgement is, "Is it good?", rather than correct; and it needs to be fast. In fact we have a slogan, "Fast Help is Good Help". People don't ask, "Are you entitled?" but do it – and ask after. They say, "Do your best, do it now".'

The attitude that service is about doing it well, rather than 'correctly', is echoed by Guy de Panafieu, Managing Director of Lyonnaise des Eaux, 'If we see something needs doing [with a customer], we do it first and discuss "who pays?" afterwards. We are in it for the long-term and this [attitude] is a sound investment. But such values are not shared by everyone. We always used to steer clear of becoming involved in construction work, because we saw the contractors as "hunters" who were interested in making a "kill" and then moving on. Essentially we are "farmers", though maybe given the attitudes in construction and the long-term nature of our business, "conquerors" and "foresters" are better analogies; we know we will be here tomorrow and that we have to live with the results. However, more and more we are realizing that even when customers start a project, of say, building an office, they don't want to be "hunted"; they want to get the value of the investment over the lifetime of its use – a "farming" concept. So we have gone back into construction [with the merger with Dumez], but this time as part of the service, so that there is no break between building and the running of it afterwards. That's a big cultural problem we have to tackle. To integrate the values of service into the initial construction of a project – whether it's a new waterworks, or a new bridge – and create a unity out of both this [construction] and the service maintenance, once it has been built.'

Woolworths probably has a bigger task than most – and the greatest ambitions – starting from a point where not only were its financial results poor and its High Street presence clearly no longer in tune with customer expectations, but its staff were also held in low esteem. 'People [used to be] spoken of as dirt – they were scared,' said one middle manager who had lived through the change. Mair Barnes, Managing Director, recounts her first store visit, where the manager asked as a quick aside when she arrived, 'How do you want me to refer to you?' Unsure if the question concerned whether she preferred to be Mrs or Ms or how her name should be pronounced, she replied, 'Some call me Mrs Barnes, but I'm happy to be referred to as Mair.' 'Oh, no,' replied the manager, 'we call directors "Sir" and I was unsure whether we should say "Ma'am" or "Madam".' Little wonder that personnel director Leo McKee commented, 'We found that few managers really understood what they had to do to implement our plans. We have had to go back and work harder at that.'

Handelsbanken management say, 'It was tough at first; some managers failed to adjust'. 'It took some years.' 'We still have to work at it.' (after 20 years) and, 'We [still] have to be prepared to deal with people who cannot measure up to the values of responsibility – probably much more than most organizations have to elsewhere.'

Organizations which have built their success over many decades by growth from a strong national basis or from a local culture or family influence look to the future with some concern. They appreciate that the very strength of their past success has the potential to frustrate their need to create changes in the way people work. One Lufthansa manager said, 'We have been almost too effective in delivering a reliable service. Trying to be more responsive, to meet competition from previously backward competitors, is going to be tough.' Sainsburys' David Quarmby echoes this, 'Our characteristic is a strong, hands-on management style. But as the company grows larger, we have to empower a greater number of management throughout the organization. We must help them take risks; accept the odd mistake, and help them learn from it. That means we [top management] have to give a little too. We cannot simply put in a new "rule book". Enabling has to come from a complete change of management emphasis.'

So, while good plans are essential, the critical task of service management is implementation; taking the purpose of the business and turning it into action at the point of interaction – delivering the promise, through people, to people. The importance of this need for emphasis on people in creating new values is illustrated in the Cases 3.2 and 3.3.

Case 3.2   Creating change

Wessex Water was one of the water authorities privatized by the British government in 1990. Like most public authority businesses of its kind it had a spirit of customer-mindedness which was essentially technically based: it knew what was 'right' and the consumer was at best a fortunate target. As one long-serving manager said, 'We really did think we knew best'.

Inevitably, therefore, the organization was bureaucratic and the engineering aspects were overemphasized at the expense of building relationships, even though Wessex's history of technical excellence was good. It had the best compliance record on sewage treatment and, unlike most British water companies, it had not had to impose restrictions on water usage in dry spells.

Nicholas Hood, who took over as Chairman to steer the company to privatization and bring about the necessary changes in the business says, 'I was pleasantly surprised at the quality of people I found. However, they had been "protected" from the market, not only by their position as a public authority but also by management attitudes. Management, top management, were not visible and one of the first things we did was to reduce the layers of management from 7 to 5. Then we started the process of making engineering the servant of the customers, and not the other way round – and of getting people to be open about the problems.'

Managers echo this down the line, 'We have been given more responsibility and are beginning to understand it's OK to learn through mistakes,' and, 'Even if we don't have the responsibility officially, and we can see that if it needs to be done, we can take [the decision].' But the cultural difficulties in doing this in an open environment are illustrated by another comment, 'We really did take pride in being the 'silent service'. Now we have pulled out concerns about quality and we inform and educate customers. It's a big change. We are more public in the private sector than when we were in the public sector!'

Nicholas Hood and his colleagues have attempted to tackle this with a series of parallel efforts:

continues

continued

- Defusing rumours by working quickly through staff communications and the union and setting up a 'rumour' hot-line. Anyone can ring a member of top management and get an answer. 'We can't stop the rumour machine,' said one manager, 'but at least we show we are not ducking the issues.'
- Introducing a reward system which emphasizes involvement, profit, personal responsibility and the long-term nature of the business.
- Emphasizing quality and the teamwork necessary to achieve this.

'We still have a long-way to go. It will take years,' said one senior manager, 'and we are still inclined to arrogance – "Wessex is best" – but we feel we're in something which is progressive and getting somewhere.' Another added, 'We have an enthusiastic group at the top but down on the ground, in middle management, we still have a lot to do. They are trying to take responsibility and improve efficiency but it is such a fast rate of change to get used to – and with that dedication and loyalty goes a certain amount of bureaucracy and autocracy. We could retreat into complacency.'

Nicholas Hood doubts this, '95% of Wessex staff own shares in their own company and most of them used their own money to do this. So they share in the success or failure, the praise or the criticism – and all their neighbours are Wessex customers, too.'

Case 3.3   A story of change

One of the major Woolworths sites is the distribution depot in Castleton near Rochdale. Housed in an old cotton mill, the building is still undergoing refurbishment. The personnel staff at Castleton – Christine Bridge, Claire Schofield and Carole Shepherd – relate how the change in people has taken place, too:

'People are much more relaxed now. There used to be bells for everything. It was like a schoolroom, lino throughout, and people felt like battery hens.

Change happened gradually but really started when the split with the US operation came in 1982. There was then a less paternalistic, "here for life" mentality about the board.

In the old days, anybody could get a job – and did. They would drag people off the street. You had to ask permission to go the toilet and were timed. There was instant dismissal if you were found running in the corridor.

continues

continued

Only managers were allowed to smoke. There was no give and take. If the bell went for a break when you were on the 'phone you couldn't come back from a break a few minutes late. "We abide by the bell." Mr/Mrs/Miss, no first names. Now it's first name terms, friendly and relaxed.

But that old regime did give security and reassurance. There was always a Christmas party and a director on site. A lot of older women still say Mr and one or two [of the men] still prefer to be called that way. There is an element of nostalgia for the past. Long servers have had to struggle through change.

They are now into setting objectives, added value and contribution. The pay review is only one way of recognition. People are recognized as doing well by the way they are treated.'

A personality approach

It was Oscar Wilde who said, 'It is personalities not people who move the age', and it seems too that services with a strong personality will be the ones to succeed. This link between personal and organizational behaviour and attitudes is mirrored in the fact that cultures are essentially personalities. As the research indicates, being clear about what you are – and having the insight to relate this to market need – is more important than anything else in making services successful.

One interesting insight into the parallel between different individuals and company culture is given by the use of the personality analysis method, 'Personality Structure'.[6] Briefly, 'Personality Structure' is designed to help individuals understand how their personality impacts on their relationship with other people and is, in turn, impacted upon by the personality of others.

Work carried out in Germany and Switzerland by the originator of this method, Rolf Schirm, has also shown that it can be applied to the 'personality' or culture of organizations: 102 factors are fed into the model and the 'image' of the organization is then shown in the form of a polar chart, with three colours making up the whole. Each of these colours has a value:

- The green part of the models signals warmth, humanity and sympathy but also reliability, traditionalism and consistency, though with a tendency to resist change;
- The red part signals dynamism and ambition, but also aggressiveness and a tendency to quick solutions;
- The blue part signals rationality, detached objectivity and forward planning, but also complexity and a tendency to perfection.

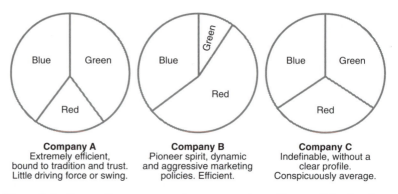

Company A
Extremely efficient,
bound to tradition and trust.
Little driving force or swing.

Company B
Pioneer spirit, dynamic
and aggressive marketing
policies. Efficient.

Company C
Indefinable, without a
clear profile.
Conspicuously average.

Figure 3.6 Personality structure and company culture. (*Source:* © Institut für Biostruktur – Analysen AG (IBSA))

Some examples of such models are shown in Figure 3.6.

Schirm says, 'It might be supposed that the ideal organization would come from a balance of all three areas. This has been proved wrong. Equal addressing of all three areas leads to neutrality, giving an average profile. On the other hand, a clear dominance of colour (personality characteristics) indicates a strong lasting impression.... That goes for the company culture as well as for marketing programmes.'

So culture, like personality, is at its most valuable when it reflects clear strengths.

What sort of culture?

What is the right sort of culture? Apart from hard work and stubbornness, what makes a good culture?

(1) It would be a mistake to believe that it is soft. None of the successful organizations we talked to saw it as that. For example Nicholas Hood, of Wessex Water, says, 'We value service but we are not here to appease our customers, rather to serve them.' Arne Mårtensson at Handelsbanken puts it even more bluntly, 'The values of customer care are hard, not soft. You make profit from customers.'

(2) *What* culture you have is less important than the need to have a culture which is specific, strong, linked to the market objectives and consistent. You need a 'personality' which is simple, strong and clear.

(3)   Unless staff and customers are prepared to play their part, then, quite literally, the market solution does not exist. Helpful, friendly service depends on staff being helpful and friendly all of the time, or at least in the overwhelming majority of cases, and on customers responding to this and valuing it.

(4)   Similarly, not making a drama out of a crisis depends not only on staff *not* making a drama for the customer when he or she is in a crisis, but also on customers not being over-creative at dramas either! Indeed, you may have an obligation to 'educate' customers or staff may fail, regardless of effort.

(5)   To reach this point, staff and customers have to feel involved, be made accomplices in the achievement of such aims.

(6)   Being helpful and friendly, not creating dramas, these aims must be integral to the values of the organization if they are to be of commercial value, a part of profitability.

National/regional differences

Although cultures have universality there are, nevertheless, important differences characteristic of national or regional cultures. Organizational cultures are less a function of market demand, at least in the conventional sense, than of collective cultural expectations, on the part of both staff and customers, of what is right or reasonable. For example:

- We may see real and sharp differences in what is expected in restaurant service, at similar levels of price, between, say, the USA and Western Europe.
- Within Europe, a Swiss expects the 6.05 train to leave at 6.05 and finds it reasonable, in order that good time-keeping can be achieved, not to be able to board it after 6.04; an English person might see this as unfair – so long as they were there by 6.05 why shouldn't they be allowed on?

Such differences in collective expectations, in particular those between the USA and Europe, are quite marked across most areas of activity:

- American service organizations which have achieved wide success have generally done so through being routine, but then applying responsiveness (for example McDonalds or Holiday Inns). There are few surprises, if few moments of exceptional service.
- In contrast, the majority of European organizations which have achieved wide success have done so not so much through being routine, but rather by delivering from a less regulated, more flexible basis. Often this results in a degree of variability or even inconsistency, which you may see as 'charm' or 'incompetence', depending on the situation!

These are broad generalizations and there are many individual exceptions, both within Europe and in the USA. In particular, countries such as Germany or Switzerland produce a considerable number of more routine examples, and some of the exceptions to the rule are among the examples in this book However, this difference between the US and Europe runs deep, as though it were part of a profound cultural divide, and is much greater than the differences within Europe. It is interesting to note that the general thrust of American business writing on services has been toward creating structure – removing the sources of conflict between customer and staff through direct structuring of the interaction and, where possible, putting operations 'out of sight' where they can be more controlled.

European moves, in contrast, have tended to be the other way. As Jan Carlzon at SAS has said, 'We found that most costs [of the organization] were in the delivery of the service – human resources mainly. So we moved staff from the back-office to dealing with the customer where they could be of more value.' Virgin Atlantic have also stressed the unstructured element, the ability to create 'memorable moments'.

There are some compelling illustrations of this contrast from outside the world of business. Take sport for instance. Which is the only major country in the world to be unenthusiastic about the free-flowing, relatively rule- and stoppage-free sport of soccer? The USA. Americans prefer the short set-piece, the greater 'routine' of American football. Formula One car racing is less popular in the US than almost anywhere else; instead, such high-powered racing is dominated by the 'Indy formula' – where cars are bunched up behind the leader (that is, subjected to a routine) by a marshal as soon as the field gets drawn out.

So, in devising service cultures it is vital to take account of the collective cultural expectation in that country or region. The cultural research so far indicates that:

- Scandinavian organizations demonstrate overall a much greater responsiveness in implementation, linked to greater orientation towards leadership and the creation of higher levels of involvement.
- British and French organizations are similarly poised as regards responsiveness in implementation, but:
  - French organizations are more biased toward control
  - British organizations have lower scores on involvement, though this difference with France is not dramatic.
- Swiss organizations have much closer cultural cohesion.

However, the true nature of such cultural differences is much deeper than these few superficial comments might suggest. Charles Hampden-Turner, Senior Research Fellow at the London Business School and author of many works on business culture, wrote recently, about a *Harvard Business Review* 'World Leadership Survey'[7], '[The Survey] assumes that psychological factors like people's opinions and attitudes are critical to understanding larger social, cultural and economic practices. But this is simply not the way that members of many of the world's cultures think.   In particular, Asian and (European) Continental cultures prefer to start by discerning a meaning in the larger whole that is endorsed by the group and then showing how this pattern repeats itself in multitudes of small details.' He goes on to say that failure to understand this led to a failure to understand the subtleties of differences between cultures, because, for example, it changes the attitudes towards and reaction to concepts such as competition, free trade and what signifies cooperation. This has important implications for anyone attempting to replicate a service in another culture.

In conclusion

There are, therefore, a number of significant factors to recognize with regard to culture in a service business:

(1)   All service organizations have a culture. The only question is whether or not it is recognized and forms a distinct 'personality' with clear values.

(2)   The link between internal culture (what happens within the organization) and customer perceptions is direct.

(3)   Top management is a key part of this. It is their failure to see themselves as *part* of the change – not simply authorising it – which accounts for most service failures.

(4)   Just as the internal culture is a result of the attitudes, behaviour and beliefs of both management and staff, so the external culture is a result of the attitudes, behaviour and beliefs of both organizational personnel and customers.

(5)   Because of this linkage, customers help shape the culture. They participate directly in the final processes of forming the service they receive, and their expectations and reactions are a key part of conditioning performance. As any actor will confirm, different audiences can elicit widely different performances.

(6)   The result – which is of profound consequence at both a strategic and operational level – is that your culture is a key part of what the customer buys.

(7)   The value of any culture is a factor of:
   • The market values – the expectations and perceptions of the market, relative to your business and national characteristics;
   • The position you need to occupy in that market – whether you need to be a highly routine-based organization;
   • The ability to match internal cultural, and specifically management, values to effectively directing the implementation, creating customer experiences which meet or exceed expectations;

(8)   These key values need to be simple, clear and direct and should be shared by everyone as part of their own beliefs as well as perceptions of the company's aims.

Whatever your culture, it is most important that it is strong and clear in these values and that you attain them on a consistent basis.

References

1.   British Institute of Management (1990). *Beyond Quality*
2.   Hampden-Turner, C. (1990). *Corporate Culture for Competitive Edge*. London: Economist Publications
3.   Argyris C. (1989). *Strategy, Change & Defensive Routines*. Pitman
4.   KIA Management Consultants, confidential client work, 1992
5.   Normann R. (1984). *Service Management*. Chichester: John Wiley & Sons
6.   *Personality Structure* (Struktogramm) is C. Institut für Biostruktur-Analyzen AG (IBSA), Zug CH, and is reproduced by permission of the licensees for the UK, KIA Ltd
7.   Hampden-Turner C. (1991). World Leadership Survey. In *Harvard Business Review*, September/October. © 1991 the President and Fellows of Harvard College, all rights reserved

4

The importance of vision

- For a service to be successful in the long-term, there is a need for a vision, a sense of mission, which is not only shared by all but stems from their own beliefs.

- This vision should help employees to see their tasks in terms which create worth to others.

- To break down the barriers to creating a vision, it is necessary to create a framework, using an understanding of 'our' culture.

- The vision should be expressed as a mission statement which must reflect and explain this vision in terms everyone can understand and subscribe to and which can guide their daily activity.

Creating a vision

The existence of a vision – the organization's view of itself beyond the immediacy of existence – is a critically important feature of almost every service which people generally admire. McDonalds and British Airways – to name but two – are organizations which have created a clear vision to direct their activity and guide their actions. Of course, this carries penalties. British Airways found that if staff – and customers – have bought into a strong vision, then they expect the organization to live by it. For BA, their recent traumas have been most felt by staff, who see their trust, *their beliefs* (for they have come to see them as theirs too) betrayed, as letters in numerous issues of the BA staff newspapers have testified. McDonalds are arguably handicapped by the very strength of their vision, a standardized, technological approach which reduces the 'interference' of people – staff and customer alike – but delivers consistency and value for money. As markets become more demanding and individual, there are signs that McDonalds' formula will work against them. But then few formulae have perpetual acceptance.

Maybe it was this which led John Major to say recently to a group of American students, 'I am not sure I agree with vision. People with vision have often done as much harm as good'. Of course, in one sense he is right since if visions are powerful then the wrong vision will be powerfully wrong or will act as a constraint. But whether that means that visions, *per se,* are wrong is questionable and indeed there is strong evidence to suggest that Britain's problems, not just those of the current Government, are due to a lack of vision, as was seen, to an even greater degree, in France in 1945–56.

Such visions formed a key constituent of the companies in our research. However, not all visions are necessarily written down or are articulated well, but without there being a key character, almost always as Chief Executive, to provide a clear embodiment of the vision (as in our research with Jerome Monod at Lyonnaise des Eaux and Richard Branson at Virgin Atlantic) then a written vision is likely to be a vital influence. This is because without a symbol, not enough people will be able to share a sufficient understanding to carry the vision forward. Indeed, in Lyonnaise des Eaux there were clear signs that it was difficult to transmit the vision to full effect through a large organization without greater effort (despite Monod) and in Virgin Atlantic the official mission statement fell short of the vision that everyone knew, accepted and worked to. (For a fuller insight into Virgin Atlantic's vision, see Chapter 11.)

However, whatever the weight to be attached to the part of the Chief Executive, there can be no doubt the creation of the vision for an organization is one of his or her key tasks to be undertaken in conjunction with his or her fellow leaders. Without a vision it is difficult, if not impossible, to create that sense of unity of purpose which will overcome functional and personal differences. The absence or presence of the role ambiguities and conflicts discussed earlier is heavily dependent on some clear centralizing purpose, which must be expressed in a way which others can understand and commit to as if it were their own creation.

In some cases, Sainsburys for example, this vision, like the culture, of the business is deeply rooted in the history of the company and in the driving ideals of the founders. The problem is to maintain this in an updated form which matches market and employee perceptions and beliefs, itself a difficult task and one the company is tackling as a high priority. However, for most organizations it is going to be a question of either developing such a vision from scratch or refining it from existing or previously stated positionings. This is, or should be in turn, the central core of a framework for the entire business; the culture which controls and drives the way it works, and which provides guidance as to the organizational imperatives in daily execution. Such a framework is to be found in some mission statements.

However, the mission statement must be more than just a document. It is simply the tangible expression of a deeper sense of belief in the vision of the organization (as we have seen with Virgin Atlantic). The mission statement has also formed the basis for the success of organizations as diverse as Handlesbanken and Saga. Further, it is the development of vision which lies behind the transformation of Televerket, Wessex Water and Woolworths over the past few years, and to take a quite different example, it is seen by the originator of the Swatch, Nicolas Hayek, as the basis of its success. To him this success is not simply because the Swatch is a fashion item, but lies in the fact that, 'we are offering our personal culture. If it were just a fashion item, it could be easily copied, but Swatch have tapped deep into the roots of change, to respond to feelings of wanting to be identified with what you do'. How much more important this is, then, for a service.

A way of living

For a service to achieve this, the vision must also be a 'way of living' which pervades the whole working of the organization, and provides a sense of fulfilment. As we saw in the early chapters, 'Employees who work in settings that are more in harmony with their own service orientation experience less role ambiguity and role conflict and, as a result, are generally more satisfied.'[1] Where this harmony and low levels of role ambiguity and role conflict exist there is not only greater employee satisfaction but, directly connected to this, increased customer satisfaction since most people give of their best when they feel that they are achieving something worthwhile.

A factor working in Falck's favour was that everyone viewed their job as 'doing good'; they felt they were achieving something worthwhile. In fact this was a strong link between all four of the utilities studied (Falck, Lyonnaise des Eaux, Televerket and Wessex). However, it was noticeable that in Televerket and Wessex it was only since they had embarked on a programme of 'market-mindedness' that this had come to be expressed as customer concern, rather than as a slightly superior, inward attitude of, 'We are technically excellent and know what is good for you'. Perhaps because it was so much less expected, this faith in themselves as achieving their ends through doing good for others rather than simply doing a job was particularly pronounced in Lyonnaise des Eaux and formed a key part of both the philosophy and specific objectives of the company.

But not every organization can have such clear social goals as these utilities. Or can they? An overriding characteristic of long-term success is dedication to the customer. So, a successful strategic objective involves doing something worthwhile for and with your customers and not simply treating them as 'punters' who must ultimately be the losers whilst you are the winner. The struggle in organizations that have only recently embarked on change – and three to four years is nothing in this context – all too evidently centres around trying to focus on the customer and to develop a 'listening' culture. Woolworths is an example of this, where the struggle is toughest and where ultimate success will be worthy of the highest praise.

This sense of something above and beyond simply work has been noted by other researchers too, and the presence of such vision is more widespread than might at first be thought. For example, Andrew Campbell and his associates[2] have found, 'A sense of mission occurs when the values of the company are attractive to employees, that is when the employees find their work fulfilling because they are using it to act out some deeply held values', and they go on to say, 'Two aspects of organizational philosophy need to be managed by executives. They need to help employees cope with conflicts that arise between their personal morality and the organizations' collective morality; and they need to create an inspiring philosophy or morality to which employees can attach themselves'.

In Case 3.1 we saw an organization which had failed to create a vision, a *sense* of mission which people identify with. Rather, they had written down a few reasonable statements about themselves, which in some ways reads like the Virgin Atlantic mission statement, 'As the UK's second long haul carrier, to build an inter-continental network concentrating on those routes with a substantial established market and clear indication of growth potential, by offering the highest possible service at the lowest possible cost'.

However, the 'real' vision of Virgin – their sense of mission – is not expressed in a statement but in the personality of their charismatic leader, Richard Branson, and also through the everyday writings and discussions of Branson and his colleagues in management. It is more properly summed up in a sentence, such as the one below, written by Richard Branson as the opening to a small booklet for all staff entitled *Our Airline*, written as part of a drive to keep up the momentum in the 1990s. (For a fuller discussion of this, see Case 11.1.) The sentence reads, 'We have always said that we wanted the airline to be one that people like us would want to fly,' and on the second page goes on, 'most airlines do things in more or less the same way. Right from the start we knew we were going to do things differently.'

Virgin Atlantic's success is that it is an extension of the ideals and feelings of its founder and the people he has gathered around, as with Hayek and Swatch, and its appeal to customers – those for whom it has appeal – lies in sharing these ideals and feelings in a relationship. In their own way in their own markets – and with inspirational rather than charismatic leaders which is a much more common situation – Saga, Televerket and Woolworths are doing this.

Mission statements as a framework

Creating this relationship is also the task that faces PSVR (Chapter 3). But that vision also needs a framework, whether called a mission statement or something else, which takes the core ideal through to practical identification of the 'what'. In PSVR's case, given the rather bureaucratic field in which they work and the clear picture of the culture which we get from the CVO research, the way forward needs a strong vision and a firm framework but not fresh rules, standards and suchlike, at least not at the start. Such a vision and framework needs to be both practical and compelling and it needs to show 'what' has to happen. The result is shown in Box 4.1. It should be compared with the original statement in Case 3.1. Not only is it more explicit but the key factors that will make it effective have been clearly identified.

In a few months this mission statement has played a key role in releasing the energy of that company and is used – as mission statements should be used – as a practical guide at meetings and in development, and as a means for more junior managers to challenge more senior colleagues, through statements such as, 'How is that course of action, that refusal, helping to achieve our strategy?'

Box 4.1 PSVR Mission Statement

It is our aim to be a successful marine insurance company operating at world-market level and achieving our success through a reputation for providing solutions that make our customers successful.

We will provide this distinction for PSVR through personal contact, at all levels, with our customers. This will also ensure that they may have full confidence in our operations.

To achieve this, wherever possible we aim to engage in a long-term partnership with our customers in a manner which is mutually beneficial, supporting our customers in the achievement of their objectives and meeting the needs of our staff and shareholders for a dynamic, secure and profitable organization.

Objectives

To fulfil our mission, we must achieve the following objectives:

- *Customer satisfaction*   In a changing world, the long-term viability and distinctiveness of PSVR will be best assured by ensuring that we understand our customers' requirements fully. Our services and solutions must actively help them to achieve their objectives. We will therefore

continues

---

continued

build such relationships by demonstrating that we are an organization that understands them and is there to provide a valued and responsive service.

- *Security* In order to guarantee security, we must maintain our financial strength through adequate capitalization and the continuation of that through profitable underwriting, information and the full backing of our shareholders.
- *Motivation of staff* Staff are our major asset in any such achievement. We must motivate them through clear leadership and empowerment towards the fulfilment of our corporate goals. Our concern for the satisfaction and well-being of the staff must be evident.
- *Reliability* Reliability means fulfilling our promises and our obligations to all of our partners (customers, staff, shareholder). It must be an integral part of our internal culture and of our dealings with our customers and our shareholders.

To achieve these objectives means we must adopt these key values:

- *Teamwork/cooperation* To achieve our objectives on a continuing basis, we must all work together as a team, freely exchanging information and sharing concerns and problems, with respect, recognition and trust in and for each other's contribution.
- *Personal contact* Through regular personal contacts, our partners will get to know the persons in our company to whom they may turn with all their queries. To this end, we will ensure a continuity of personal contact.
- *Technical excellence/professionalism* We must ensure that we establish, maintain and practise a high level of professionalism. This must be part of the distinctiveness that sets PSVR apart from others. We must be seen as an insurer who uses these skills to help others to be successful.
- *Value* For us quality stands for the optimal fulfilment of our services and whilst doing so we bear all the needs and requirements of our customers in mind.

The barriers to vision

We can see that the concept of vision, a sense of mission, which pervades and infects the true service company is in fact bedded in culture because, as defined in Chapter 3, 'culture is the set of beliefs which form the basis of collaborative behaviour, that is the values which govern and direct our activity'.

Why, then, if the creation of a vision based on culture is such a critical part of success, is it not seen as more central to achievement by more managers?

There are probably as many reasons for this as there are such situations but research and experience suggest that the common threads running through such reluctance or failure are:

(1)   The difficulties of weighing the factors involved and putting them into balance with other harder facts. In fact, most managers would prefer to see mission statements in terms of business definitions and competitive positionings rather than 'the creation and maintenance of a satisfying culture'. [2] Yet our research would suggest that the very reasons for long-term success in a service are a clear vision with a strong customer focus and a cohesive culture working towards this focus. Further, that missions which are only, in effect, abbreviations of a strategic statement, are unhelpful in creating a shared unity.

(2)   The lack of recognition of the fact that developing a culture is not simply about 'others' but about ourselves, and that changes in direction and method involve 'us', or even more pointedly 'me'.

(3)   The defensive routines adopted by managers, particularly in dealing with the disturbance and threats of change, which shut off the chances of development. (See the comments by Argyris, quoted on page 48.)

Research can go a long way towards overcoming points one and two. It can also help with point three, but it will only increase defensive routines and erect new and more formidable barriers to change if it is not part of a plan. To quote Campbell again, 'Mission statements frequently do more harm than good because they imply a sense of direction, a clarity of thinking and unity which rarely exists.'[2] Further, as we saw with Case 3.1, top management cannot stand back from the change because they are a critical part of it, and maybe even a 'barrier'.

However, it is invidious to identify any one point and see that as *the* barrier. Rather, it is necessary to provide a framework for success using a thorough understanding of culture, including the barriers to acceptance of its value and the defensive routines that threaten its implementation.

Culture as a basis for vision

Looking back over the research we can see why this is so:

•   Services are about relationships and successful services are about creating successful relationships;

•   In turn, such successful relationships externally will be repeated internally (the triangle) otherwise, where there was a large gap between the two, it would have led on to an erosion of impact;

- Being clear who you are and having a sense of direction are key ingredients in closing this gap. So, long term success in a service business is related to a strong culture, where people know where they stand and what is expected of them;
- Such harmonious settings create less role ambiguity and role conflict and are more satisfying to staff;
- Such satisfaction is in turn positively related to customer satisfaction.

The two projects illustrated in Case 4.1 illustrate the importance of these links.

Case 4.1 Contrasts in culture

This case study illustrates the effect of two quite different cultures on two companies operating in a similar field of business. Both pieces of work were centred around the same time (February 1992).[3] Their real names have been withheld because of the ongoing and confidential nature of the work.

James Hope & Partners

James Hope & Partners (JHP) are a London-based firm of international insurance brokers. In common with most brokerage firms they are very sales orientated and sensitive to immediate customer reactions. Acquired by a bank a few years earlier, they have been undergoing substantial change, moving from being simply an aggressive group of like-minded but highly individualistic people, towards being consistent, professional players building deeper relationships in the market – a response to both perceptions of market change and the demands of their parent.

Although the market sector had been showing a decline in profitability in the last two years, JHP had managed to maintain profits in value terms, though this was, nevertheless, a declining percentage of income. At the same time, the Managing Director, Colin Wyatt, had been able to start a process toward a more planned approach to the business, both through better financial controls and market analysis. However, despite substantial enthusiasm throughout the management team for the changes, progress was slow and, apart from some better financial controls, little had been achieved. Even with finance, there was resistance on the part of managers to 'putting our progress in a straightjacket'.

So, Colin Wyatt decided to carry out a thorough analysis of the company culture, assess the reasons for success and the barriers to change, and design

continues

continued

and implement a route forward. The CVO research was used as a core for the analysis and the results are shown in Figures 4.1, 4.3, 4.5 and 4.7. This was linked to parallel in-depth interviews with selected managers and staff and a review of market positionings, using internal and external research.

Allison Blair & Co.

Allison Blair & Co. (ABC) are also a London based firm of insurance brokers, but operating almost exclusively within the London market. Originally British owned, they have been the subsidiary of a continental European broker for many years. Although the owners have put little pressure on ABC to change, nevertheless the Managing Director, Robert Scott, had felt for some time that substantial internal change was needed if ABC were to both understand and take advantage of market opportunities. However, his colleagues – and in particular the Director responsible for marketing, Richard Owen – felt that talk of change was overstated. For Richard Owen it was simply that the 'insurance cycle' was against them; given time and effort it would be alright again. There was no fundamental change in the market, nor was one required of them, and there was certainly no need to carry out any special exercise to analyse this. After all, 'Profits [measured in cash terms] are not down, despite the current difficult markets,' as he pointed out.

Despite this opposition, Robert Scott decided to go ahead. Not least he was concerned that a recently initiated, and expensive, programme of management development seemed to be yielding minimal results. Again, the CVO research was used as a core technique for the analysis. The results are shown in Figures 4.2, 4.4, 4.6, and 4.8. As with JHP, it was linked to parallel in-depth interviews, etc.

Results

Despite the similarity of their business these two firms provide a stark contrast in culture. This started with the response ratios: over 82% with JHP, despite being a worldwide random sampling; only 45% with ABC, despite the fact that all staff were in one location and everyone was invited to respond.

continues

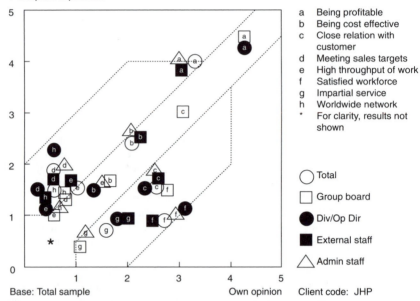

Figure 4.1   Service objectives: primary factors for success. (Service Matrix Analysis
© KIA Ltd 1991)

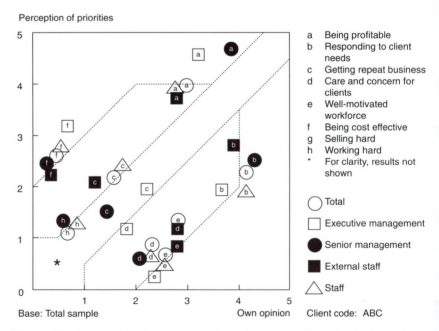

Figure 4.2   Service objectives: primary factors for success. (Service Matrix Analysis
© KIA Ltd 1991)

continued

Service objectives

(Note, although the criteria used are broadly similar, there are variations to reflect the different stated objectives, etc.) JHP (Figure 4.1) is in marked contrast to ABC (Figure 4.2).

- There are no JHP results outside of the centre channel or the shoulders to this, whilst those for ABC are widely scattered;
- In particular with ABC, there appears to be a direct conflict between responding to clients' needs (b) and being cost effective (f), a conflict which is shared by everyone, even Executive Management;
- There is little to choose between them in terms of 'grouping' of results between levels, though they are slightly more grouped in ABC, but JHP Group Board are persistently different.

Service values

The visual contrast between the two is graphic. JHP (Figure 4.3) has a remarkably close set of values, both in terms of relation to each other and congruence of 'our opinion' and 'perceptions of priorities'. On the other hand ABC (Figure 4.4) seem to share very little, except a general tendency to see matters in terms of 'I think this but they think that'. In particular we see that:

- Virtually without exception, all JHP respondents have chosen and rejected the same two sets of values;
- Almost the only figure in JHP away from the centre channel is 'good teamwork' (b), for administrative staff;
- JHP Group Board are the least in line;
- There is almost no consistency at all within ABC, with few results in the centre channel and many at extremes;
- The Executive Management of ABC have made five surprising 'statements':
  - they perceive 'quoting lowest prices' (a), being 'technically excellent' (b) and 'strong leadership' (j) of strong or moderate importance to the 'Company' but *not at all* to them;

  whilst:

  - their opinions that 'good team work' (d), to a great extent, and 'high standards of integrity (e), to a lesser extent, are important but are not *shared at all* by the others.

On the basis of these four figures, and linked to the understandings gained from parallel interviews, it is possible to see that:

- JHP has a strong sense of shared values with effectively only three points of possible concern, the Group Board positioning relative to others, the difference of view about teamwork on the part of administrative staff and the comparative lack of a few overriding objectives;

continues

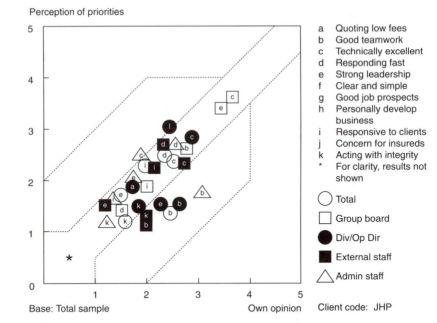

Figure 4.3   Service values: support factors for success. (Service Matrix Analysis © KIA Ltd 1991)

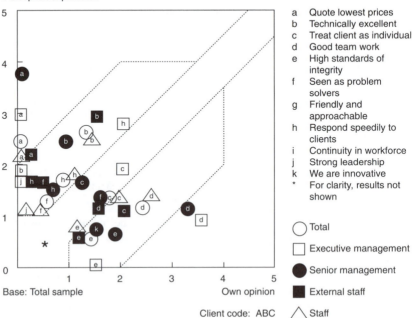

Figure 4.4   Service values: secondary factors for success. (Service Matrix Analysis © KIA Ltd 1991)

continued

- ABC, in contrast, seems to be house divided against itself with little in the way of clear shared objectives or values. Executive Management, in particular, seem to be unclear about a great number of issues.

Service structure

Looking at the other figures we can see some further surprising results. JHP (Figure 4.5) is not nearly so 'close' as ABC (Figure 4.6). In particular we can see:

- The Group Board of JHP positioned 'north', seeing the business as much more responsive than anyone else;
- A 'two-culture' company, with administrative staff seeing it as much more routine;
- Whereas in ABC only senior management have a (mildly) different view from others on implementation.

Service management

ABC (Figure 4.8) is tightly grouped with the exception of senior management – who are well away in the 'aimless' area – whilst JHP (Figure 4.7) are more loosely grouped but with a slight drift away on the part of management (Group Board toward 'involvement' and senior management (Divisional and Operational Directors) toward 'leadership').

The way forward

Linked to the earlier charts – and the observations – it was possible both to analyse the problems and design a way forward.

For JHP:

- The Company has a sound value base but lacks clarity of direction.
- In particular, the Group Board is failing to take people with it in the period of change from the old partnership situation to the new.
- Senior Management are reacting to this by 'drift' (as we saw with Bank J in Chapter 2) and unless given more direction, leadership and help, will continue to drift, destroying the culture, which is obviously a key ingredient in success to date.
- There are definite signs of a 'hands-on' tendency on the part of management, an unlikely way to control people who clearly have such 'strong' values.
- Two cultures are tenable – many such strongly 'sales-orientated' companies have this feature – provided they are recognized and constant efforts made to bridge the gap. The result in Figure 4.3 on 'teamwork' (b)

continues

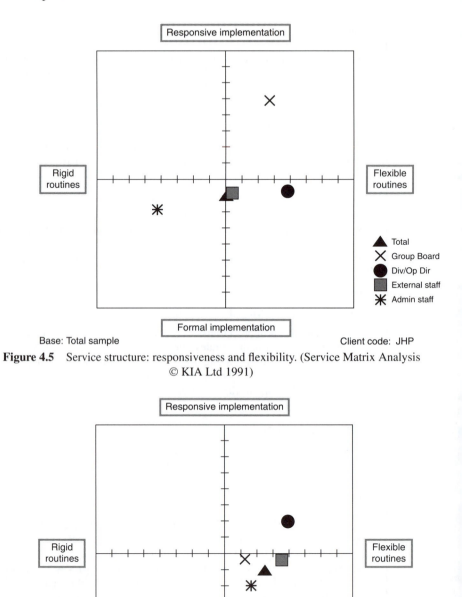

Figure 4.5   Service structure: responsiveness and flexibility. (Service Matrix Analysis © KIA Ltd 1991)

Figure 4.6   Service structure: responsiveness and flexibility. (Service Matrix Analysis © KIA Ltd 1991)

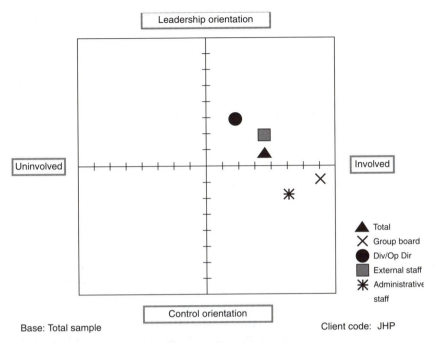

Figure 4.7   Service management: leadership and involvement. (Service Matrix Analysis © KIA Ltd 1991)

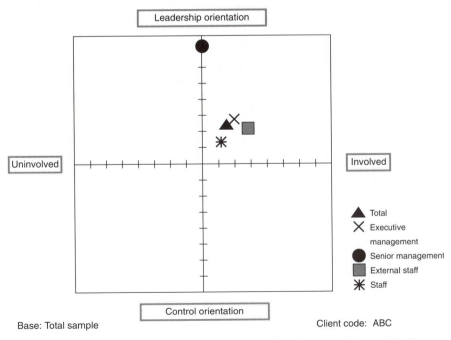

Figure 4.8   Service management: leadership and involvement. (Service Matrix Analysis © KIA Ltd 1991)

continued

suggests that may not be true in this case, however. (In fact, the more detailed analyses within divisions etc showed conclusively that this was a key problem, as pressures of change resulted in middle managers seeking to protect their role.)

The route forward had to include:

- A clear statement of vision, through a mission statement.
- Help for the Group Board to adjust their behaviour in support of this.
- A crash development programme for senior management.
- A widespread programme to release the energy of the organization towards meeting the new vision, adapting and abandoning old practices.

For ABC:

- The company has neither a sound value base nor a sense of direction.
- Differences amongst management are mirrored throughout the Company and senior management are 'drifting'.
- The sense of cohesion in Figures 4.6 and 4.8 is more an outcome of apathy and clinging-together than any shared dynamic. This was strongly supported by the parallel discussions and visual observation – people looked apathetic and only seemed released when they finished work. Not surprising, perhaps, if you have no clear direction to your work and share almost no values; it goes almost beyond role conflict or ambiguity. This is supported by the low response rate of 45%.

The route forward had to include:

- Shock tactics with the Executive. The CEO had to face them with a stark choice of accepting that no change was necessary and they could go on living for today, for a time, or they had to accept that they themselves had to change. The Executive accepted the challenge, for the Company and for themselves.
- So, the major development programme for management was adjusted to reflect these new needs and directed more at the Executive than previously.
- A key first part of this was the development of a shared vision. This was of crucial importance. It is very easy at this point to choose the wrong set of values, for everyone to defensively seek out internal values which sound fair but are technical, inward-looking or simply don't touch the buyer. This is a particular problem in the insurance industry.
- The setting-up of a project group to look into all aspects of the operations – including recruitment – to capture key individuals and opinion formers to change and to develop specific new activities.

Missions, objectives and values

As we can see, in both of the illustrations in Case 4.1, an early necessity was to agree on 'where the business was going'. However, merely adopting the convention of 'defining our business' and 'our position within that selected area' would never touch on the cultural changes which clearly underpinned existing attitudes, behaviour and performance and needed to be taken into account if change was to happen.

Further, such an approach would not only fail to address these aspects but would also fail to address those issues which managers see as a 'threat'. We will look more deeply at the processes involved in Chapters 8 and 9, but first, what is involved in the creation of a vision of a mission statement, if it is to be of use in providing a framework?

For a mission statement to fulfil this function of providing both a vision and a framework, it must:

- Link the definition of our business and the definition 'who we need to be'.
- Be capable of clear articulation in simple terms which can be understood by everyone.
- Be capable of providing a clear statement of the organizational imperatives, the values, 'the way we work', such that in the heat of the moment – at the moment of truth – the action that is taken is that which the individual knows will receive support.
- Act as a framework or guide for all strategies and all plans, by providing a focus for questioning 'how does this activity, this plan, help us to achieve our mission?'
- Act as a framework for stimulating new strategies, and plans where existing activity fails to meet the needs.

It is the failure to do all this, either in written form or verbally, which leads to the rejection of mission statements as being simply 'wallpaper'. Indeed, vast numbers are simply statements of such obvious truth and, not uncommonly, breathtaking banality that they are of no value.

You will find examples of more valuable statements used throughout this book to illustrate key points (Royal Albert Hall in Chapter 8, Saga in Chapter 9, Woolworths in Chapter 10) but of the two companies in Case 4.1, JHP has been the most successful in articulating 'who' they are and setting in hand a programme to make it all happen. An adapted version of their mission statement is given in the box. Note that it goes well beyond the conventional mission statement, but nevertheless has an opening section which can stand on its own.

Box 4.2 James Holt & Partners Mission Statement

James Holt & Partners (JHP) aspires to be the first choice in the provision of risk analysis and containment services. These will be of the highest professional standards and integrity and will be provided worldwide to industry and larger commercial enterprises. In achieving this aim we will always be mindful of the need to think long term and to reflect the aspirations of our customers, staff and shareholders.

Objectives

To fulfil our mission statement necessitates our achieving the following objectives:

- *Customer satisfaction* We must identify the needs we intend to satisfy, set clear targets and measure our achievement against these expectations.
- *Motivation of staff* Staff are our major asset in any such achievement. We must motivate them, through strong and clear leadership, toward the fulfilment of our market task.
- *Cost effectiveness* Our customer orientation means that we should concentrate resources on the achievement of their expectations. We should eliminate costs not aimed at meeting this objective.
- *Profitability* Profit is the necessary ingredient in achieving our long-term aims and the availability of capital to meet the needs for such investment.

Values

We will only achieve the right balance of our objectives if we have a clear set of values which we all share and see as guiding our day-to-day behaviour. These are:

- *Responsiveness to customers* Our customers will recognize us for what we do and how we act, not what we say. We must ensure that at all times our behaviour, our language, our response recognizes that we have understood their problems.
- *Concern for people* Our business is based on trust and the integrity of our relationships. People form the key ingredient in these and our concern for them and their needs and ambitions must be evident.
- *Teamwork* Responsiveness and concern will only be effective within a spirit of teamwork at local, national, and international level. We will actively foster this through the free interchange of information and respect for each others' contribution.
- *Technical excellence* We have a unique blend of skills and back-up teams to match. We must ensure that we maintain and use our level of skill to a high level of professionalism, externally and internally.

continues

continued

Explanation

Our mission statement has been developed only after careful thought and widespread involvement. This section is intended to help you to understand why and what it means.

Our mission

Why aspires? Surely we *will* be the first choice! Yes, we believe we *will* be, but we won't achieve our overall goal by complacency or arrogance. We believe our success will be better based on realism and hard work than on grand claims – and anyway, it is for our customers to say, not for us.

Risk analysis and containment – our business is increasingly more than purely insurance broking. We must offer sufficiently broad services to meet our customers' concerns, not simply focus on one technical element.

Professional standards and integrity – the Group's market position has been built on our professional standards and integrity; these must always be maintained as we grow.

Worldwide – this does not mean that the Group will have an office in every country in the world, but rather that we will provide a worldwide service that is at least the equal of our major competitors.

Clients, staff and shareholders – our business will only remain healthy and grow if we recognize that the reasonable expectations of clients, staff and shareholders must be satisfied, and kept in balance with each other.

Our objectives

Our objectives pick out the four things we have to achieve if our vision is to become more than a dream. These are the aims we have to strive for, each day and every day, whoever we are!

Customer satisfaction   All businesses have to ensure they are truly satisfying the needs of their customers; ours is no exception. We all believe this, and that the standards we set must be those of our customers – and their customers too. At all times we must put ourselves in their shoes – 'what would I expect if I were them?'

Initially, we have selected two measures and we will develop research tools to ensure we monitor our progress against them. They are to establish with all employees:

(1)   That the James Holt Partnership are the preferred suppliers of risk analysis and containment services.
(2)   That the reason for preference is that we understand and meet their needs.

In other words, we do not, for example, want to be chosen simply because we are 'cheap' or seem as 'technically good but remote'.

continues

continued

Motivation of staff Motivation comes from both being kept informed and from feeling recognized as an important part of the business. We have to improve this. We also have to ensure that the same degree of purposeful leadership is provided by the management of all the divisions.

Initially, we have again selected two measures and will develop research tools to ensure we monitor progress. They are to establish with all employees:

(1) That they feel that we are an excellent employer.
(2) That they feel this is because we provide a stimulating and rewarding work environment.

Obviously, each of these words will be open to interpretation, but out aim is to build teamwork through enthusiastic involvement in which individuals feel they have a part to play.

Cost effectiveness This does not mean that we will run the business on a shoestring. It is rather that we will be critical of where we spend money and ensure that it is always in line with our objectives and, particularly, client satisfaction. This will benefit not only our own profitability but also our clients, by helping to keep our fees at a reasonable level.

Our measures will include:

(1) A cost/return ratio which is better than the average of our competitors.
(2) A 4 to 1 ratio for the fees earned by marketing staff related to all salary costs.

Again, we will seek to monitor our achievement.

Profitability Only by being profitable can we secure our future. Although this is clearly understood, it should flow from our other objectives, but we always need to bear in mind that we can only expect continued support if we show a return on investment. To do this we will:

(1) Expect each subsidiary within the Group to achieve the agreed return on sales target.
(2) Only invest in new ventures if they will be profitable within four years.

These key strategic objectives may alter from time to time, in answer to our need to adjust performance against our mission, either because of external shifts or our own business results, whether successful or otherwise.

Our values

Each of these values will be used as a basis for developing our business, especially our training and development programmes. However, it is how each of us personally responds to them which is most important. Read them carefully and think what you can do to contribute to their fulfilment.

continues

continued

Responsiveness to customers   Through the organization – amongst management, sales and administrative staff – everyone must recognize that we are a service business. This means that our main task is always to respond to the needs of our customer, however pressing internal issues and deadlines may be.

Concern for people   We will put people at the top of our agenda. It will be the basis of our customer satisfaction and the achievement of objectives.

Teamwork   Everyone in the Group must understand that good teamwork is essential if we are to provide high-quality service to our customers. This applies not only within each office, where sales and administration staff must work together closely – each recognizing the others' pressures – but also across the various divisions of the Group.

Technical excellence   The technical excellence that people throughout the Group bring to their jobs is the foundation of our success. Yet the technical skills required from the Group by our customer are always changing and we must ensure that we develop these skills to meet our customers' needs. Effective training will be of the principal means by which we can continually build and adapt our technical skills.

   We believe our success comes through people. This means both placing the customer first in every decision and action, and supporting our staff, to bring out the best in everyone. But concern for people cannot simply be taught – it is a way of working that comes from the heart.

Note that:

- The simple statement of mission, the vision – often all that some organizations produce yet usually too bland to provoke any response beyond 'yes, of course' – is then focused into a set of clear objectives and clear values.
- These objectives and values are small in number. In fact, experience suggests that four of each is the very maximum. These are all anyone can remember, particularly in the heat of the moment.
- Further, they represent the 'organizational imperatives' – they are the yardsticks by which we can judge whether the action we have to take is right in terms of 'what (we) management, want you to do'.
- In turn these objectives and values are explained clearly so that everyone knows 'what we mean by that'.
- The objectives can be clearly measured and there is provision to update these measures in the light of experience.

In conclusion

It is vital to have a vision which taps into the real beliefs of the people in the organization so that role conflict and role ambiguity are kept to a minimum. The culture of a service organization is integral to the success of this. Understanding the culture will not only help to explain success, or failure, but also provide insight into what action is appropriate to achieve change. This is vital in a service, because change can only come about through people who must be persuaded to play their role.

Further, the internal organization will govern the external culture. It is vital, therefore, that there be a synergy between these. The vision needs elaboration in the form of a mission statement which should encapsulate this vision and create synergy between culture and strategy, providing a clear framework for action. We will return to this link when we discuss strategy in Chapter 7.

References

1. Schneider B. and Bowen D.E. (1983). *Employee and customer perceptions of service in banking: replication and extension*. University of Maryland
2. Campbell A. *et al.* (1990). *A sense of mission*. London: The Economist Books

5

The customer as focus

- Treating customers as more than a target is a characteristic of good service.
- Customer focus needs to be designed. This not only requires planning but may mean rejecting some traditional techniques, amongst them the marketing mix.
- Using the service mix as a basis for planning the elements of competitiveness in a service.
- The service as a process – designing the service as a whole with the customer as participant.
- Using discontinuity theory as a way of planning both marketing and your response.

The customer as participant

That vision, which we have seen as so important in the last chapter, will be unlikely to create success if it is not directed externally. As Adam Smith observed more than two hundred years ago, 'Consumption is the sole end [purpose] of all production and the interest of the producer should be attended to only so far as it may be necessary for promoting that of the consumer.'[1] So, not surprisingly, a strong characteristic, common to all successful service companies, is a feeling that a customer is someone who is more, much more, than simply a target. This customer focus is a key issue for services, not simply because of the need for market orientation but because the customer is a participant in the interactions. He or she forms a part of the 'product' and lives with the provider of a service. In our research those organizations which had either achieved long-term success, or appeared to be successfully negotiating change, have a simple and overriding dedication to the customer as an integral part of thinking.

Some, like Televerket (see Case 5.1), had attempted customer orientation for years without really achieving it, just replacing one set of technically-based values with another. Whilst they had become more market friendly, they were not truly based on the customer and as a result had not really achieved a breakthrough in terms of customer perceptions of improvement. Only in 1987, seven years after first starting down the path, did Televerket see that technical excellence in itself was nothing if it was not accompanied by a real, and deeply held, belief in the customer's own perceptions. Now you can see quite different results, although, as Bertil Thorngren admits, 'We still have some way to go before we see the level of result we need, though the latest research (1993) shows we are being seen as comparable for service delivery with SAS (Scandinavian Airlines System), for long the "service leader" in Scandinavia.'

This technically orientated approach to marketing is, in fact, commonplace, pervading most financial services, especially insurance, as well as IT, telecommunications and a number of other industries. Many managers are aware of this shortfall but it is a neglected area, with very little literature comment. Those articles that do exist tend to see the customer as a sales target.

As a result, the importance and involvement of customers is more likely to be related to failure (customers talk readily about dissatisfaction) rather than to success (customers less commonly talk about satisfaction). Maybe one of the reasons this shortcoming is not recognized more clearly is that most customers never complain or make any comment to the supplier, but merely go elsewhere, or will do when the chance arises. Indeed, a recent survey of 11 European service companies[2] showed that, while only three per cent of these companies' transactions resulted in specific complaints which were logged, 15% caused dissatisfaction and the complaint was made verbally at the time, and a further 30% were dissatisfied but simply walked away.

A further reason is that customer focus is not easy and it is this feeling which is missing in those organizations whose hold on success is tenuous or where change has had mixed success. Box 5.1 shows some of the contrasts noted during our research and drawn from statements by the management and operatives of respondents. In one set of quotes the customers are remote; they are people who are seen to act capriciously, even unreasonably. In the other set they are real, and because the relationship is clearly valued the company sees itself as having a responsibility.

Case 5.1   *Changing the focus*

Televerket is like every other telecom organization in having to face up to competition after decades of protection affording little choice to the consumer. The spur of both technical innovation and deregulation – which are in fact highly interlinked – has brought about a world barely imaginable a decade ago. And although Televerket claims that it has never been a monopoly, effectively it was and most Swedes would be surprised to learn otherwise.

Bertil Thorngren, head of corporate planning, says, 'The atmosphere bred a sense of technical excellence. We didn't have to pay high salaries to get good engineers to work for us because it was very stimulating, a bit like a university. And like a university, it was difficult to get promotion unless you had papers regularly published.'

Morgan Svensson, currently a deputy director but an engineer in those times, agrees, 'Technically we were excellent, and our first responses to being 'customer' orientated were based on this and we set targets for excellence which meant nothing to the customer – like 55% of repairs in eight hours. But what if you [the customer] were continually in the 45%? Now we realize we should worry less about the tools and the systems [of quality] as they serve to confuse. Instead be crystal clear about simple objectives for the organization; be equally clear about the role each person has to play to achieve that; make sure the rules reflect this. Get the culture right and the rest will follow.'

Even today, a number of Swedes will still laugh at the thought of Televerket and quality, because a few years of concentrating on quality, as the mass of customers see it, have yet to establish Televerket firmly as a company that does care. It also has to overcome the legacy of *saying* Televerket had quality and was concerned, but in truth meaning 'We know we're good and we're going to make sure you know too!'

Bertil Thorngren, again, 'It's a bit like the usual complaint about Volkswagen car heaters; in truth not bad but they don't feel warm! [They know about that sort of thing in Sweden.] In truth we were not bad but we didn't feel good to our customers. Partly that was due to our large number of big international customers. They forced us to change but we saw the market through their eyes, not the ordinary customer. But even with our big business customers we failed to provide feedback. We might well have done something significant to put a problem right or meet a particular need, but they might not know. This is of particular significance where the original complainant is not the 'contact' person for Televerket. We also concentrated on average performance and this hid pockets of persistent failure. So some customers got a raw deal and some engineers 'played

continues

continued

the system', achieving their averages through bypassing difficult problems. Now we have both average targets and absolute minimums – at any time of the day, on any line.'

Stig-Arne Larsson, Senior Director Finance, echoes this and adds, 'Invoicing is one the few times we have a chance to make a non-routine contact with our customers. By allowing them to decide when they wanted to pay the bills, so as to match their income and other monthly payments, we were able to show a human face. Our investment in this area has been well worthwhile.' Marianne Nivert, Manager, Gothenburg area, stressed the impact of personnel and the amount of time and effort put into their ambitious leadership programme, 'But of course we were able to work with the unions, who understood the need for change and were prepared to cooperate.'

Televerket still has a long way to go, but already it has made substantial inroads into changing the focus of service from its own perceptions to those of the consumer. For example:

- The target of 55% repairs in eight hours has been replaced with 'all by latest next day'. You either succeed or fail and the promise is clear to both customers and staff.
- If a coin box is full of coins, then calls become free. Customers are no longer frustrated by the problem – and the incentive to keep the boxes emptied is very strong.
- All home calls are booked to within an hour, say 'between 10 and 11'. So people don't have to wait in all morning or afternoon. Where Televerket fails to meet this deadline, it pays compensation.
- Wherever possible, all repair work etc is the subject of a follow-up call within three days. The key point is to make sure everything is alright now, but it is also to ensure that the customer *knows* the work has been done.
- All businesses have their 'own' repair man, so they feel they can control their situation or at least talk to someone they know. Where there is a complaint, whenever it is possible or allowed, the original complainant is identified and contacted to make sure all is well.

As Tony Hagstrom, Director General, says, 'We have to recognize that our service is basic and people depend on us. We simply cannot permit problems that don't take account of this.' Morgan Svensson again, 'We were a traditional culture of proud engineers but we failed to learn from the market. We got a lot of satisfaction from being good but now you can actually see the joy, the pleasure, people take from seeing happy customers. We were colourless; this focus gives us colour.'

Box 5.1   Contrasts in focus

Successful organizations

Organizations with success unproven/doubtful

'We feel we are so positive with our customers because they recognize we are doing something good for them.'

'We would like to be fair to everyone, but how can you when there is a small minority which cheats?'

'If a customer is acting stupidly, you really have to ask yourself "what are *we* doing wrong?"'

'We have tried to show all employees we are on the same side, so as to sell more to the punters.'

'Customers should know how to get what they want from an organization. It's *our* failure if they are frustrated.'

'Customers are a pain in the neck with their special requests. We do try to be polite.'

Source: KIA/EU research comments.

Customers are demanding

This gulf between our feelings as a customer and our feelings as an employee runs deep and is a crucial block to our ability to create a customer focus. Rarely do you hear people say, as in the quote above, 'If people act stupidly, you really have to ask yourself what are *we* doing wrong?' Yet, as a customer, most people would instinctively assume that they were the centre of the activity; that every act performed, every comment, was directed at them or intended to have an effect on them. This is because they have matched not only their expectations but, very likely, their promises to others to a particular level of performance. So, for example, the absence of polite forms of address may make someone feel less important in front of others or, if they are unsure of themselves, confirm their own feelings of insecurity or unimportance. A flight delay may break a promise they have made to not be late or to attend a meeting. But the design of our service will typically treat this as secondary. Indeed, it may play no part at all. The gulf we have to bridge is starkly illustrated in the two examples given in Box 5.2.

Example 1 makes the point clearly – a point which is central to this book and is also the basis for most consumer-based developments – that you have every right as a customer to be treated as the focal point of the 'offer'. In our personal lives we believe this should be so, even if we resignedly say,

'But it's never true,' or 'It's very rare'. Example 2, however, shows how many react when it is their job which is under criticism. It is the sadder – and the more telling – for being a quote from a company which had already made the decision to become more customer focused. You can imagine the difficulty the writer of Example 2 would have in dealing with the customer in Example 1!

Box 5.2   Contrasting attitudes

Example 1

You can get good service if you fight for it. A revolution can start with a single individual. When second-grade teacher Carole Gilmore drove her 1930 Model A Ford into a Phoenix gas station one bright May day, a revolution began. The pump station was self-service so she filled her tank with gas, but as she was replacing the nozzle she suddenly noticed the price on the pump. It was two cents higher than the posted price on the huge sign on the street. Carole, the customer, pointed out this discrepancy and asked how much she owed based on the price advertised on the sign.

'Sorry, lady,' the station attendant said, and shrugged his shoulders (shoulder shrugging is a certain clue that the curtain is about to go up on 'It's not my department'). 'The price just went up a few hours ago and I haven't had a chance to get up there and change the sign yet.'

This is where the world ends for most customers; beaten, discouraged, and depressed, they dig down deep and come up with the difference. But not Carole. In her best 'class-if-I-have-your-attention' voice, loud enough so other customers lining up behind her could hear her perfectly, she announced, 'Young man, look at me.' And then she did a revolutionary thing.

She held up her right hand and made a letter C with her thumb and fore-finger. Then she moved the 'C' sign up to her eye and looked through it straight at the attendant.

'I am the customer,' she continued, 'and this C stands for customer. I refuse to be victimized by you or your sign or your system around here. You certainly had a chance to change the prices on the pumps, but if you'd thought about it, you'd have changed the road sign first, in honour of your customers.'

'You have two choices. I am willing to pay you either your advertised price right now, or else you have exactly three minutes to get that gasoline back out of my tank before I drive out of here without paying you anything. Which is it going to be?'

The chastened attendant cowered before the 'C' sign and accepted the advertised price. He thought she was a bitch. Carole knew she was a customer.

continues

---

continued

It was a mystical experience.

The 'C' sign is the sign of the customer, and it can also be sign of the revolution. Wouldn't it be wonderful if we were a nation of fighters, if 250 million Americans started rioting for good service, for caring enough to carry out a breathtaking revolution?

(*Source*: Peter Glen, *It's Not my Department*, William Morrow & Co. Inc. 1990.)

Example 2

The satisfied customer is an excellent advertisement for any company. The satisfaction comes from many sources: being fairly treated, receiving individual and courteous attention, being treated as a person and not a number, being helped. He or she quietly talks to friends and sometimes even tells us. The unhappy customer tends to make more noise. He – most of them tend to be male – never allows his voice of complaint to grow hoarse and his memory is elephantine. Usually, his grumbles are due to someone rumbling him – his greed, his pomposity, his unreasonable demands: occasionally, very occasionally, his complaints are justified.

Our reputation today arises from the knowledge of our customers of all kinds that the word of our Company stands for a special kind of service. We are reliable, reasonable and responsive. We are also aware that complacency is the first staging post on the road to disaster.

(*Source*: Extract from a company internal newsletter on *Customer Care* 1990.)

The gulf between customer and employee will not be bridged at all, indeed we may actually make it wider, if we do not recognize that:

(1)   The demanding aware customers of today are more difficult to satisfy. As we saw in Chapter 1, economic progress and the emphasis on individualism, on 'me', means that customers are less deferential toward authority and perceived standards of polite behaviour as exemplified by institutions.

(2)   Advertising good service tends to heighten this, raising levels of expectation but doing little to educate the customer.

(3)   Staff have a legitimate viewpoint. They are often treated badly by customers and if they are to work to overcome this – to win over the Carole Gilmores (see Box 5.2) – then they need more than training; they need continuous help, support and understanding.

(4)   Finally, this cannot be in a vacuum. The culture of the organization has to be customer focused and has to reward the achievement of customer support.

To simply say that the 'Customer is King' or the 'Customer is always right' is insufficient.

You have to help people to:

(1)   Understand *why* customers behave as they do.
(2)   Appreciate that the awkward customer is telling you something of value. You may not like what he's telling you – and even less his manner – but it contains a truth you need to know. Indeed, it may only be the awkward customers who will tell you. It may personally hurt to say, 'thank you, that's very helpful' but it is often advantageous and should be reinforced. (See also Chapter 11 for a development of the views on difficult customers.)

Above all staff need a leader who understands the problem and shows by example how to handle it and by manner that the effort is appreciated.

Internal marketing

It is important here to touch on internal marketing, that is the involvement of middle management and staff at the development stage and in planning the implementation. Simply telling them about it before the launch is not marketing but selling, and moreover product selling. All of our respondents stressed the time and effort put into such activity and there was no doubt that the three Scandinavian respondents, together with Saga and Virgin Atlantic, had carried this through with substantial thoroughness and consequent success. However, what really seemed to set them aside from some of the others was that they always stressed that the focus was the final, external customer, not a colleague. In fact, in both BP and Woolworths managers actually made comments to the effect that they either thought an internal stress was producing negative results or was distracting or even annoying. 'As if we were incapable of seeing the customer through the store,' as one distribution manager at Woolworths said.

It appears that the balance that needs to be found is to ensure that the effort to help colleagues, to be of service to others, has a point. Where there is a chance to make this a part of the drive to meeting final customer satisfaction, then clearly it has the advantage of providing a unifying goal. Where this is not possible, or is too tenuous to be viable, it seems that internal marketing will work best where it is not only related to helping others but taps self-interest. The success of Sainsburys' 'Backways Management' is related to getting those in distribution to see how much easier their life will be if they can help the stores.

Self-interest is a powerful tool in creating a climate for change, but it must be remembered that this is a two-edged sword. It is the customer's self-interest that is the key to success. Creating a culture in which the object is the self-interest of those involved internally does not simply blur this fact but makes it difficult to face the Carole Gilmores of the world and accept valid criticism, especially when it is loaded with emotion – the customer simply becomes seen as 'greedy, pompous and unreasonable', as in the second example in Box 5.2.

Designing a customer focus

Although all of the successful companies in the research were notable for their high degree of customer focus, the link between the organization and its market was particularly noticeable in the Yorkshire Bank. (See Case 5.2.)

However, for most organizations, it is going to be less a matter of inheriting such a strong situation and more one of designing an approach to customer focus. This must include matching staff to customers. Venues, such as the Royal Albert Hall (see Case 7.1), which mix events like boxing and symphony concerts, need different front-of-house staff because the expectations and behaviour of these audiences are so different. They are seeking a different experience.

There are a number of steps to this; each one acts as a discipline and can be used by itself, or they can be used together:

(1)   Be specific about what the customer is buying.
(2)   See service as a process, not as a product plus service.
(3)   Integrate the activity around this concept with the interactions – the moments of truth – as the key points within the process.
(4)   Create a service structure.

We will look at the first two of these in this chapter, and the other two under organization, in Chapter 7.

Case 5.2   To profitability from pennies

Founded in 1859 as the Yorkshire Penny Bank, the bank remained a small regional savings bank (any loan over £2 had to be referred to Head Office) until the 1950s, with the name change to Yorkshire Bank in 1959 and major expansion from 1960 on.

'In earlier times, we were the laughing stock of the High Street banks,' says Graham Sunderland, the recently retired General Manager of the bank, 'but we had a strong local basis and a clear image. We were brought up to believe the customer was important and have kept to this.'

Indeed, despite having grown, profitably, in the last 30 years, the bank has remained remarkably close to its market of thrift-conscious industrial customers who feel at ease in the bank's branches. As one branch manager said, 'Most of our staff have the same background as our customers. We have never tried to deny our roots and they can wear overalls in here and feel OK.'

These comments are echoed throughout the bank. For example, Lynne Taylor, a former branch manager, says, 'I am sure our success is just a question of getting it right. The emphasis is on a friendly service and we prune our costs to the bone. If we can get the morale right we can achieve it.'

'Friendliness' ('We built a bank on it'), 'being simple' and 'talking commonsense' are words which constantly recur in conversation and might be no more than words but for an often added – and even more obvious – statement such as, 'Our customers are people just like us, same background, same values.'

Although the bank prides itself on being highly structured ('One thing we're good at is writing operating manuals,' said one senior manager), in fact it has a loose organization with few levels of management and, like Handelsbanken in Sweden, a concentration on the branch.

This focus has meant that, despite its having now spread well beyond its original Yorkshire territory, the bank retains something of the dour spirit of that county, unpretentious and in some senses a little dull, but also enjoying a great spirit of relationship with its customers. In the current difficult economic climate this shows through very clearly in a much more constructive attitude toward customers in distress than is shown by some other banks. 'The banks cannot deny their share of responsibility for a situation in which many companies have become overstretched,' Michael Allsopp, AGM Group Services and subsidiaries was quoted as saying recently and, going on to talk about some specific customers, 'everyone will lose if we pull out now even if it is a possibility, rather than a probability, that they will pull through.' Nor is Yorkshire Bank's record in this respect simply wishful thinking. Independent research (1993) has shown that for small businesses 'understanding business problems' is the key criterion for judgement and such research has consistently endorsed Yorkshire's superior performance to competitors in this respect.

'Organizations that are strong are ones which know their strengths and don't get distracted away,' says Graham Sunderland. Yes, indeed, and the Yorkshire Bank shows that being closely focused can be very profitable, for supplier and customer alike.

What is the customer buying?

Putting customers in focus and determining what it is they are buying might seem to be the most marketing orientated of all of the aspects of service strategy but, paradoxically, it is often made difficult precisely because of the marketing approach. Conventional marketing theory emphasises price and those non-price variables which are hard. Such marketing would suggest that four variables control the company/market interface: price, product, promotion and distribution (or place for those who prefer alliteration to accuracy). For tangible products this is largely true.

Buyers of manufactured goods will rarely encounter activities of the manufacturer that lie outside those contained within this 'mix'. Choice will be based on a consideration of the product itself, which will be the key focus of conventional marketing activity, and its immediate presentation: price, relative to substitutes they might consider or choose and the communications, for example through advertising. Buyers will also be affected by distributors and their employees – the places they buy it in, from or through – though research suggests both distributors and their salespeople, for example, will be seen as 'separate' from the product. In other words, a Mars bar remains a Mars bar even when the shopkeeper is rude. In such a situation, successful management of the traditional marketing mix will probably lead to marketing success. Put another way, the traditional marketing mix is about balancing and maximizing activity on the right-hand axis of the service triangle. (See Figure 1.1.)

Marketing a service, however, is a much broader task than this. It is not simply about choosing customers and then planning a product, but about bringing these together and, above all, about what happens at this interaction. Indeed, as we have seen (Chapter 1) the customers internalize their choice of services, 'What will this do for me? Do they understand me enough to make it work?', rather than objectively assessing the product. It is most often at these interactions that customers reach their conclusions and are satisfied with the purchase of a particular service or will form a disposition to buy or use it again. It is, therefore, also true that it is largely at these interactions that a service organization will be able to add value and a sustainable competitive difference to the core idea or product.

Services provide lots of opportunity for developing the relationship between the market and the organization – between distinctive competence and customer need – but the traditional marketing mix does not come anywhere near to providing a method of managing this situation. Indeed, the very attempt to impose the traditional mix as a working tool leads to the belief on the part of many experienced managers in service organizations that 'imported' marketing techniques are irrelevant. More importantly, they may go on to reject the marketing approach in its entirety. Significantly, not one of our respondents saw the marketing mix as a way of developing or controlling business but instead used some broader concept involving people and giving more emphasis to distribution.

In his pioneering work on service marketing, Grönroos coined a simple variation on the traditional mix.[3] He added the interaction, so that there are five elements:

Product	Price
Place	Promotion

Interaction

Since then others have, again for the sake of alliteration but with even more loss in meaning, changed 'Interaction' to 'People'. Yet others have gone on to add even more elements to the mix, so that there can be up to seven, as for example [4]:

Product	Price
Place	Promotion
People	Physical Evidence
Process	

The problem is that not only are all of these replacements complex to use but they miss the cardinal point about services – the uniquely significant nature of the interaction as an *outcome* of the other aspects, a point which is especially noticeable with the success of Handelsbanken, Saga, Televerket and Virgin Atlantic and which was the central moving idea behind the transformation of both SAS and, in turn, British Airways.

To achieve this you have to move away from the straightjacket of simply providing a list and shift the focus to the key area for a service organization – that is, the meeting with the marketplace. From this it is possible to construct an entirely new approach to the marketing mix which reflects this.

It is precisely this which underlies the model shown in Figure 5.1 where the interaction is the focus of the business and the elements that go to make for success surround this focal point and interact at it. This starlike formation acts as a basic control both for stating the elements of the mix and for setting them into context and balance. These five elements are the marketing mix in a service, the elements which, if properly balanced one with another and in relation to a defined market, will make for success. More properly, this is the service mix, for it encompasses everything that is involved. The focus may then be seen as the encapsulation of the vision into a simple, overriding statement of the imperative at this critical point.

Unlike the marketing mix, the service mix does not create a distinction between revenue-earning elements – the elements of the traditional marketing mix – and cost-incurring elements. In a service, all activity is integral; costs and cost expenditures or savings have a significant and direct impact on

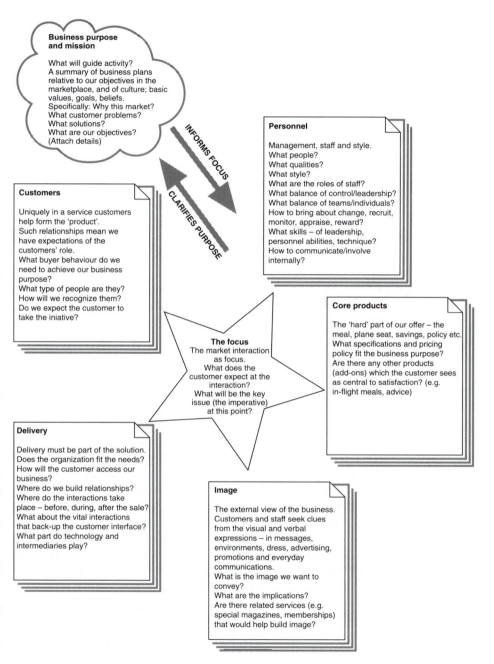

Business purpose and mission

What will guide activity?
A summary of business plans relative to our objectives in the marketplace, and of culture; basic values, goals, beliefs.
Specifically: Why this market?
What customer problems?
What solutions?
What are our objectives?
(Attach details)

INFORMS FOCUS

CLARIFIES PURPOSE

Personnel

Management, staff and style.
What people?
What qualities?
What style?
What are the roles of staff?
What balance of control/leadership?
What balance of teams/individuals?
How to bring about change, recruit, monitor, appraise, reward?
What skills – of leadership, personnel abilities, technique?
How to communicate/involve internally?

Customers

Uniquely in a service customers help form the 'product'.
Such relationships mean we have expectations of the customers' role.
What buyer behaviour do we need to achieve our business purpose?
What type of people are they?
How will we recognize them?
Do we expect the customer to take the iniative?

Core products

The 'hard' part of our offer – the meal, plane seat, savings, policy etc.
What specifications and pricing policy fit the business purpose?
Are there any other products (add-ons) which the customer sees as central to satisfaction? (e.g. in-flight meals, advice)

The focus
The market interaction as focus.
What does the customer expect at the interaction?
What will be the key issue (the imperative) at this point?

Delivery

Delivery must be part of the solution.
Does the organization fit the needs?
How will the customer access our business?
Where do we build relationships?
Where do the interactions take place – before, during, after the sale?
What about the vital interactions that back-up the customer interface?
What part do technology and intermediaries play?

Image

The external view of the business.
Customers and staff seek clues from the visual and verbal expressions – in messages, environments, dress, advertising, promotions and everyday communications.
What is the image we want to convey?
What are the implications?
Are there related services (e.g. special magazines, memberships) that would help build image?

Figure 5.1   The service mix: using the service star to put the customer in focus. The figure summarizes the elements of the service mix relative to the focus of the business – the interaction. (*Source*: The Service Star © Ken Irons 1984, revised 1991)

Figure 5.2   The cost trap. *(Source*: Grönroos, Strategic Management and Marketing in the Service Sector (1982))

performance. Indeed, it may be seen that much traditional marketing is potentially dangerous. In a manufacturing situation costs may be seen as a largely internal issue. In a service, however, there is almost always a direct link between costs and market performance. Attempts to achieve profitability at a time of competitive pricing pressure may well simply lead to a deterioration of the service at the point of interaction or discontinuity, and so decreased satisfaction. You may recognize the 'vicious circle' that is shown in Figure 5.2.

The service mix is a fundamental tool for ensuring that planning is based on a customer focus and not on a product focus. A real-life example is shown in Figure 5.3. Constructed by a reinsurance company, a highly technical field where it is easy to lose sight of the essentially people-based nature of the business, it shows how the tool helps to put the product, and technique, into context. A further example for a small, passenger ferry company is shown in Figure 5.4. Again it helps to emphasize both the elements of the service mix and the need for them to balance at the focus – the interaction – and to reflect the purpose or vision of the business.

The task of designing a customer focus is a 'chicken and egg' situation. The creation of a focus from the mission statement and a balanced service mix, will be a starting point, but it will require refinement in the light of subsequent steps. In particular it is necessary to recognize that a customer's relationship with the organization is dynamic, with typically a large number of interactions

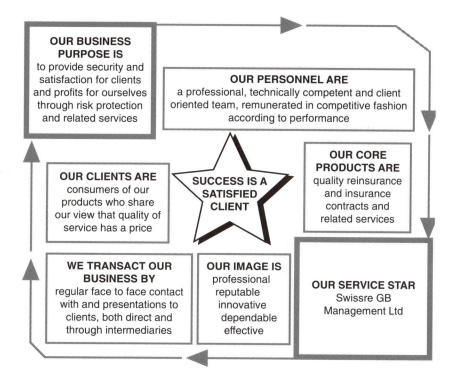

Figure 5.3   Service Star I. (*Source:* © Ken Irons 1984/1988)

happening over a period of time. Putting the customer in focus therefore requires not only that a specific identified person, or group of people, is in focus but that it is clear what is to happen at the point where they and the organization meet. Organizations with clear answers to the questions, 'Who is the customer?' and, 'What is he/she buying?' have a significant advantage here.

So, for example, both Lyonnaise des Eaux and Saga have structured their business around both a clear customer definition – 'local authorities' and 'people in or approaching retirement' respectively – and have treated technical considerations as secondary. Rather, they have concentrated development on their customers' needs, a task which has become easier because the buying behaviour of a clear customer group is more readily discernible and capable of linking to interactions. So, for example, Roger De Haan, Chairman of Saga, says, 'Once we had become clear about our target market, life became much simpler. Everyone knew much better what they had to do. We put great emphasis on understanding and supporting the customer at the points of contact (interactions) because we recognize these are absolutely critical to them and to our

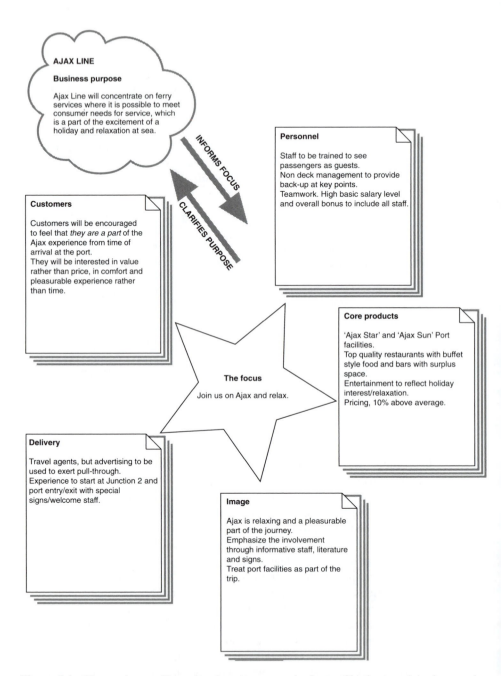

AJAX LINE

Business purpose

Ajax Line will concentrate on ferry services where it is possible to meet consumer needs for service, which is a part of the excitement of a holiday and relaxation at sea.

INFORMS FOCUS

CLARIFIES PURPOSE

Customers

Customers will be encouraged to feel that *they are a part* of the Ajax experience from time of arrival at the port.
They will be interested in value rather than price, in comfort and pleasurable experience rather than time.

Personnel

Staff to be trained to see passengers as guests.
Non deck management to provide back-up at key points.
Teamwork. High basic salary level and overall bonus to include all staff.

The focus

Join us on Ajax and relax.

Core products

'Ajax Star' and 'Ajax Sun' Port facilities.
Top quality restaurants with buffet style food and bars with surplus space.
Entertainment to reflect holiday interest/relaxation.
Pricing, 10% above average.

Delivery

Travel agents, but advertising to be used to exert pull-through.
Experience to start at Junction 2 and port entry/exit with special signs/welcome staff.

Image

Ajax is relaxing and a pleasurable part of the journey.
Emphasize the involvement through informative staff, literature and signs.
Treat port facilities as part of the trip.

Figure 5.4 The service star II: putting the customer as the focus of business activity in a service.
(*Source:* © Ken Irons 1984/1988. Copy based on an example 1986)

long-term success. So, we have specially developed training packages, to allow our staff to cope well with the particular demands of older customers on the 'phone; responding to their needs to talk and feel listened to yet not allowing costs to get out of control. We 'over resource' – by the standards of other operators – our customer assistance during the journey to the holiday destination (for example unusually at both the departure and arrival airports) because we know this is an important point of contact – a key experience – for our customers.'

The service as a process

These comments from Saga highlight the next point. In service organizations, production processes happen together with consumption processes – and usually sales processes, too. In fact, process is a good description of what is happening. Whilst most suppliers are inclined to view service as an addition to the product, a series of, maybe optional, add-ons which can be altered, varied or dropped as pressures dictate, in-depth research into customer attitudes toward service businesses and service purchases suggests the consumer sees the service as an integral process, to which there is a start (the beginning of involvement) and a finish (the end of that involvement). The core product is simply a part of this.

This view of a service as a process is a direct reflection of services being made 'face-to-face', at the time of consumption. They are a series of 'one-off' production runs. Although the analogy between a manufacturing process and a service process is strong, it is only an analogy. Service processes are different because:

- The consumer is a participant in the service process;
- A service is less capable of structure and control than manufacturing, though the amount of control can be varied, depending on the market and internal factors;
- The output is transient, leaving only memories or promises.

Such definitions of the service process are also those of a relationship, and that is the most productive way of viewing a service business because in this it parallels human relationships. The life of a business relationship may be seen as analogous to a lifetime, with the progress between start and finish being substituted for the journey between birth and death. Both are punctuated by discontinuities or breakpoints – such as a Saga customers' main-line station transfers – and it is this analogy which has given rise to discontinuity theory as a method of identifying both the process as a whole and the key breakpoints (see Box 5.3).

Box 5.3 Discontinuity theory

The basis

For every individual, life can be seen as a continuum between the two great discontinuities: birth and death. But only a moment's reflection will show that the continuum is in fact punctuated by a number of major discontinuities. Some examples are illustrated in Figure 5.5. Closer examination would show that even the intervals between any of these major discontinuities are in fact punctuated by a host of minor discontinuities.

The life of a relationship between a company and its customers is also a series of discontinuities, some major, some minor. These discontinuities are essentially another way of expressing interactions, those key points when our business idea is finally turned to success or failure with the customer. As can be readily seen, it is at these major discontinuities, for example buying a house or a new car or a major business initiative, that customers are most exposed to new problems, need new solutions and so may seek alternative suppliers of services. Indeed, research suggests that in between such breaks in life customers are not prone to seek out new sources of advice, help or satisfaction.

Taking this further, you can see that it is at these points of discontinuity that you may find new customers. However, the changes in society (for example, the growing strengths of the 'discriminating aware consumer' mean that customers want – and will increasingly expect to get – a total or seamless solution to their needs at this point. They will expect to be treated as an individual, not as a target for a series of possibly well meant, but essen-

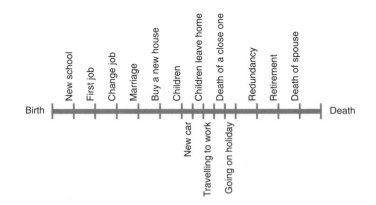

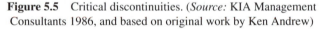

Figure 5.5 Critical discontinuities. (*Source:* KIA Management Consultants 1986, and based on original work by Ken Andrew)

continues

continued

tially uncoordinated efforts from a bewildering array of difficult to understand suppliers of various technically-orientated products.

Practical applications

Life discontinuities

A major life assurance company was interested to develop innovative approaches to distribution and product development. Research among the key target group of customers (age 45–60, married, middle income) showed that:

- There were clear categories of discontinuity in their lives;
- Preparedness for and reaction to these discontinuities varied from category to category but there was an overall feeling of helplessness/ unpreparedness;
- In each case, there was a primary area of effect which dominated their reactions and was the key to 'entry';
- There was enthusiasm for a source of planning for, and support at, these points.

From this it was possible to construct detailed, quantified research into specific aspects of distribution and product development and also to give more focused sales training.

Service process discontinuities

An airline carried out a study to determine the most important elements for the customer in an airline journey. They found that five critical discontinuities determined whether customers felt that they had received good or bad service:

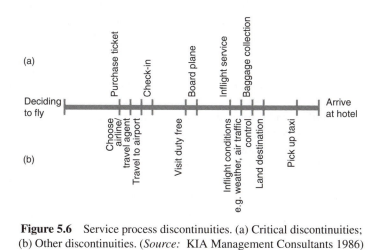

Figure 5.6 Service process discontinuities. (a) Critical discontinuities; (b) Other discontinuities. (*Source:* KIA Management Consultants 1986)

continues

continued

- Buying the ticket
- Check-in
- Boarding the plane
- In-flight service
- Baggage collection.

Figure 5.6 illustrates an airline journey in terms of discontinuity theory.

The study concluded that, provided the airline ensured that sufficient attention and resources were applied at these points, there was a very high chance of satisfaction and that the customer would choose to travel with them again.

One of the problems here, of course, is that not all of the critical discontinuities are under the airline's control, for example baggage collection. Nevertheless, the customer still feels and believes that the airline 'owns' the problems at these points. Airlines therefore try to find ways of exercising control at baggage collection by having their own 'terminals' at major airports.

Seeing the service as a process and the discontinuities as the key points and then selecting those that are most important to the customer – rather than you – can transform both the way the business is run and the results in terms of customer satisfaction. Televerket, for example, have recognized that very often they get a bad image because the originator of a complaint within a customer company does not get to hear about the quick repair or good service. For him or her – both in personal as well as business life – Televerket have simply failed again. Quick response and quick recovery mean nothing, because they never get to hear about it. So, as we saw, Televerket now take great pains to ensure that wherever possible the person within a customer company who originally requested a service call, and not just the immediate contact person, is identified and informed of the outcome by the Televerket employee assigned to that company.

Virgin Atlantic have even sought to create such discontinuities, providing key experiences which enhance the customers' perception of service. 'Every journey should be made up of unforgettable pleasures and surprises,' they say. So, for example, they provide ice-cream in mid-flight, 'just when people feel a need for something refreshing'. This goes beyond expectations to provide a superior experience.

In conclusion

The vision of a business has to be rooted firmly in the customers and their perceptions of what is important. This vision is realized at the interaction and it is necessary to put this at the centre of your planning. Then the resources at your disposal – as defined in the service mix – need to be brought together in balance at these points of interaction.

These points can be seen as discontinuities within a total process which, if looked at from the customers' viewpoint, often suggest a different order of priorities. In turn, this is going to have an impact on structure and organization and we will look at that in Chapter 7.

References

(1)   Smith A. (1777). *The Wealth of Nations.*
(2)   Quoted by Claire Penfold of Avis at a Market Research Society seminar, 1991.
(3)   Grönroos C. (1982). *Strategic Management and Marketing in the Service Sector.* Helsinki: Svenska Handelshögskolan
(4)   Cowell D. (1984). *The Marketing of Services.* London: Heinemann

6

Strategic management

- Strategic management is about turning the vision into a two-way link between 'our world' and the world of the consumer – 'their world'.

- What happens at the interaction is not simply the outcome of strategy but, in a service, it *is* the strategy.

- Strategic management is not just strategic planning but is the key to giving direction in a service.

- Being clear about strategic objectives – the strategic positioning of an organization – makes it easier to be clear about what needs to be done and how to organize for this.

- The 'virtuous link' style of management allows a high degree of authority at the interaction without loss of central control.

Strategy and service

Many organizations in our research reacted to questions about strategy by saying that they did not have one. This was primarily because they saw strategy, from experience elsewhere or from textbooks or consultants, as being a complex document written to please planners and not to achieve anything worthwhile commercially. Yet, in fact, they always did have one and it was, in effect, a vision or mission statement – a core set of beliefs rooted in the market and the business. Most often it was written and was primarily narrative in nature. Whether by intent or default, they had adopted one of the basic principles of strategic management.

As we have seen, such an approach is a critical part of developing a successful service and is interlinked with the existence or creation of strong and cohesive cultures, for having an aim is fundamental to providing a common purpose, and from this the 'clear personality' of such cultures emerges.

But service management needs to be more than simply a vision or mission statement if it is to have real impact. It must give that vision practical effect and, in doing this, take particular account of two almost contradictary needs:

(1)   To give strong direction.
(2)   To allow the implementation – itself a production process, but largely run away from direct supervision and with direct customer interference – to mould as events unfold.

In a service, therefore, strategic management needs to be about both the creation of the central purpose, the sense of mission, *and* the guidance and direction – but not immediate control – of the implementation, together with effective feedback to allow that moulding to happen without anarchy.

In all of this the mission statement plays a role beyond that of simply being a statement of good intentions. It should also be the principal guide and we saw this with the JHP document (see Box 4.2).

So, for example, Saga have a mission statement which forms a key part of their five-year group plan and provides guidance to the Group Board on key decisions, such as direction of investment and parameters for Divisional Management. However, the mission statement is also used directly in the development of implementation. The Chairman uses this as a base document for briefing the buyers of hotel space – obviously a key component of the service mix – so that in negotiations they may have in mind not just price or 'good' service but 'relevant' service. This is putting expectations and experiences at the heart of strategy.

The creation of service is a strategic matter in which many of the traditional separations between planning and implementation have no part. Strategy is never a completed task but is continuously being developed and recreated from the very fact of its being used. It must constantly pull together 'our world' and 'their world'; that is why strategic management is a task and not simply a plan.

Service implementation

Strategic management, rather than strategic planning, approaches are becoming increasingly accepted. However, it is not new. Most thinking about strategy was first codified by the Prussian general Clausewitz in his classic book *On War*. It is instructive to read his comments on implementation. 'As [strategy] to a great extent can only be determined on conjectures some of which turn out to be incorrect, while a number of other arrangements pertaining to details cannot be made at all beforehand, it follows, as a matter of course, that strategy must go with the Army into the field in order to arrange particulars on the spot, and to make the modifications in the general plan which incessantly become necessary in war.'[1]

This emphasis seems to have been a lasting legacy, since Max Hastings, in his book on the Normandy campaign in 1944, *Overlord*, comments on how the German army were able to put up a significant resistance in the face of overwhelming superiority of material and numbers simply because, at NCO level in particular, they had a better understanding of objectives beyond the immediate and were prepared to take the opportunity as it arose. As a result, they built on and exploited weaknesses in the Allies' attack.

There are many reasons for this effectiveness, but in the light of current attitudes toward middle management it is interesting to note Max Hastings' comments, that a key difference between the structure of the American and German armies in Normandy was the high percentage of support staff and full officers in the American army. Some American units had only 65% fighting men whilst their German equivalent had 90%. Moreover, the number of fighting men in the German army included a much greater proportion of non-commissioned officers and, 'the [German] army laid particular emphasis upon NCO leadership'.[2]

Few service organizations are about something as terrible and destructive as war, but the basic lessons of service strategy (for an army is a service) are relevant and strong; the strategy needs to be implemented not only through people, but by them. It must capture their commitment so that they respond to events as they unfold.

The comparisons are also relevant in that they demonstrate that individual acceptance of responsibility and hierarchy are not necessarily incompatible. One of the most service orientated of the organizations that played a part in the research for this book was Falck. 'Fast help is good help' is their slogan and one of the crewmen said quite spontaneously, 'We always know we need to get the job done and help people'. But Lars Nørby, Chief Executive, who comes from an insurance background, observes, 'Although they are less bureaucratic [than an insurance company] they need symbols and structure. To my surprise, and even more that of my family, I have to wear a uniform on some occasions. We have parades and a New Year Day speech. [In the insurance company] people were studiously casual but in Falck it can be almost militaristic.' On the other hand, supervisory management are leaders not managers. 'My job,' said one shift manager, 'is to provide support. I would only tell someone what to do if he didn't know – but in nine years I've never had to.' What the research showed was that Falck had an outstanding leadership situation, linked to a culture based on highly routine procedures.

The points of commonality in this are that you must:

- Have clear, simple objectives, which can be understood and endorsed by everyone involved;
- Allow individual judgements on interpretation to be not just an accepted part of the work but encouraged; emphasize that it is failure to act which is the problem;
- Ensure top management share the principles and *openly and visibly declare themselves* as sharing the same priorities as their middle management and staff;
- Ensure middle management see themselves as leaders (see also Chapter 8) and become a focal point in providing support at the key point of consummation, the interaction.

The excessive belief in hierarchy and pyramid control structures is a great hindrance in achieving this, causing top management to be cut off from the critical part of strategy implementation, the interaction.

Strategy as the link

Strategy is critical to providing this link between the idea and its implementation and the control necessary to achieve decentralization without creating chaos. As we have seen, strategy has been derided by some managers in recent years because it became associated with excessive planning – putting into neat boxes a future which never happened. But strategy as a vision of the future and as a method of controlling where the business goes in relation to this – not being just a collection of 'nice little earners' – is of particular significance because changes in society (see Chapter 1) mean that the future shape of service organizations will be radically different from those that predominate today. Responding to the increasing pressure for customer focus, the service business of the future will be an organization which provides seamless solutions to particular – indeed, often highly specific – groups of people with similar needs. Such changes destroy traditional concepts of markets, as the boundaries of each industry are unknown and unstable; sometimes it is hard to distinguish between customers, suppliers and competitors.

In such a situation recognizing your 'core competencies', relative to a specific market or markets, rather than technical considerations, becomes essential. Two of the core respondents in our research are examples of this new type of business: Lyonnaise des Eaux-Dumez (see Case 6.1) and Saga. Saga has built an enviable record as a supplier of services to older people, primarily to people in or approaching retirement. Starting with off-season travel for pensioners, it is now also involved in special interest holidays, publishing,

Case 6.1 A strategic focus

Lyonnaise des Eaux is one the oldest established water companies in the world but today the focus is not specifically water, or any other technical skill, though it has them in abundance. Rather, the Company has defined that its distinctive competitive skills, its market edge, lie in 'dealing with local government and the parallel structures of central government' and more particularly within this 'environmental protection'.

'Because we had a visionary Company, and were prepared to articulate this, primarily due to Jerome Monod (our President),' said Guy de Panafieu, Group Managing Director, 'we realised long before it became fashionable that there was a need for an organization which could do more than provide services but could look at the environmental issues involved as a whole. Such a vision also helped us to fight off nationalization in the early 80s (when much of French industry was nationalized, including all the major banks and insurance companies) and show that Government involvement would provide no added value.'

Indeed, Lyonnaise is a visionary company and more recently (1990) has gone on to realize that the achievement of this aim means that capital investment and its subsequent operation are increasingly inseparable; that the traditional builders' view of 'build and go' is not acceptable. In this, maintenance and building are two sides of the same coin, so Lyonnaise bought Dumez, a construction company, and will integrate their cultures, so that the customer will benefit from seamless service.

Guy de Panafieu comments, 'It has not been an easy time to get involved in construction but we are creating a synergy which is having results already. For example, we won a major contract in Buenos Aires just recently (1993) because unlike the other tenderers we had competence across the range of activities needed, and an established construction record in Argentina. We still have much to do to achieve the cohesiveness we seek, but we are steadily building up a service mentality and management in the Dumez operation and Jerome Monod is a critically important figure in this.

We still have a creditability problem with some individual shareholders and with the press, who have yet to really understand 'why' we did this. They see it as merely a grandiose dream, to be simply bigger. But we are confident, indeed much more so now than last year when the construction problems were at their worst. Now we can see both real growth of activity – five to ten per cent a year – and the real fruits of our vision, in many parts of the world.'

financial services and retirement homes. But the vision of the Company is uncompromisingly 'service to these people in or approaching retirement'. Chairman, Roger De Haan, says, 'But, such a clear strategy is also constricting. For example, we have not been able to work with traditional property developers on a joint basis [on projects such as retirement homes] because their focus has been on building; ours is a continuing relationship of service. For us, that is the crucial issue.'

As Case 6.1 shows, the experiences and ambitions of Lyonnaise and Saga, have interesting parallels. So, it is companies like these and Falck, with their tradition of care and concern, that will be the key to the future. Companies that aspire to this will need to develop a culture of leadership rather than simply control. If employees are to act like Falck employees ('We just concentrate on the job (and the customer),' said one employee) then they have to have a culture where that concentration is possible.

The Royal Albert Hall, too, has been able to successfully create change. The key to this was a shift of focus, not simply to the customer but to what the customer gets from the whole experience. The Royal Albert Hall is there to provide success (for promoters) and a sense of excitement, of occasion (for the public). To achieve this, everyone has to be able to share the customers' experience and be able to respond to it. This is more fully outlined in the next chapter, in Case 7.1.

The fault of most organizations is that they see such developments as a purely marketing activity, as operational or tactical decisions, *an outcome of business strategy*, whereas in fact such vision in a service, *is the strategy*. Your mission statement creates a market position. Whilst such a strategic positioning should always be an important part of strategy, in a service it is vital. Without it, plans may either be incapable of translation or become so degraded in the process of implementation that they cease to have meaning.

The reason for this is that in a service environment, the translation of strategy into reality is totally dependent on the translator for effectiveness, indeed for it happening at all. Even cost effectiveness has to be something people *want* to achieve if it is not to be mere efficiency, unrelated to effect. The transiency, the involvement of people not merely as salespeople but as an integral part of customers' perceptions of what is satisfactory or unsatisfactory; the finalization of the 'product' in front of and with the customer; the 'one-off' nature of the 'product'; the influence exercised by the customer – all of these mean that strategy in services is uniquely different from manufacturing because of the differences in implementation. *But it is too late at the implementation stage to consider this.*

This aspect of strategy is critical to success. Yet it is not simply a commonplace problem to see strategies – often good strategies – ineffectively implemented in a service business; it is normal, with good execution the exception.

We will return to this question of implementation later in this chapter, but first we should clarify what we mean by strategy.

What is a strategy?

In essence, service strategies are no different from strategies for any business. The purpose of strategy is to identify future needs and to marshall resources to create solutions to these needs, whether in the short or long term. It is not a budget or any other form of operational plan.

In their purest form, strategies are about clarifying what is to be achieved and how to achieve it, against a background of an understanding of the pattern of external events, and the threats and opportunities they represent. Winston Churchill summed this up neatly in the first volume of his book, *The Second World War.* 'Advantage is gained in war and also in foreign policy and other things by selecting from many attractive or unpleasant alternatives the dominating point. American thought had coined the expression "Overall Strategic Objective". When our officers first heard this they laughed; but later on its wisdom became apparent and accepted. Evidently this should be the rule, and other great business be set in subordinate relationship to it. Failure to adhere to this simple principle produces confusion and futility of action, and nearly always makes things much worse later on.'[3]

Annoyingly for the Americans, the British still found this difficult to accept, Churchill included, as the historian Correlli Barnett records so graphically in his history of the Royal Navy in the war[4], almost failing to achieve any one thing with the slender resources available. Nevertheless, it is fascinating to see, after the idea of concentration on an overall strategic objective (or two) really began to take hold, how much more effective the Allies' war effort became.

So, strategy must provide both an overriding aim to activity and guidelines concerning how this is to be achieved. As part of this, the strategy must define how this relates to the external environment – how it relates to the needs of customers, relative to the alternatives they perceive as relevant. So, in effect, there are three parts to a strategy:

(1)   The ultimate purpose, the vision or mission statement.
(2)   The strategic guidelines, or the outlines which will allow for the evolution of the vision, taking account of changing circumstances and immediate problems, yet retaining an element of sufficient control from, and feedback to, the centre.
(3)   A justification – 'the reason why'.

The ultimate purpose

This is the cause everyone is working for. It will act as a rallying point and give everyone a clear objective and an equally clear reason for their effort. Some of the terms that are used to describe this are, overall strategic objective (as in the

Churchill quotation), strategic positioning or, as we have used so far, vision or mission statement. The document may be a few very simple statements or just a few pages. The illustration from the Royal Albert Hall in Case 7.1 is a good example of positioning. A further example, based on the work of an insurance company, is shown in Case 6.2.

A further form can be that of the Service Mix Model (Figure 5.1) and this is a valuable way of summarizing thinking. Whatever form it takes, the statement should be:

- Simple to understand.
- Unifying in its concept, that is it should serve to unite everyone behind an agreed common cause which also reflects of their own perceptions of what is right.
- External in its emphasis, that is it should strive toward achievement outside of the organization and not be simply a self-satisfying internal statement such as, 'We are the best' (this merely serves to confirm everyone in their own view and possibly classify any critical outsider as not understanding the real, that is 'our', problems).

Being simple is of particular importance. A strategic objective needs to be capable of creating a clear focus for everyday work. It should be easily repeatable, maybe even recreated pictorially. The very simple, 'We Try Harder' of Avis – probably the first time anyone had dared to advertise they were less than supreme in the marketplace – is still one of the best examples ever. Using the Service Mix Model, the vision would form the critical part of the 'Business Purpose' and the reduction of this the focus of the 'star'.

The strategic guidelines

Once the positioning is established, it may be necessary to produce a more detailed document or series of documents. These will not be detailed plans, but will show *how* the strategy is to be achieved, setting parameters for action. It may be written at the same time as the positioning or later. It may be broad (that is at the organization-wide level) or specific to a task. As an example, in the last chapter, we saw how James Holt & Partners had developed their mission statement. This is a good example of how a 'Strategic Guidelines' document can be developed to provide guidance but not close down too tightly on, for example, divisional thinking.

Case 6.2 Selling security

Developing a strategic position

Insurance companies are under particular threat. Like all financial organizations their previously protected position is being eroded, and not just by
increased competition (the 'supply side' of insurance, money, is something
which is easily 'turned on', not only by competitors but by buyers, too, who can
self-insure), reduced legislation and technology. Their 'product' – indemnity in
the event of unexpected accident or catastrophe, funded by the contribution
of the many to protect the few – has been overtaken by events and is seen by
customers, who increasingly want to be treated as individuals, as out of date.

Research shows how very critical this is. 'We sell security,' say most
insurance companies. 'When I have a crisis, the insurance company is a part
of the problem, not the solution,' say most consumers.

Cornhill Insurance, a hitherto conventional medium-sized UK company,
has taken a radical view of this (and carried out much research and development). Their conclusion is that real security must be provided and to this end
the company has adopted a clear positioning to provide not only insurance but
related services in order to achieve this. Only time will tell the result, but the
objective cannot be in doubt from the strategic positioning it has adopted.

'Cornhill's objective is to expand its business in a profitable and dependable manner by concentrating on meeting customers' needs for security. This
will be achieved by building relationships, not simply by issuing paper
products. This requires the development of a service culture at every level
which delivers and demonstrates care and concern for customers, intermediaries and staff.'

Currently, this is now being developed in terms of specific strategies for
identified markets where providing security has commercial value, but is also
being expanded into a wider set of definitions of values which the company
needs to have to rule its business decisions.

However, even at this stage, it shows that the ultimate purpose of a
strategy should be in a form which relates to the market and 'its' perceptions,
not the inward-looking definitions of technique or suchlike.

A justification

This will set out the reasoning, either for change or for the status quo, based
on what consumers need. In other words, it will outline 'demand change'. It may
be an extensive document and will almost certainly have some back-up docu-
mentation (for example some market research and/or an analysis of external

and social change as it affects the market). The sort of factors outlined in the Box 1.1 are of particular significance in understanding real change, not least because services are particularly affected by such external and social change.

Strategies and budgets

From a business control point of view, budgets can be an important tool, but for strategic management they are not simply insufficient, they are misleading and dangerous. This is because they have a number of significant defects:

- Being money driven – and indeed largely cost driven – they tend to ignore the market potential, either overlooking opportunity or simply failing to take account of market pressures, especially local variances or competitive moves.
- Being short term, they most often accentuate the short-term return and so cloud the effort needed for long-term change, a key issue in services.
- Being numbers driven, they tend to be unattractive to anyone other than finance people and thus are seen as a chore to be completed quickly, not as an aid.
- With a focus on a 'point in time' and the current year they are likely to fail to emphasize the value of customers over time, and the need to link resource usage – particularly the key service resource of time – directly to the central tenet of service philosophy, the relationship.

It is important to emphasize that strategic management is not simply a synonym for long-term planning. It is a particular form of planning and is about giving an aim to action and employing resources to achieve the organization's mission or end purpose. As such, timescales and conventional planning procedures, while not irrelevant, take secondary importance. The differences between conventional, budgetary-based planning and that underpinning strategic management are illustrated in Figures 6.1 and 6.2. Figure 6.1 is typical of many strategic or long-term plans. It is simply a form of extended operational planning, typically based on the budget. Such plans, having usually started out as a success, become embellished with step-by-step extrapolations of existing, and so largely known, factors. Such plans do not present arguments for change or for selecting from alternatives the course or courses most likely to achieve overall objectives. Further, step-by-step plans are often difficult to review because they are overtaken by events before they can be fulfilled and are too light on narrative to stimulate debate or understanding, let alone conviction in their outcome. Such an approach to strategy can be readily identified, for it will usually have page upon page of largely meaningless figures, each passing year showing an even greater apparent accuracy in the shape of a growing number of decimal points.

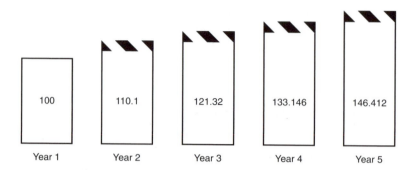

Figure 6.1   Strategic planning – the wrong way. (*Source:* Based on original work in the Eastman Kodak Company, Rochester, NY)

In strategic management, however, what we most need to have related is our specific competence to a market which will sustain our ambitions in terms of, for example, profit; similarly, production and consumption must be related and not take the form of an exercise in adding up figures. Figure 6.2 illustrates a more realistic approach to building plans linked to overall objectives using a market-led approach.

Using the principles in Figure 6.2 it is possible to:

- Think in terms of both where you are going and how you are going to get there;
- Consider alternative scenarios, either highlighting the key issues of discontinuities, which need particular monitoring because they signal you are on the road to success or failure, or alerting you to a need for change;
- Provide 'a strategic frame' – a parameter within which implementation may be developed;
- Give more objective consideration to matching internal and external efficiencies – that is you will find it easier to stand back and look at what you have as an organization and what you need for the market;
- Develop a sustainable competitive advantage;
- Have the faith to be different because you have a more clear-sighted view of what the future may, or could, bring.

Devolving power

The distinctions between strategic planning and strategic management are not merely of academic interest. For most organizations it will be the planning processes which provide the possibility to achieve change or to block it. The need is to ensure that top management can:

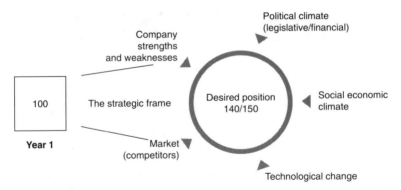

Figure 6.2   Strategic planning – the right way. (*Source:* Based on original work in the Eastman Kodak Company, Rochester, NY)

- Exercise strategic control, clarify purpose and set the broad parameters for activity;
- Yet retain influence over the implementation because in a service this cannot be entirely divorced from the plans themselves.Strategy must respond to the interactions.

As already observed, Handelsbanken has responded to this by eliminating the budgetary processes, virtually in their entirety. It has now followed this precept with success for nearly 20 years, and some of the thinking which lies behind this is expressed in Case 6.3.

Not every organization will have the nerve to carry out the radical approach adopted by Handelsbanken, but it has worked for them in terms of results, including an effective control on cost, as illustrated by one of the branch managers who recalled how, when his branch was renovated, he and his staff had gone to IKEA and bought the 'backroom' furniture to save money.

Increasingly, organizations are recognizing that budgets for service organizations should be the end result of a process which starts with the questions 'What does the market need and what can we expect to achieve with the resources we have (or could have) at our disposal? How can we marshall our resources to best effect to achieve this?' Properly organized, it may not be necessary to involve anyone but financial people in the budgetary process itself. Indeed, a number of organizations have stopped involving others.

BP Oil International, a giant of a company by any standards, has already taken steps in this direction. BPOI is the refining and marketing arm of the

Case 6.3   Dispensing with budgets

How Handelsbanken broke with convention

By conventional standards of control Handelsbanken are deficient – no strategic planning *and no budgets*. Yet they have one of the clearest strategies – a firm 'strategic positioning' in terms of the relationships with the markets rather than with products. This is all set out clearly in their internal booklet *Our Way*, and is based on the pioneering work of Jan Wallander, the architect of Handelsbanken's success today.

However, not only did Wallander believe that it was relationships and not products which created profit, but his experiences as a scientist and head of a research institution – linked to the Swedish Government and industry – had led him to doubt the value of most forecasts, he wrote, 'During my subsequent practical work as a banker...I reached the scandalous conclusion that forecasts, budgets and long-term plans often do more harm than good.'[5]

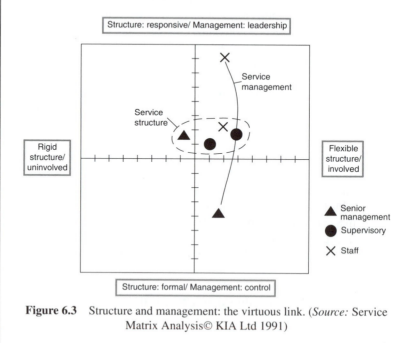

Figure 6.3   Structure and management: the virtuous link. (*Source:* Service Matrix Analysis© KIA Ltd 1991)

continues

continued

Developing this thinking, in the early 1970s led Handeslbanken to do away with most of the, then, fairly extensive long-term planning and budgeting processes. They continued to make long-term forecasts of their liquidity and interest levels, which were necessary for long-term investment. They continue to, '...always ask questions, to discuss alternative actions and opportunities [and look at] detailed and exact assessments of the future [since they] become interesting and important in so far as they illuminate these continually shifting decision situations [and] it is then, but only then, meaningful to make [decisions]' [5]. However, of greater significance is that the Bank has rejected conventional budgetary control, with all its heavy emphasis on getting the figures right and adding up. Instead, Handelsbanken has:

- Been crystal clear in its overall strategic objective of developing service relationships;
- Insisted that the branch is the focus of all activity, even where the customer is a major company;
- Based its report structure on being able to analyse branch profitability (the key 'building block' in the structure) by customer, and so by relationship;
- Put considerable faith in branch managers' ability to act in the best long-term interests of the bank, and given the support and encouragement necessary for this;
- Been quick to take action when managers failed to measure up to the responsibilities;
- Given branch management the help needed to create teamwork at the branch, and the reward system to match this (a generous company-wide profit-sharing scheme makes no distinctions of salary base);
- Created a culture of leadership, where both regional and head office management see themselves as resources to the branches;
- Kept open the channels of communication between levels of management, so that everyone may learn from one another and customers need never be more than two layers away from the top.

This single-minded application of the logic of service thinking shows up graphically in our research and, although illustrated anonymously in Figure 2.16, is illustrated again in Figure 6.3. Clear, clean controls allied to visible presence and open channels of contact produce the 'virtuous link'. Staff feel they have leaders; management are in control.

BP Group and is one of BP's four main businesses. The International Management Project (IMP), which was set up to simplify management processes, has considerably increased divisional financial discretion and reduced the number of levels required to review large financial documents from 14 to 3 signatures. Some of the early results of BPOI's change are illustrated in Case 6.4. However, it is also necessary to note that planning and planning controls are not all that make for such success. True service, true customer focus, mean that management must be available to lead and to solve problems.

Case 6.4 Focusing control

'BP Oil – A Global Strategy' – the words are grand and suitably reflective of the size and power of a major oil corporation. But grand ideas in large companies have a habit of disappearing without trace and BPOI had many reasons for following this path:

- For all its size and world coverage, BPOI was fragmentary;
- The centre was seen as concentrating more on control than on strategy: more as a negative force than a positive one.

BPOI's strategy was to be in the forefront of the international oil industry through the concentration of effort on a few clearly-defined success factors (motivation, health, safety and environmental programmes, strong branding of the BP name as synonymous with quality and service, concentration of investment in growth markets and a determination to be more effective in everyday, existing activity) and through the creation of a 'BP style'. This style, although still evolving by consultation with BPOI employees, encompasses:

- Respect/trust/openness
- Being responsive to customers
- Building quality
- Integrity (ethical/forthright)
- Adaptability/innovation
- Clarity
- Long-term orientation not short-term responsiveness.

It is easy to dismiss it as words, but Jorge Tavares, who took over the leadership of the Planning and Control units in 1989, was determined to make it work in his area of responsibility, because if this function continued to exercise merely as a 'control' function then the BP strategy was doomed – the centre would remain passive.

continues

continued

'My experiences as a manager had taught me to believe that people are immensely honest and I was determined we would have a system that would reflect that, encouraging local management to make their own judgements. Our first step was to do an overhead value analysis of our Head Office in London. It showed that much of this work duplicated other activity. In many ways this was natural, because we had good people – some of the best in the business – who often did have great knowledge and experience, but they created a feeling of interference with operating managers.

The second step then was to define clearly the roles of key players and in particular to make distinctions between 'accountability', 'responsibility' and 'contributions'. [For definitions see end of this Case.]

It became clear we were getting too much information at Head Office, that we took on too much in the way of commenting on what we got – we were passing judgement rather than inviting constructive input and so creating helpful dialogue – that we had too many layers and people, and finally that few outside the centre knew what we did and where we could help.

So we made radical and far-reaching changes. Three critical areas were:

- We made it clear who had 'responsibilities', who would be 'contributors', but above all who had the 'accountability' for developing and implementing business plans (the latter being the line management);
- We classified information so that only that designated as 'core' came to Head Office; business information was for the operation of the business [for definitions see end of this Case and Figure 6.4];
- Commentary on performance – the judgement as to what results meant and what needed to be done – was the responsibility of those who were accountable, not us in staff functions.

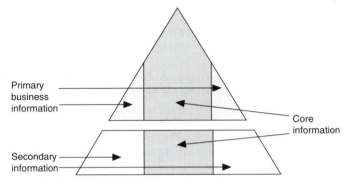

Figure 6.4   BP Oil's classification of information. (*Source:* BPOI 1990)

continues

continued

We also issued a brief booklet which stated clearly the principles and values by which we – the Management Services Group and no longer 'Oil Planning and Control' – would work and showed clearly each of our responsibilities and contact numbers, etc.

The results to date have been very encouraging. We have found people more friendly and prepared to cooperate because they are clear about both their role and ours in our ongoing relationships. They see that the control focus has shifted towards strategy *implementation* by line management (and *not the business plan* at Head Office level).

The outcome is a lighter strategic-control management style, where accountability for day-to-day management clearly rests with the operating units. Head Office staff numbers have fallen to around 100 people for a $10 billion capital-employed business.

Definitions

Accountability   The key elements of accountability are responsibility for achieving a result, together with sufficient authority and power to take needed actions and a degree of measurability of the result. In general these are found in line management positions.

Responsibility   Responsibility alone means that results are to be achieved without the direct authority and power to issue orders. All managers may have responsibilities outside their line accountability, but responsibilities are most often found in staff roles.

Contributions   A contribution to achieving a result may be required from any manager. It concerns the provision of information, assistance and advice to those with the accountabilities and responsibility. Within the document we highlight those from whom a significant contribution may be expected.

Committee   These are a few remaining necessary discussion and decision-making groups.

Network   Networking is sharing information between experts. This is a forum for discussion and not decision. People will be asked to join a network because they have information skills to contribute. The decisions are taken by the line manager accountable. The idea behind networking is a revolutionary change for the company. You join a network because you have something particular to give as needed, not only on the basis of a job title. For example, Retail is an international network for Retail Marketing, and International Technology Teams are specialist Management & Services networks. Networks do not necessarily require physical meetings, communication can be effective through electronic systems.

continues

continued

Core information This is the common currency of BP Oil throughout the world. It is built up within Divisions and International Businesses for circulation to senior managers and the Group Centre. Its ultimate focus is the Chief Executive.

Primary business information This is the specialized information required for a specific BPOI network. It is used primarily for strategy formulation and review, and is focused on the Business Developments Units. Along with core information it is the common currency of the BDUs and Divisional Businesses which together form the international business network. Similar arrangements apply for functional networks such as Human Resources, Health Safety and Environment, Research and Development, Tax and Information Systems.

Secondary business information This is the everyday information used at the operating level to run the business. It is focused on Operating Units (OPUs) and forms the common currency of the OPUs and Associates at the local level. It includes orders, despatching, invoicing and credit information, prices, stocks, payroll, general ledger and local reporting information.

In conclusion

Devolving power – creating a framework whereby individuals can respond to individuals at the interaction, the focus of the business – requires a strategic management approach in which strategy is, 'the evolution of the original guiding idea according to continually changing circumstances'. [6]

It is necessary to set a view of your positioning relative to the market. This will be linked to a view of the long-term prospects for that approach, but will free up the activity from the tyranny of short-term planning linked to budgets. Indeed, budgets are intended to be precise in allocating control and responsibility: used as strategy they will tend to emphasize financial figures and other, often internal, measures. As a result they are usually precisely wrong, when what we need in strategic management is to be approximately right!

For this to work ideas must be able to travel up as well as down. Administrative structures are, literally, a separate issue as many organizations

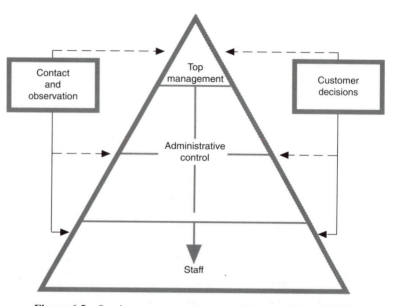

Figure 6.5 Service management contact. (*Source:* KIA Ltd 1990)

are now separating customer-based decisions from administrative control, and top management must be both involved in and aware of implementation. This is illustrated in Figure 6.5.

It will seem disturbing to many managers, reared on notions of hierarchy, but it is the form of 'control' which underlies the 'virtuous link' style of management. Traditional hierarchical structures would mean that everything goes through the levels, cascading down or percolating up. In a service, there must be contact across all levels and a fast channel for quick decisions. In this situation, middle management's key role is that of team leaders and facilitators. The implications of this are discussed in the next two chapters.

References

1. von Clausewitz K. (1832). *On War*
2. Hastings M. (1984). *Overlord.* London: Michael Joseph
3. Churchill W. (1948). *The Second World War*, Vol. 1. London: Cassell
4. Barnett C. (1991). *Engage the Enemy More Closely.* London: Hodder & Stoughton
5. Wallander J. (1979). *On forecasts, budgets and long-term planning.* Presentation published by Svenska Handelsbanken
6. von Moltke H. (1858–79). Writings when Chief of the German and Prussian General Staffs

7

Organizing for the market

- Creating an overall framework is critical to maintaining a customer focus.
- Integrating external and internal activity. Segmentation needs to be of the total service – the process – and not simply of products or customers.
- Service structure – designing the structure around the process not the product.
- Traditional functional organization can cut across this demand for customer focus and create chaos – the organization is at variance with the objective.
- The barriers – why services are not designed around the customer.
- Services across frontiers – what allows a service to travel?

The impact of customer focus

As we can see from the previous chapter, strategic management is not simply about planning but about the whole question of organizing ourselves around a vision, focusing on what we wish to achieve externally, not solely on the creation of plans designed to meet our internal drives. Handelsbanken have to be the most extreme example in our research, since they have taken the principles of service to the ultimate – decision making close to the customer, authority to make and carry through these decisions, a flat organization with easy access to top management on operational matters and a belief that staff roles are, first and foremost, to serve rather than control. But others had also created organizations which gave the customer priority, in particular Falck, Saga, Televerket and Virgin Atlantic. Sainsburys and Woolworths, too, were adjusting rapidly their previously hierarchical structures.

All of this is essential if the customer is to be the focus of activity. Those with whom the customer deals must also be in this focus and must act within a framework which reflects this as a reality of the way the organization is structured. They must have sufficient expertise and authority at their level to match the objectives and, in turn, they need both the knowledge and the confidence to act responsively. You cannot make people give service, but you can help them to give that little bit extra of themselves – from the heart and not just the mind – which turns the average into the individual.

However, such situations necessarily are unstructured, and may even tend toward the anarchic, and most managers:

- Put more emphasis on control systems than 'free response' to such haphazard stimuli;
- Are ill-equipped by both experience and training to cope with such freedoms on the part of subordinates;
- Are working, or are used to working, within a structure which emphasizes functional control rather than customer control.

Although service is our focus, we are also reflecting a fundamental change in the way in which we have to organize and manage businesses generally if we are to survive. This is not simply for services, as the following quote from the Chief Executive of Nissan Motor Manufacturing UK stresses, 'As organizations we must become increasingly able to change quickly and painlessly. This means overlap of responsibilities and functions, building on and around people's abilities rather than limiting them for the convenience of easily recognized roles. With this approach it becomes easier to accommodate constant change because it becomes part of the everyday life of the business. If we are to cope with the world we will face, we must learn to create structures that are sometimes messy, short-lived and temporary but aid the process of change. Those businesses that develop this ability will be those that survive and prosper into the next century and the challenge facing tomorrow's business leaders is to instil this culture in a fluid internal environment.'[1]

Merging 'our world' with 'their world'

If we are to succeed in creating customer focus, we have to recognize that the service demands of living with the customer mean that 'our world' and 'their world' must be able to merge at the interaction. In turn that means that we have to move away from the rigid hierarchical structures and adopt structures which

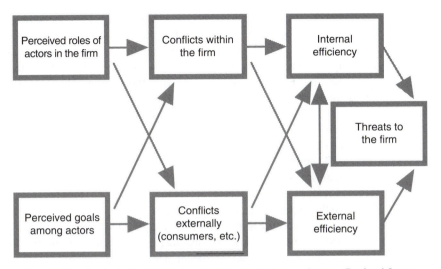

Figure 7.1   Interrelating internal and external efficiency. (*Source:* Derived from a figure in E. Rhenman and B. Stymne, *Företagsledning i en föränderlig värld*, Aldus, Stockholm, 1966, p. 92)

are not only flatter but allow for greater fluidity, more teamwork and more contact with others on a basis of need, rather than job. So, for example, Virgin Atlantic are increasingly seeing more general approaches to job descriptions linked to more task forces as a key to the future, with, to quote Chris Moss, '…jobs more and more built around the individuals and their capacity than as a straightjacket into which an individual has to be fitted'.

However, there are two barriers to this; our own defensive mechanisms and the very basis of so much conventional management thinking. We will deal with the first point in Chapter 9, but the critical block in translating service management principles into organization is, again, the traditional basis of strategic planning. In this, there are three distinctive – and distinct – elements:

(1) *Product/market efficiency.* Most strategic planning is concerned with this aspect. It involves the key questions about the overriding or ultimate purpose, deciding which services are to be provided to which markets, agreeing on product or other development and segmenting markets.

(2) *External efficiency.* This is the organization's ability to serve agreed, specific markets. It includes functional strategies such as marketing, research and development and distribution.

(3) *Internal efficiency.* In a service, this is primarily related to administration, accounting and finance.

As Figure 7.1 shows, internal efficiency as well as external efficiency problems may cause threats; both may cut across product/market efficiency. 'Our world' and 'their world' merge. So, for example, a restaurant may attempt to meet a perceived market need by developing a menu which cannot be effectively prepared or served with the existing staff. An airline may specify a level of service which the cabin staff – controlled by a different department – simply cannot cope with in the time available. In both cases the customer will become involved and directly feel the impact. These internal/external and internal/internal conflicts are commonplace (both the examples given here are real) and are often caused simply by a lack of clarity about common goals and common values. A mission statement, however uplifting, will remain a piece of paper if the real barriers to providing that service are not removed; they will not be removed if strategy is not capable of being carried through the organization, on a non-functional basis.

However, even amongst our respondents, few service companies have tackled this issue in any fundamental way. As a result it will be increasingly difficult to sustain success at a satisfactory level. Despite enormous investments of time and money in initiatives of customer care or 'putting people first', results will fall off, after an initial burst. The residual impact will often only be the replacement of one set of rules, designed to structure the activity into easily managed and consistent routines, with another. We will deal with such routines in more depth in Chapter 9, but in organizational terms the objective must be to find a way of providing a framework which gives enough control for direction but leaves open enough flexibility for both development of the strategy and implementation – the exercise of strategic management.

For many companies, interrelating 'our world' and 'their world' – creating a set of routines which match market need in flexibility and allow for the development of responsiveness in usage, to revert to the principal components of structure as shown from the research – is made exceptionally difficult because there is no real match between the customers' expectations, as a defined group of customers, and those of our staff who 'live with them' as a defined group of staff. There is a high potential for role ambiguity and, even more, role conflict.

For Saga, this is a key part of their success and Saga's experience and approach (see Case 9.1) demonstrates that successful matching of the expectations of staff and customers is behavioural as well as structural. Nor can this be seen as surprising given the importance of expectations and experiences, which obviously have a large behaviour content. But for Saga this is relatively easy because they have such a defined market, it is one of the reasons companies such as Saga, with a customer group focus and not predominately a technique focus, will prosper in a service environment – they can match the two worlds more effectively.

But in more conventional, technique-dominated, companies, where the market audiences being addressed are diffuse, especially as regards behaviour due to different expectations and experiences, it is difficult to bring the elements of market demand, structure and management abilities together. The conflicts between internal and external culture grow. Staff, in particular, cannot switch easily from one set of expectations, in effect one 'demand segment', to another; management find it difficult to control, or even accept, the resultant situations.

Service segmentation

To create a structure in which service can be effective it is necessary to have clear service segmentation but this is not the same as the conventional 'brand management' approach of product segmentation or customer segmentation (which are just the right-hand axis of the triangle). Instead there must be *segmentation of the whole organization around its chosen market,* so that it can deliver a seamless solution, without undue divergence between the internal and external cultures. Dynamic stability, as with Saga, is achieved by grouping all internal and external issues around a specific market. Where an organization is dealing with widely differing markets – an airline or a bank for example – then this may require a segmentation which cuts deep, because the task of managing these segments may be quite different.

This makes new models for such planning necessary; models which allow the relationship inherent in the triangle to be profiled. One such model – using a circular graph to reduce a multi-dimensional situation to just two dimensions – is shown in Figure 7.2.

Figure 7.2 shows, in a simplified form, the overall service comparison of two customer types (professionals and artisans) for a retail bank, using 12 key criteria. Being small businesses, both segments have similar conventional product characteristics (criteria 5 and 6) but, as the charts show, the overall service demands are starkly different. In fact, they are both part of quite different segments, so far as a service business is concerned. Whilst they require similar core products, they require quite different delivery and personnel, maybe even different images, and certainly have different expectations of customer behaviour. To illustrate this, in Figure 7.3 the profile for small artisan businesses is matched with that for over 65s. Despite differences on product criteria, the overall service pattern is an excellent match across the service mix. In fact, these two types are both part of the same service segment.

Using such profiling it is possible to take account of all aspects; there are no specifically desirable shapes, just a need to identify those shapes which match with each other, so that it is possible to structure all of the service elements coherently, relative to a specific market.

The importance of such coherence is that organizations and staff – and their managers – can function effectively, relative to the market and to each other, only when the range of options is narrowed, when organization and market can identify and live with each other in a 'balanced world'. That is, when the organization, or division, has reached a point of dynamic stability relative to the issues of market demand, structure and management, as we saw with the Yorkshire Bank in Case 5.2 and as is the case with Lyonnaise-des-Eaux and Saga. In this we may see an analogy with the creation of a brand in manufactured goods. Branding provides a simple and coherent shorthand

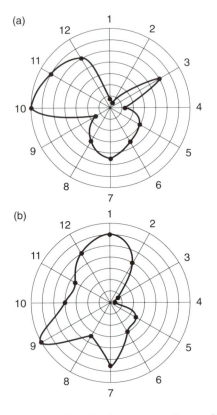

Key

1	Branch usage
2	Transmission needs – paper
3	Transmission needs – technology
4	Transmission needs – international
5	Product complexity
6	Staff – technical skills
7	Staff – customer skills
8	Staff – high/low level
9	Staff – time usage
10	Customer involvement
11	Heavy/light consumption
12	Price strategy – high/low

Figure 7.2 Service segmentation profile: comparison I. (a) Segment professional business (self-employed); (b) Segment small artisan business (primarily self-employed). (*Source:* © Ken Irons, 1984)

for what the customer may reasonably expect. But the stronger and more successful the brand, the higher the expectations of the consumer. The more they rely on the brand, the more their uncritical acceptance – in service terms, their expectations – of its good values, but equally they will be highly critical if they experience any failure or shortcomings with the brand.

So a brand cannot have 'sometimes' elements. It must be consistent. In terms of a service, therefore, a brand must be a consistent balance of all of the elements of the service mix – core products and price, personnel, image, delivery and the customers themselves. A premium service, for instance, must be premium in all respects; the pride or status that comes from the purchase of a 'premium' will be dashed by an 'ordinary' delivery or by other 'ordinary' customers.

Indeed, reverting to discontinuity analysis, it may well be that it is precisely at breakpoints that the buyer will most seek, or value, premium treatment. For example, priority in getting through immigration or customs, such as Air Portugal provides to business class passengers at Lisbon, may save

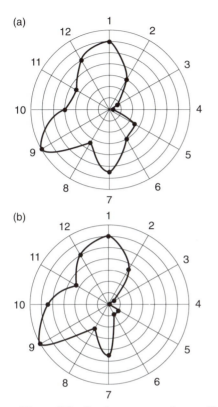

Key

1   Branch usage
2   Transmission needs – paper
3   Transmission needs – technology
4   Transmission needs – international
5   Product complexity
6   Staff – technical skills
7   Staff – customer skills
8   Staff – high/low level
9   Staff – time usage
10 Customer involvement
11 Heavy/light consumption
12 Price strategy – high/low

Figure 7.3   Service segmentation profile: comparison II. (a) Segment small artisan business (primarily self-employed); (b) Segment 65+, individuals. (*Source:* © Ken Irons, 1984)

more time than a speedier flight or make up for air traffic delays. Similarly, the impact of other customers as an element in the service mix – a part of your distinctiveness – may be that sharing social time with like-minded people may be more important than the perfect golf course.

So segmentation by the whole process of the service – in which products and both staff and customer behaviour play parts – is critical to integrating activity. With this integration, it is possible to focus resources and to reduce role ambiguities since everyone is working with a more clearly-defined structure which, paradoxically but critically, allows for greater responsiveness.

Such segmentation also points to profitability because the reduced level of ambiguity will ensure that costs are more clearly identified in relation to end value. It is also often a hidden factor in profit. For example, a recent piece of research using the technique described here, showed that the key determinant of profitability for a reinsurance company was customer behaviour. There was a direct relationship between different segments, defined by behavioural characteristics, and the long-term level of profitability of the customer in those segments.[2]

Service structure

Having identified the customer relative to the process it is necessary to create a structure. As we saw in Chapter 2, any service organization is a balance between bureaucracy and enthusiasm; although the emphasis of either of these is less important than a consistency of belief and purpose at all levels. Further, and most importantly, where there is harmony, there is a correlation with a positive customer response. That is to say, where people work in a 'positive' culture, with a clear value system, then customers are 'positive'. Role ambiguity and role conflict are lessened. What the more recent research has shown is that achieving long-term success involves more than just a simple balance between bureaucracy and enthusiasm. Instead, it depends on a cohesive attitude both to routines and to their implementation.

The routines

Following through on the factors in the research, we can see the value of routines. You cannot run any business without a degree of routine. For example:

- Railway timetables
- Emergency routines
- Administrative procedures
- Menus
- Booking procedures
- IT systems.

In particular you will see more systemization/procedural bias in:

- Larger or complex organizations;
- Organizations with a core business centred around a firm procedure (in our research putting out fires is an example) or a timetable (such as an airline);
- Organizations depending on rapid throughput, and so generally low added value per sale and hence profit through volume. Many retail organizations fall into this category.

Cohesion of management and staff perceptions along this axis is important for sustained success since failure here would suggest the organization is unclear about a basic fact, specifically do employees who deal with a customer have much or little discretion within the systems? Clarity about these imperatives in relationship to a specific market, and at each level of management and staff, will help to ensure that both staff and customer expectations are clear and free of uncertainty or ambiguity about 'what?' The questions that were used to identify the positioning on this axis help to highlight the issues involved (see Figure 7.4).

Whilst it remains largely true that successful organizations are those with closely clustered results, nevertheless what is even more true is that with successful service organizations the service structure is in harmony with a specific market demand. Two examples of bureaucratic organizations are shown in Figure 7.5. A is one of the most successful retailers in Europe and B is one of the most successful insurance companies in Europe – both highly profitable, both currently have highly rated shares. In both cases it is their very certainty in the eyes of their market which is the bedrock of their success, though it is worth noting that it may also be the stumbling block to achieving change; the very solidity of the business may make it difficult for those involved to accept change or be prepared to take the risks. A number of observers have suggested that McDonalds faces just such a problem.[3] As markets change – and the overwhelming tendency is towards looser, free situations in which there is dialogue, a relationship, and not simply sellers and buyers – this will become more accentuated as a concern.

---

(1)	(a)	It is important that we deal with as many customers as possible.
	or	
	(b)	We should spend as much time as is necessary with each customer.
(2)	(a)	Our work procedures should be flexible enough to satisfy all our customers.
	or	
	(b)	Our work procedures are standardized but meet the needs of most of our customers.
(3)	(a)	It is important to treat each customer individually.
	or	
	(b)	We make sure that customers know that they are all treated the same.
(4)	(a)	Customers need to fit in with the way that we work.
	or	
	(b)	We need to fit in with the way our customers work.

Figure 7.4   Questions on routines. (*Source:* KIA/EIU research, 1991, C3 question)

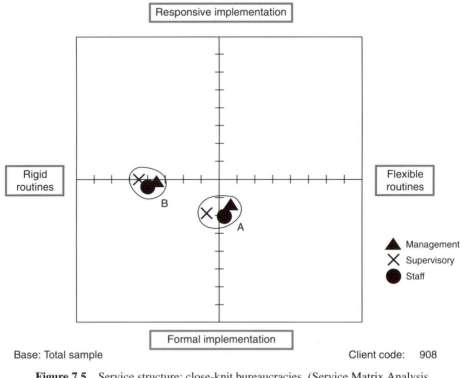

Figure 7.5   Service structure: close-knit bureaucracies. (Service Matrix Analysis
© KIA Ltd 1991)

Implementation of routines

On its own, an analysis of routines would have only limited meaning or value
– everyone could agree that the task is simply to run the trains on time as an
end in itself, or to have perfect, well-functioning booking procedures, with
little thought, and maybe even no consideration, being given to the customer.

So it is necessary to look at the business in a further dimension – how formal or responsive to external pressures is the implementation? Unfortunately,
many service organizations lack market responsiveness. For some, this is due
to monopolistic or legally protected positions. This applies, for example, to
many utilities, banks, insurance companies and airlines. Market responsiveness
needs a real and deep belief in the customer, not some routine repetition of
catch phrases. 'The customer is king,' says the poster on the wall, while the
staff continue to apply routines which demonstrate clearly this is untrue. The
staff usually know that, but no one listens.

Here we can see from the research that success is strongly linked to the cohesion of the patterns of perceptions. It is of little use for management to see the organization as flexible, if staff – who have to deal with the customer – do not; staff are inhibited from responding to the customer if their management do not see this as a priority, or even as having commercial validity. Significantly in our research, management were more inclined to see 'responsiveness' in their business than were supervisors or staff – suggesting a lack of realism. However, the successful organizations did not share this discrepancy to the same degree. Indeed, it was on this dimension that they were most noticeably close to each other.

The questions used to identify the positioning on the axis (Figure 7.6) reveal the possibilities for this variation and why it is that management can be unrealistic in their assessments.

Creating such situations is essentially a strategic problem yet, often, strategic objectives are set without regard to such concerns. Maybe they are not even seen as relevant or worthy of discussion, yet they can be, and often are, the cause of serious shortfalls in achievement in a service. Those whose task it is to bring about change – real change where it matters most, at the interaction – are simply unsure what is expected of them or cannot perform because of barriers of organization, current practice or even commonsense. In other words there is role ambiguity.

It is vital to recognize that the different extremes are of themselves 'value-free'. It is not important that you would like to be dependable, for example, rather you need to:

- Know what the market wants;
- Be able to structure the routines to reflect this (there can be immovable barriers, such as laws);
- Be able to deliver with and through your raw material, people;
- Above all, have cohesion around the values of the chosen positioning. This cohesiveness was shown in earlier charts on service structure, in Chapter 2, and some further examples are shown in Figure 7.7.

---

(1)   I often feel prevented by our procedures from making sure the customer is treated properly.

(2)   I feel I am not allowed to make mistakes.

(3)   It is more important for me to be flexible in my approach to work than to always do things in the same way.

(4)   My day-to-day routine is never the same.

(5)   Nothing can be done without filling in a lot of forms.

Figure 7.6   Questions on implementation. (*Source:* KIA/EIU research, 1991, C1 question)

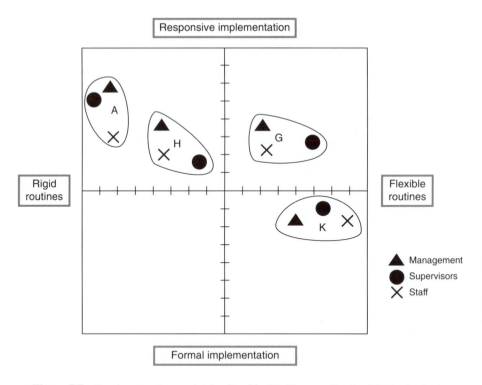

Figure 7.7   Service structure: cohesion is critical I. (*Source:* Service Matrix Analysis © KIA Ltd 1991)

In Figure 7.7 A is Falck, the Danish company operating fire engines and ambulances; G is a successful retailer; H is a successful travel operator; K is a bank which has achieved an above-average result for the sector in the past few years, although it has yet to demonstrate this over the long run.

This bank shows that it is possible to be in the bottom right quarter and still have the potential for success. But the difficulty of a positioning in this quarter is – essentially that of a mechanistic carrying out of routines, however flexible – that long-run success may be postponed unless everyone can agree on the place and role of customers in the priorities. In a sector such as banking, if the importance of the customer is ignored, it may work, but it will always be under threat from competitive manoeuvring because there is no strong link with the customer. Indeed, in this case an analysis of the results of our questions on 'own' priorities for success versus 'perceived company' priorities, shows that the overall result is due to an above-average cohesiveness on 'internal' questions (for example profit) but below-average on 'external' questions (for example customer satisfaction).

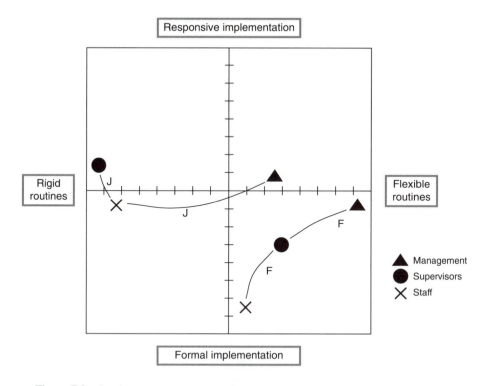

Figure 7.8   Service structure: cohesion is critical II. (*Source:* Service Matrix Analysis
© KIA Ltd 1991)

In Figure 7.8 are two further outlines, this time of organizations with no clear cohesion: F, a bank, and J, a travel operator without a clear strategy and only modest short-term success. Looking again at answers on 'own views' versus 'perceived company' priorities, there are no clear patterns, other than that neither staff nor supervisors are convinced that customers are a priority.

The implications for structure

There are a number of important implications for the structure of a service organization, not least because functional splits in organizations will only obscure the customer focus. Many of the functional splits in organization which are taken for granted in manufacturing are often used in a service without regard to the different circumstances. This is positively dangerous. Robert Townsend caught the feel of this in his book *Up the Organisation,* which recounts his experiences in bringing Avis back from the brink of extinction. He states, '"Marketing" departments – like planning departments, personnel departments, management development departments, advertising departments, and public relations departments – are usually camouflage designed to cover up for lazy or worn-out chief executives. Marketing, in the fullest sense of the word, is the name of the game. So it had better be handled by the boss and his line, not by staff hecklers.'[4]

In other words, marketing cannot be left to the marketing people. The implications do not stop at marketing, however. Human resources are a critical part of all aspects of service. Indeed, by referring back to the service star in Figure 5.1, it is possible to see that there is very little that is not a part of the service mix. This is because, on average, 10% of a manufacturing company's staff have a direct impact on the customer, whereas in a service this figure is

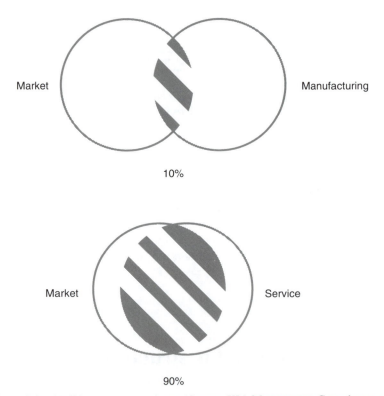

Figure 7.9 Staff impact on customers. (*Source:* KIA Management Consultants and based on the work of Christian Grönroos. *Strategic Management and Marketing – the Service Sector.* Svenska Handelshögskolan, Helsinki, 1982)

Figure 7.10   The market bridge. (*Source:* KIA Management Consultants and based on the work of Christian Grönroos. *Strategic Management and Marketing in the Service Sector.* Svenska Handelshögskolan, Helsinki, 1982)

90% (see Figure 7.9).[5] This in turn has a major impact on an organization because conventional management theory assumes a 'bridge', as in Figure 7.10, between the organization and the market, largely peopled by the 10%, a mostly consumer-driven group who can, or should, be relied on to match the company to its market.

However, in a service organization, marketing often does not exist at all as a separate entity, nor does it have such a narrow and well-defined consumer interface. Further, many marketing departments in a service organization have less direct contact with the market than those who make up the 90%, nor will they control most of the elements that achieve service distinction at the interactions. Finally, this 90% are, for the most part, a largely task-driven group who may even be uneasy with consumers or wary of contact, since they may be technicians or introspective people who have chosen an office life specifically because it does not entail high levels of personal contact. The relationship created by this bringing together of the majority and the market is illustrated in Figure 7.11.

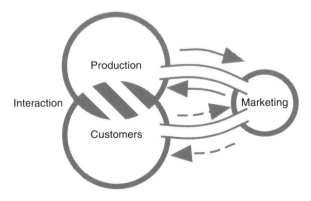

Figure 7.11   The company – market interaction. (*Source:* KIA Management Consultants and based on the work of Christian Grönroos. *Strategic Management and Marketing in the Service Sector.* Svenska Handelshögskolan, Helsinki, 1982)

Using this type of analysis, Handelsbanken has eliminated its marketing department, keeping just two people to provide a central coordination and information activity. As Arne Mårtensson, says, 'We don't believe that products can be the difference nor do we believe in much advertising; it is people who are the difference with the decision making at low level – but not with low level people!' This point about products not being the difference is not simply one for banking, as the illustration in Case 7.1 shows.

Case 7.1   Living with a national monument

The Royal Albert Hall was completed in 1871 and is not only one of the great landmarks of London but also one of the great concert halls of the world. Its elegant round shape may have provided an acoustical nightmare and added to maintenance problems, but these have been largely overcome and it is a venue with character and history.

By 1989, when a new chief executive, Patrick Deuchar, was appointed, the Hall was having difficulties. It still attracted promoters because it had such stature, but the standard of customer service had fallen to an all-time low. Promoters found themselves the centre of opposing factions, making 'their night' a matter of uncertainty rather than celebration.

The public – concert-goers, boxing fans and all the others – was equally unhappy, so much so that there were even articles in the daily press on the bad manners and rude behaviour of the staff.

Central to these problems was the fact that the 'core product' – the Hall itself – had become an easy way both of excusing inefficiency ('What can you do with a place like this?') and of doing business ('Do you want to be privileged to use our historic building or not?'). In addition, there was often a feeling of unprofessionalism about the running of the Hall, with only security staff gaining the upper hand.

But what to do? The Hall, with all its merits and faults, could not be changed. Using specialized service consultants to help with a review and analysis, Patrick Deuchar came to the conclusion that the answer was to refocus the activity of the staff not simply towards the customer but towards what the customer needed from the Hall. The focus was to become the inter-action with the two key audiences – the promoters who would make the decision to book the Royal Albert Hall as a venue, and the ultimate customers, the public.

continues

continued

With each audience, a clear positioning was adopted, worded in terms of what was to happen at the 'interactions' in the relationship with the two groups:

(1)   *With promoters:* the Hall is dedicated to the success of their functions. This is to be demonstrated through pre-function analysis, support in promotion, at rehearsal and 'on the night' and with post-function debriefing.

(2)   *With customers (the public):* the Hall is an exciting place to visit. This is to be demonstrated through preliminary material, bookings, the appearance of the Hall and the individual reactions of staff at the event, who must share this sense of excitement and take pleasure from its fulfilment.

Four years later, Patrick Deuchar knows that they are on the right track. With a 38% increase in rental charges – and so a substantial increase in the money available for reinvestment, the only profit criterion for this Trust – the Hall is experiencing:

- An almost total elimination of customer complaints.
- A continuing high level of bookings from promoters. During 1992, a bad year for London venues, not only have rents been held but long-term bookings of the Hall have increased.
- A big increase in 'year in advance' contracts and 'multi-year deals', allowing for more planning ahead.
- A steadily increasing quality of show, and with it quality of audience, which is in some ways the most important of all for the Hall's prestige and staff morale.

But it is not just the management of Royal Albert Hall who are pleased; promoters, too, are delighted with the change as the following quotes show:

- 'Yes things have definitely improved. More often than not the shows we do now are a sell out. Early hiccups with the box-office computerization have been sorted and it is now very efficient.'
- 'The stage manager is good, the marketing department helpful, stewards, charming and competent and staff very cooperative. It is still a bit grubby with badly fitted dressing rooms but now [1992], even these are being taken care of.'
- 'In general the RAH seems more able and willing than other venues to discuss each event, from when it can be held to an after-show debrief. It's a big change.'
- 'It's just good to have someone you can turn to for continuity.'

As Patrick Deuchar relates, 'Probably the single most important change in all this was getting everyone to see that enjoying the experience at the Hall was the critical issue. But of course it was more than that.' Charles Haines, himself an ex-show manager and now Technical Director adds, 'We have moved 'show management' centre stage, and key elements, such as security,

continues

continued

now all provide back-up for this, so that our approach to staging events is coordinated, to the benefit of promoter. We have provided a focal point for promoters. Once a contract is signed, they are assigned a show manager who knows a lot about staging shows. He or she does not cut-off contact with the specialists in our organization, but monitors progress, makes sure everything we said would happen does happen and is always available to the promoter to sort things out. We have set up post-show debriefings. It is my personal responsibility to contact the promoter after the show and set up a meeting with the Chief Executive, myself and other key people to find out what we could do better and how we can help to tackle a future show. It is, perhaps, a measure of our success that there is now only about a 25% take-up of this offer. Most promoters simply say, "We don't need to talk, it was fine!"

We have made the recruitment of professionals who know their job a key point. So, ticket sales, reception etc are now all in the hands of dedicated staff. But more than that, it is imperative they are service-minded staff, who share our values. We don't just want people who agree with service but people who embrace it. As an example, we have recruited an ex-airline purser to look after the stage door.

We have delegated responsibility, structuring the organization so that people know what they are responsible for. We have also improved the physical conditions – for the audiences, for promoters, for artists and for staff.'

The Hall is also more financially secure, as David Elliott, Finance Director relates, 'In addition to spending approaching half a million pounds on routine annual maintenance, we are generating sufficient cash to spend more than one million pounds annually on major changes, including major refurbishment of public and performer facilities, the creation of a new restaurant, and investment in modern stage equipment. This not only allows us to attract new shows but speeds turnaround times, so we can have quite different stagings on successive days.'

Karen Booth, Sales and Marketing Director, is also an enthusiast for the change, 'We have some way still to go, and we have a ten-year time horizon to achieve all we want to do. But we are getting there. We have got rid of the feeling that we are there to preserve a national monument and instead there is a feeling we are there to use it to create enjoyment. And we are beginning to see the first signs of real competition over bookings for dates at the Hall.'

Certainly the Hall has a different feel four years on. Not just visually, though the smarter corridors and newly fitted function rooms and dressing rooms are a stark contrast to the old. But even more noticeably, the people have an obvious and deep fund of enthusiasm and willingness to help. Not just the new people either; many that have been there for years seem different people, but all of them clearly are not just proud of the Hall but pleased to share it with you.

The barriers

There are many reasons why service organizations are not designed in a way which makes customers central:

(1)   It is easier, and less emotive, to concentrate on and build service around the core product. It is professionally satisfying and it is measurable and non-reactive. But this technical basis is rarely the aspect used by customers to distinguish one supplier from another; in fact, to the customer all technical (core) products seem much alike.

(2)   Not enough is known about the customer to be aware of true needs – the expectations – at the point of interaction. Nor are experiences analysed against these.

(3)   Management fear the disruption, the problems with organization and with unions, staff and management, that such a focus will bring.

(4)   Management do not feel responsible for all of the events which condition customers' responses. To take the example of an air traffic control delay, the airline may feel that it is not its fault, but the customer will certainly feel that the airline 'owns' the problem for two reasons:

   • Customers feel, unfairly maybe, that 'surely something could have been done' (and they are often right). The truth is, the more you try to distance yourself from a problem, the more you may be felt to be involved, to be trying to edge away from taking responsibility.

   • Regardless of any question of right or wrong, any residual feelings of 'failure' or 'dissatisfaction' spill over and colour customer perceptions in subsequent dealings, at later interactions or with the 'memories' (all that may be left!). A previously happy journey can be blighted by lost luggage.

A further point of concern is the impact customers have on one another, reinforcing good or bad perceptions both through 'third-party' comment and by 'conditioning' the interaction for others by their reaction. So, someone complaining about a lack of information regarding a delay, for example, will infect others. Indeed, in the research quoted earlier, it was said that an unhappy customer affected twice as many other people as a happy customer. If there is real reason for the complaint, it can rapidly build up into a mass discontent.

Services across frontiers

A further consideration in customer focus in services is their transferability across frontiers and, within these, across regions. In Chapter 4 some of the differences in national cultures were highlighted. These have a profound impact on the perceptions not only of customers but of staff. Localized, specific delivery is critical to consumer perceptions and satisfactions. The core idea may be the same, but to varying degrees everything else may need to flex and change. If this change is considerable, one is almost certainly talking of a different business with entirely different values. So a credit card may be a humble method of payment in one culture, but a sign of prestige and influence in another; each will need different strategies, and therefore implementation, to be successful and to build that relationship so critical to a service business.

In Figure 7.12 this concept of the change required in the transfer of a service is shown in the form of a circle with a series of concentric rings. Progressively, as you move out from the centre you will need to consider change. Indeed, in most cases you will be too inflexible if you make no changes in the outer rings. The elements which go to make up the categories in each ring are shown in the Box 7.1.[6]

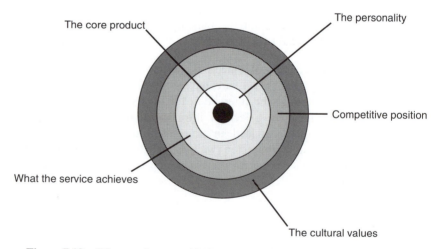

Figure 7.12   What services travel? (*Source:* KIA Management Consultants and developed in cooperation with Judie Lannon, former Research Director, JWT Europe.

Box 7.1   What services travel?

The core product

The 'product' and its specific function. This will rarely vary, except in terminology.

Examples: a plane seat; an hotel room; a savings account; a mass-market but quality clothing store.

The personality

The personality of the service and the values goals and beliefs that underpin this. The basic attributes to be seen in the service.

Examples: prestige, health, relaxation, security, thrift, international (cosmopolitan).

Equally importantly, the basic management qualities and tone. Rank and order will vary more than content but more than a small variation would indicate a possible mismatch.

Examples: integrity, quality, conservative, aware, large, friendly, leadership.

What the service achieves

What the service and its various elements will do for the buyer. This will reflect the basic emotions people feel. These will not be a major variable but the tone and method will respond to local beliefs and preferences.
The closer these are from territory to territory, the easier it will be to 'manage' the service in a common way.

Examples: a symbol of position (in life) an opportunity to improve health or well-being, ensuring protection, being smart.

Competitive position

The position of the service in relation to other services and the ways in which it will be delivered to the (ultimate) consumer.

This would require detailed decisions on, for example:
- frequency of use/visit/purchase
- whether the concepts (as in the inner circle) are new or established
- the expectations of services that support the central idea, for example:
  - limousine service[†]
  - organized excursions
  - money transmission
  - credit facilities
- the role of the customer, for example what they will do to build the relationship.

continues

continued

The cultural values/delivery

The values attaching to the service and the expectations of people in the particular situations which arise in the course of introducing, selling, executing and supporting the service.

This would directly affect the focus at the interaction, so that the final 'delivery' of, say, a tourist hotel concept or a savings account could appear different in different cultures, or a clothing shop may not need changing rooms in one culture but would find them essential in another.

It would also affect:

- the emphasis in personnel selection/reward and in image creation;
- physical positioning of, for example, branches.

† An interesting example of how a seemingly small element of the service mix can change the whole relationship is quoted by David Tait, executive vice president of Virgin Atlantic, in connection with the introduction of their limousine service. 'It has cut "no-shows" down to virtually nil,' he says, 'because it is easy enough not to turn up at the check-in but very embarrassing to have to send away a limousine.' Although not the original intention, this change has subtly altered the balance in favour of the supplier, yet to the real apparent advantage of the customer. Those suppliers of service who complain about 'lack of responsibility' should note that you can create it.

Seeing the service at the five 'levels' shown in Box 7.1 helps to sift out the balance of change required to maintain local presence without losing the essential nature of the original core idea. It also helps to emphasize that services are about customers in a way which is specific – it is the customer's involvement and his or her expectations and experiences which are central.

In conclusion

Putting the customer in focus is a vital first step in setting a service strategy; indeed, it is a distinctive mark of successful service businesses. However, it is vital to see that this is more than simply defining 'who'. It also involves defining the dynamic process which governs the relationship between the organization and the customer.

Having made such definitions, it is critical that all aspects of the strategy – internal and external, product and markets – be integrated in a way which permits focus on clearly related segments. Otherwise staff responsiveness will be poor and control difficult; the differing requirements will tend to lead to an inability to 'individualise'.

Finally, don't be fooled into believing that organizational change alone will bring the answer. Organizational change should be a response to change, not a substitute. That it may also give merely an illusion of change is evidenced by this quote:

> 'We trained very hard, but it seemed that every time we were beginning to form up into teams, we would be reorganized. I was to learn later in life that we tend to meet any new situation by reorganizing and a wonderful method it can be for creating the illusion of progress, while producing confusion, inefficiency and demoralisation.'

> (Gaius Petronius, Roman general, c.AD 66.)

References

1. Gibson, I. (1992). *Diamonds and Mud* in *London Business School Alumni Review* based on a presentation to the school's Summer Congregation, 16 July
2. KIA Management Consultants (1992). Confidential client work
3. For example see Schlesinger L.A. and Heskett J.L. (1991). In *Harvard Business Review* September/October
4. Townsend R. (1971). *Up the Organisation*. Hodder Fawcett
5. For a fuller and more detailed treatment, see Grönroos C. (1982). *Strategic Management and Marketing in the Service Sector*. Helsinki: Svenska Handelshögskolan
6. Developed in cooperation with Judie Lannon, former Research Director, JWT Europe

8

Developing leadership

- Changing from a control to a leadership style has to be a revolution, otherwise the idea gets lost on the way.
- Attitudes toward leadership are ambivalent and the necessary changes put a squeeze on middle management.
- Yet middle management are the only people who can deliver service objectives – they control the interaction.
- The barriers to achievement need to be recognized:
  - a change of roles by all management is required – not simply new skills
  - implementation must be treated as integral to planning
  - defensive routines must be overcome and ideas must be subject to criticism and change
  - perceptions and roles of middle management and the way they are treated must be changed.
- The dialogue required to overcome these barriers has to be planned – involvement has to be designed not just expected.

Evolution or revolution?

The stress on service success being realized through 'customer focus', allied to the need for strategy 'to go with the army into the field', [1] means that responding to the customer as an individual, devolving power to the frontline and letting knowledge be widely available are all key issues in a service organization. Inevitably they create a need for fundamentally different approaches to management; approaches different enough to remove the key causes of conflict in pursuing a more fluid interaction (which may be unstructured and cause disruption) with the customer – that key determining event, where the majority of satisfactions and dissatisfactions are generated. However, unless the change to this focus is planned properly – and seen as a strategic issue – there will be a potentially negative clash between the 'old' way and the 'new' way; an attempt to be evolutionary in the face of revolution, to control change so that you don't really have to come to terms with it.

Yet it is primarily those organizations which have been prepared to face up to the implications of revolutionary change that have succeeded. Tom Hedelius at Handelsbanken is emphatic, 'Organizations only have a problem with chaos [caused by change] when they fail to implement customer focus completely. Then chaos is caused by conflict. At Handelsbanken, we only have the customer as focus, not the product.'

But few organizations have been prepared to see this as a revolutionary process in management. Woolworths is an example of an historically formalized organization that is determined – not least because it has to be – to move to a position of greater flexibility and market mindedness. 'But it has to be evolutionary not revolutionary,' said Mair Barnes in 1990. However, creating the change necessary at Woolworths has meant a change in culture which can only be described as a revolution, with a massive investment in management development (seven million pounds in 1993) particularly on the 'Managing Better People Better' programme (see also Case 10.1).

This stress on evolution is very common, especially with organizations which are more rigid in their culture. However, given that management face a service revolution, it has to be an open question whether or not evolutionary change will suffice. 'Swinging the staff behind the objectives necessary to achieve the new objectives and developing an approach to management which permits this,' to quote one of the opening sentences of Chapter 1, means facing up to the fact that you can only have on board those who want to go the journey. While commitment to the principles cannot be partial, the revolution need not be violent.

The changes at Handelsbanken were not bloody, but there has been a steady turnover of senior talent that cannot be described as evolutionary. A cool look was taken at the market and it was realized that real and substantial change was necessary; the Chief Executive accepted personal responsibility and forced issues through. This was true, too at SAS and something of the spirit of the current SAS approach is contained in the Box 8.1. It is interesting to note, however, that the early work of SAS to bring about change was hampered by the failure to bring middle management into the change process sufficiently. The appeal to staff to be customer minded, which was made without involving middle management, created not simply resentment but, more importantly, confusion and uncertainty.

Box 8.1   Revolution at SAS

'Nothing short of a revolution in leadership will deliver the results required fast enough for SAS. It is the goal of the SAS Leadership College to ensure that, in 1991, there are well over 1000 SAS leaders whose performance demonstrates that they have both the commitment and the competence required to deliver the results the company requires. We have re-emphasized our commitment to customer orientation by our commitment to performance improvement for each individual leader. Traditional management styles now have to give way to the challenges of tomorrow's professional high-performance leadership.'

(Jan Carlzon, Chief Executive, Scandinavian Airlines System.)

Tackle the fundamentals

The need is to both manage change and change managers – clearly two of the key factors in turning service ambitions into reality. As we have seen, the evidence suggests that the overwhelming majority of initiatives fail to meet their objectives. For most, results have fallen off after an initial burst despite enormous investments of time and money. Frequently the effort merely leads to an overburdening of the structure, complicating the routines rather than releasing potential and maybe more importantly, just disturbing management without giving that 'push' which allows for real change to come about.

Developing leadership is not a task which is easy to achieve by cautious steps. The vast difference between the relationships involved in 'control' and 'leadership' styles of management is too great to be bridged by half-hearted change. Creating leadership where there was control is revolutionary and must be tackled in a revolutionary way, otherwise the weight of passive resistance will prevail. That this is nothing new is illustrated by the extract in Box 8.2 on the problems of reforming the medieval church.

The management problem is that most operational initiatives (such as customer service, quality, marketing) not only miss the fundamental points of flexibility and fluidity involved – and, therefore, the potential to create an opportunity for control – but also make matters worse by trying to operate within the same framework of management as before. But, as Saga have identified, giving authority, creating responsiveness with the customer creates a 'dynamic tension between management's desire to control and (the need for) greater latitude and discretion'.

Simply creating a fresh set of easily managed routines – whether they replace others or overlay them – is not going to work because not only is it

Box 8.2   Lost on the way

The older conception of churchmen working hand-in-glove with lay lords was never entirely supplanted, reiterated as it was in daily life with the parson paying his respects to the lord of the manor, and the bishops sitting in council with the king. The new ideas transformed but did not overthrow established ways of thoughts. They were like the arrested dawn of a rainy day. The underlying purpose of the reforming movement failed to gain general understanding or widespread support. It did not even gain the comprehending devotion of a majority of the clergy, who might acknowledge the propriety of papal instructions, but whose vested interests kept their feet moving along the old paths. The implications of the reform movement had to be modified to meet their passive resistance. Ideally the dissociation of the clergy from worldly cares should have meant the surrender of the landed estates which brought them within the framework of feudal society; but to try to meet the impossibility of persuading the clergy to do this by allowing them to retain their estates but at the same time requiring them to disavow the obligations to secular lords that were carried with them, was a prevarication doomed to failure. As often happens with mortal men, the incidental features of a great idea gained the day, but the idea itself got lost on the way.

(Source: W.L. Warren, *King John*, Methuen, London.)

impossible to be entirely predictive about these interactions (even a company as systematic as McDonalds has been able only to minimize the uncertainty), but ultimately the result would be unproductive. *For individuality needs at least some degree of unpredictability,* and the more there is a need to deliver high added values through service, the more there is a need for individuality, some unpredictability and, therefore, an element of chaos.

In such situations there has to be considerable allowance for making mistakes, yet our research showed that the fear of staff – and often of management and supervisors too – about making mistakes was one of the clearest indicators of poor cohesion in service structure. Overall, 39% of all staff in the survey 'strongly agreed' or 'agreed' with the statement, 'I feel I am not allowed to make mistakes', but this varied widely across respondent companies from 64% (33% 'strongly agree') – a cross-channel ferry company with poor results overall – down to nil (Handelsbanken) and 4% (Club Méditerranée). Flexibility – dealing with the customer in a way which makes the customer feel individual – heightens the opportunity for mistakes. So in those cases where 'mistakes are not allowed' change is inevitably stillborn.

Table 8.1 Attitudes to leadership and its importance to success.

(% seeing leadership as an important factor for success)

		All			Banking			Retailing			Travel			Utilities		
		Mgmt	Super	Staff	Mgmt	Super	Staff	Mgmt	Super	Staff	Mgmt	Super	Staff	Mgmt	Super	Staff
'Own'	%	31	24	13	31	24	6	35	18	11	30	29	16	25	23	16
opinion	Ranked	3=	6	8=	4=	6	7=	2=	6=	8=	3	4	6	4	6	8=
Perception of	%	31	24	22	35	33	18	35	24	16	22	19	26	21	19	24
company view	Ranked	3	3=	4	2	2	7	3	3	7=	4	6	3	6	5=	5

Source: KIA/EIU research, 1991, B2.1 and B2.2 questions.

Bewildered managers faced with such an erosion of their expensive service plans are tempted to ask, 'Is it all worthwhile?' but may at the same time feel they have little alternative, since they still want to achieve the original aims.

Is such a shortfall inevitable? Can it be overcome? Can service success be sustained? As the charts in various earlier figures show, an emphasis on leadership qualities is a necessary ingredient in achieving responsiveness. Yet our research also showed a high degree of ambivalence toward leadership. Table 8.1 shows there is considerable inconsistency of belief in its importance, and that staff generally tend not to rate it highly.

Further, in the qualitative research there was in an uncertainty felt by top management in many organizations regarding the middle manager: a questioning of the need for them and, even more, of their role. Although there was a recognition of the need for change, 'Yes, I realize I can't go on managing in the way I have in the past,' said one senior manager in one of the bank respondents, in some organizations there was almost fear about its consequence: 'How can we retain the control we need, if we let go responsibilities to others?'; 'Our management have already demonstrated they are not capable of carrying that burden.'

A general trend

However, the changes needed, and already witnessed, in management are not confined to services or simply the result of the service revolution. Just as the service revolution is itself the result of dramatic shifts in the make up and ambitions of society – particularly the shifts toward individuality, femininity and economic independence – so too is the shift in management styles from control to leadership.

John Harvey Jones, formerly Chief Executive of ICI, has written, 'I believe absolutely that in the future it will be the company that conforms to the individual that attracts and motivates the best people. Companies will have to be more flexible in their demands, to accommodate more and more the individual's different hopes, wishes and ambitions.' [2]

Jack Welch, chief executive of General Electric in the USA, talks of the 'transformation' of management and the need for 'business leaders' rather than managers. Welch is, 'championing a company-wide drive to identify and eliminate unproductive work in order to energize GE's employees.'[3] It is neither realistic nor helpful, Welch argues, to expect employees of a 'decidedly leaner corporation' to complete all the reviews, forecasts and budgets that were standard operating procedures in more forgiving times. He is, 'Developing procedures to speed decision cycles, move information through the organization, provide quick and effective feedback, and evaluate and reward managers on qualities such as openness, candour and self-confidence.'

Welch stresses that this is not primarily a systems or organizational change but is a, 'redefining [of] the relationship between boss and subordinate. I want to get to the point where the people challenge their bosses every day: "Why do you require me to do these wasteful things? Why don't you let me do the things you shouldn't be doing so you can move on and create?" That's the job of a leader, to create not control.'

Saga, too, believe they have an educative style of management but that, 'Open and informal though it is, this is still our area of greatest need – leadership development'. Their aim is to achieving a situation where, 'My job as a manager is to take away the barriers that prevent you achieving,' says Roger De Haan.

The squeeze on middle management

These pressures in manufacturing are even greater for service companies because the target is not things but people. It is the ability of both staff and customers jointly to convert ideas into reality which is the final and decisive part of the process. In such a situation, middle management in particular can easily adopt negative attitudes and be seen as a block to progress. In Chapters 6 and 7, the discussion of strategy and organization also highlighted this 'squeeze'.

As we saw, top management cannot allow their role in creating strategy to become divorced from implementation; a sense of leadership and involvement requires that top management are visual and inspirational. Apparently, the middle manager no longer has a task; he is 'squeezed' out. Yet the paradox is that it is only middle management – particularly first-line or supervisory management – who can deliver service objectives, since the final 'production process' can only be carried out in the field, face-to-face with the customers. It is impossible to anticipate every situation, to lay down rules for every eventuality. Instead it is necessary to rely on at least some degree of interpretation. If operators are to feel secure in doing this, they must be able to seek guidance without losing their individual initiative, and, if top management are not to be swamped with uncontrollable amounts of information and requests, then they must rely on middle management to provide this guidance.

Again, resolving the paradox inherent in the last two paragraphs is difficult if it is seen as purely evolutionary, since it calls into question many of our most entrenched beliefs regarding the role of managers. To achieve change, the traditional 'command and control' model – the view of a manager controlling a group of people to achieve his or her tasks – must be replaced by the model of a leader helping staff to achieve their tasks, using coaching skills and the ability to inspire commitment to team goals; leaders who can ensure success through the affirmation of values and the achievement of unity of purpose, and who can achieve through others.

In simple terms, the change involves moving from the viewpoint:

'As a manager (or supervisor) I have a job to do and, say, six people to help me.'

to:

'As a manager (or supervisor) I have six people with jobs to do and it is my task to help them.'

The responsive system

If we are to create responsive systems and give staff the task of being responsive, we have to accept that this situation of change is inevitable. Otherwise, the idea of service – and indeed the ideals of service – will never be realized. This move toward customer focus and the authority to be responsive will tend to produce 'flatter' organizations, in which creating cohesion takes more effort, and will call for more reliance being placed on the operative to react sensibly to the situation. Yet, as John Harvey-Jones has observed, 'One of our major industrial problems is that we do not ask enough of our people.'[2] To achieve such a level of responsibility and responsiveness means we must have cohesive, harmonious cultures with strong value systems, and these need team leaders who understand more than the immediate objectives and can give support in going beyond the ordinary, who can share the problems that arise and who have access to those who plan.

However, not only do many middle managers (and top managers, too) persistently underrate their staff but such a role is alien to their background and experience, developed in an era of close control of knowledge and implementation. They need help to make the change – and to know how to cope with the resulting problems that occur upwards and sideways, not just downwards! Handelsbanken has developed the concept of management as a staff resource to a high degree. Comments from managers, almost unconsciously, support this, 'The branches I work *with*,' said one regional manager; 'We spend quite a lot of time *justifying* our ideas, selling and reselling to branch managers,' said one executive vice president.

Such responsiveness creates problems. Customers don't always fit the pattern one would like; they can be wayward and even downright awkward – yet, as we will see in the final chapter, this may be a positive benefit. The operative has to ride these situations, allocating time in response to pressures and judging each situation on its merits. For the most part, these are minor events, dealt with primarily at a subconscious level, but every so often they will present a major problem. If the operatives cannot share such problems and the attendant pressures and sometimes stress that such contact can bring, then they will simply 'shut off', ensuring that they do not get 'overloaded'.

In organizations where the daily stress is real and even serious, this may be recognized. Falck middle management, for example, see themselves as a resource to their people, standing back from a crisis, making sure there are adequate resources, encouraging and if necessary stepping in, though this last point is seen as something of a failure by most supervisors – 'I shouldn't have to do it'. But it is more than that, for they see their role as providing that leadership *before* a crisis – sharing worries and concerns and knowing the potentially weak areas and the points of stress beforehand – as well as after it. Their task is to ensure that experience is turned to advantage and to remove the worry and concern that could harm future performance. (For the record the figure on 'being able to make mistakes' with Falck in the research was 19%, compared with the average quoted earlier in this chapter of 39%. This is a surprisingly high figure, but may be accounted for by the role ambiguities caused by their ownership by Baltica at the time.)

Obviously not everyone is fighting fires, but the principles still hold good. In fact, in more commonplace business situations the difficulties can be just as great because there may not be the ready acceptance that the job can give rise to stress and strain, as there is in the case of a fireman or ambulanceman. Yet stress, even in quite ordinary jobs, is a major source of poor performance and negative attitudes.

In many ways being a middle manager in a service business is like being the manager of a football team. It is impossible to predict every event for 90 minutes, and even the most carefully thought through plans can be disrupted by the other team or by the unexpected. Rather, it is necessary to create a culture where each player recognizes situations as they arise, both as an individual and as a member of the team, and is prepared to accept responsibility for meeting them. Shouts from the touchline and criticism for taking risks can easily be counterproductive – next time the risk will be avoided or there will be a fatal hesitation. Indeed, the best football teams follow such precepts. Arsenal, for example, with probably the best long-term record of any club (more than 80 years' unbroken membership of the English First Division and only once just in the bottom half) see the expression of the individual as a member of the team as critical, and not only on the field. 'It is noticeable,' said manager Terry O'Neill who took them to their last FA Cup success in 1979, (they won again in 1993) 'how it's often the best players who don't mind carrying the bags or acknowledging others' contribution'.

This view of the middle manager as a team leader was supported in our research and also by some other recent research in which 69% of senior management respondents suggested that 'undertaking more work in teams' would be the most important change for middle management. [4]

Finally, it is a further interesting echo of the quotations from von Clausewitz and Max Hastings in Chapter 6, to note that in Germany supervisors earn a premium of 70% over operatives as against 40% in most countries, and that most German supervisors have a special, supervisory 'Meister' qualification, which not only covers technical skills but also organizational methodology, handling people and passing skills on to others. Britain's National Institute of Economic Research suggests that this fact, more than any other, underpins the efficiency and productivity of German industry. [5]

Defining leadership

So, managing in an environment that calls for leadership involves some toleration of chaos, a lack of structure and the creation of involvement. It is a very different task from that of managers working in a conventional controlled environment, who seek order and control. But this concept of leadership is little understood, though the questions used in our research to identify 'service management' help to highlight the differences.

The questions in Figure 8.1 illustrate not only the 'control versus leadership' balance, but also the basic dilemma of a service outlined in Chapter 2 – 'bureaucracy versus enthusiasm'. Just as all organizations need systems, so all organizations need control, but if those who actually carry out the tasks at the point of interaction with the customer are to feel confidence in both their own judgement and that of their superiors, they need leadership too. So statements 1 (achieving sales), 3 (procedures) and 4 (telling) are all orientated to control, while statements 2 (consideration for others), 5 (help from superiors) and 6 (trying out ideas) are all orientated to leadership. Reference back to the definitions of masculinity and femininity in Table 1.1 will quickly confirm that the need for a leadership orientation is also a reflection of changing societal values.

These statements describe some of the ways companies are managed.
Which of these apply to your job?

Rank them in order of importance from 1 to 6 (with 1 as most important)

It is important to my success:

(1) That we concentrate above all on achieving set targets (e.g. sales).

(2) That I consider the views of those I work with or who work for me.

(3) That we have set procedures which we stick to at all times.

(4) That people are told precisely what they have to do.

(5) That my immediate manager is someone that I can use to help achieve my goals.

(6) That people are given a chance to try out their own ideas.

Note: Statements 1, 3, 4 indicate control orientation.
      Statements 2, 5, 6 indicate leadership orientation.

Figure 8.1   Management style. (*Source:* KIA/EIU research, 1991, c4 question)

However, on its own the adoption of a leadership orientation would be insufficient. Indeed, as we saw in Figure 3.5, this will simply lead to aimlessness. The demands of interpretation of strategy through the interaction – an ultimately unstructured event taking place, for the most part, beyond immediate influence from above yet responsible for some 70% of customer satisfactions or dissatisfactions – mean that those immediately responsible must be involved.

Although being kept informed is one aspect of this, it also means being able to:

- Relate what you are doing to the customer and their needs;
- Reconcile your own concerns and reservations before having to convince others;
- Discuss the problems that arise.

Figure 8.2 illustrates these points in terms of the questions used in our research.

Team leadership then, is the task of leading a team to success through giving inspiration, gaining involvement and being prepared to share both the positive and the negative aspects of implementation – and acting as a champion for change.

In my work:	Agree strongly	Agree slightly	Neither agree nor disagree	Disagree slightly	Disagree strongly
1. I understand how my job helps us to be successful with our customers.	☐	☐	☐	☐	☐
2. Any personal problems I have at work are always taken into consideration.	☐	☐	☐	☐	☐
3. There is always someone for me to discuss any problems I have with the work that I do.	☐	☐	☐	☐	☐
4. I am always kept well informed about events or changes happening within the company.	☐	☐	☐	☐	☐

Note: Only statements 2, 3 and 4 used for analysis.
    All 'agree' answers indicate involvement.

Figure 8.2   Questions on involvement. (*Source:* KIA/EIU research, 1991, C2 question)

What are the barriers?

Of course, many organizations have already started to tackle such change, and a number of examples have already been quoted. But few seem to have achieved much success in creating a management style consistent with their market aims. What is the block? Or is there more than one? As the noted American writer on business organization, Chris Argyris, asks, 'Why is it that when a difficult and threatening problem is correctly diagnosed, when a valid implementation plan is designed, when the resources are available, the implementation may fall short of everyone's expectations? It is almost as if there were an army of organizational pac-men ready to gobble up actions that could overcome these defences and help organizations achieve the potential of which they are capable.'[6]

The fact is that it is often difficult, or even impossible, for middle managers to be able to operate a leadership role effectively because of the following problems:

(1) It is rarely thought through as a role change.
(2) It is not recognized that implementation is integral to the plan.
(3) It is a natural tendency to avoid being 'caught out'. (See Chapter 3 regarding management defensiveness.)
(4) Middle management's attitudes and behaviour themselves are the problem.
(5) Top management is a barrier.

Taking each of these in turn:

Problem 1: It is rarely thought through as a role change

There is an attempt simply to teach skills without recognizing the profound difference entailed in being a leader. Most often, too little time is allotted to proper learning. Leo McKee at Woolworths says, 'What is important is *how* you apply your package of change, not so much the package itself... most people want to belong and give good results... but we found that middle management simply didn't understand the strategy, so we took time out to really develop their understanding so that they could appreciate what they had to do to achieve. We have found it is necessary to do it in "steps", knowing that the initial target for change falls short of the eventual positioning but giving everyone an achievable goal.' The extract from a *Harvard Business Review* article, in Box 8.3, also accurately reflects this problem. The change to a customer focus is a major shift in the interrelationship of middle managers with their staff and with their bosses.

Table 8.2 Supervisors' attitudes toward employee involvement.

	Plant								
	A	B	C	C	D	E	F	G	Average
Percentage of supervisors responding that employee involvement programmes are ...									
Good for the company	46%	75%	44%	67%	53%	96%	83%	94%	72%
Good for employees	42	58	22	44	53	81	78	72	60
Good for supervisors	15	42	33	44	32	23	39	44	31
Sample size	26	12	9	9	19	26	20	18	139
Type of programme	Quality circles	Quality circles	Quality circles	QWL programme	Quality circles	Quality circles	Cross-functional task teams	Semi-autonomous work teams	

Box 8.3   Why supervisors resist employee involvement

This extract is from an article which concerned research into the responses of first-line supervisors to employee involvement programmes. As the extract shows, it was rare for supervisors to perceive such programmes as being as good for themselves as for the company or for employees (see Table 8.2).

'Supervisors rarely show open resistance to programs which top management initiates. After all, they are part of management, too. More to the point, few have access to formal mechanisms for voicing disenchantment, and most perceive that their job security depends in no small measure on following upper management's instructions. Nonetheless, the negative attitudes are not far below the surface – negative not only toward the proposed changes in management style but also toward the process of change itself. True, supervisors occasionally criticize a program in discussions with peers or subordinates. More often, however, they remain silent or demonstrate only mild enthusiasm, which workers quickly interpret as a questionable show of support for the program.

Understandably, the first concern has do with job security. A question often raised by the popular press – will supervisors become redundant under a system of participative management? – is on the minds of supervisors themselves. When one plant began forming semi-autonomous work teams, management guaranteed that the teams would pose no threat to the job security of hourly workers but offered no comparable guarantee to supervisors. Although none of these jobs was actually in danger, rumours to that effect began circulating.

A second area of concern is job definition. What are supervisors really expected to do, and how are they to be measured? In the plant just mentioned, management took more than three years to articulate clearly what was expected of first-line supervisors. Lack of a well-defined set of responsibilities also gave special trouble to supervisors who had to balance the egalitarian position required of them by participation in quality circles one hour per week with the authority they exercised on a daily basis.

A third concern is the additional work generated by implementing these programs, work that ultimately falls on supervisors either for short periods of time (as with team development and training) or for extended periods (as with quality circles). One group of foremen, for example, who were not allowed to pay employees overtime for quality circle activities, found that all coordination and follow-up for the program fell on their own shoulders, especially on their time off and usually without extra pay. This was particularly true for second- and third-shift supervisors. In addition they felt management expected them to do many things methods engineers had been responsible for.

Even after managers addressed the issues of job security, job definition, and extra work, some supervisors were reluctant to accept the concept of employee involvement programs. Evidence gathered at the plant level indicates that each of the five types of categories of supervisors outlined (Table 8.3) has its own reasons for opposing employee involvement programs. Although these categories are not intended to be mutually exclusive and a given supervisor may fit into several groupings they do serve a useful diagnostic purpose.'

Table 8.3 Supervisors as resisters.

Type	Why they resist	Clues to behaviour
Proponents of Theory X	The concept goes against their belief system	Comments such as 'Employees are children, not adults' and 'Employees will just take advantage of the program to get out of work'.
Status seekers	They fear losing prestige	Unwillingness to let go of behaviour associated with control. Fear of losing leadership role. Comments such as 'Foremen can't be equal members of a team; they will always be the leaders'.
Sceptics	They doubt the sincerity and the support of upper management	Comments such as 'This programme is no different from past ones. It will fade away in a few months'. 'The problem is the next level up'; and 'They don't really practise what they preach'.
Equality seekers	They feel that they are being bypassed and left out of the program	Comments such as 'Why do we have to change before the employees do?'. Non support and 'hands off' as problems arise.
Deal makers	The program interferes with one-on-one relationships with workers	Comments such as 'We've been stripped of our power' and "We have no control over the process'.

Source: ©1984 by the President and Fellows of Harvard College, all rights reserved. 'Why supervisors resist employee involvement', by Janice A Klein, *Harvard Business Review*, September/October 1984.

Problem 2: It is not recognized that implementation is integral to the plan itself

The interaction is not an outcome of the strategy but the very basis of the strategy itself. Yet this implementation is often left to the uncertainties of interpretation by comparatively junior management with insufficient guidance and insight. Implementation must be based on sufficient knowledge to allow operatives (in this sense, both supervisors and workers) to assume the necessary degree of control. In a recent survey, the authors said, 'The data from our study suggest that the ability of an employee to make a proper response [in the service situation] is largely a function of that employee's "knowledge and control".'[7]

Yet, as Henry Mintzberg has observed, 'Implementation [usually] means dropping a solution into the laps of people informed enough to know it won't work but restricted from telling anyone in power what can'.[8] Many will have observed the situation where, after maybe months of discussion and adjustment, the plans are suddenly revealed to a group of people who have not had time similarly to adjust and have had even less time to respond or suggest improvements or changes; indeed, it may be made abundantly clear that such a reaction is not expected!

The comparatively chaotic situations required for a true customer focus mean that more recognition must be given to the need for plans to have the understanding and commitment of those who will have to implement them, and to the problems of providing leadership at implementation. This is why close cultures, with reduced role ambiguity and conflict, are so essential and why in the research there was a clear correlation between close cultures and success.

It is a key part – probably the key part – of 'giving direction to the implementation of the central idea.' [9]

Problem 3: It is a natural tendency to avoid being 'caught out'

A common aspect of the previous problem is that managers feel the need to present their ideas as flawless, not only in concept but in detail. This is unquestionably an important part of the change process for Sainsburys, where their philosophy of 'retail is detail' does not make it easy to liberate spontaneity.

Many organizations put great stress on being 'decisive' and 'right'; no one wants to be thought of as not having considered every angle. To quote Chris Argyris again, 'We don't want to lose credibility by being seen as not carrying weight.' [6] But it is a fact that the more ideas are *presented* as having been thoroughly thought through, with apparently every barrier removed, the more recipients will feel unable to comment, especially if management are doing the presenting. Even where employees do raise questions, they may feel, to quote one respondent middle manager in our survey, that 'constructive dissent is unwelcome'. A common reaction is not to resist openly, but instead to engage in defensive routines 'which reduce the pain but simultaneously inhibit learning.'[6]

Problem 4: The attitudes and behaviour of middle management themselves

This is arguably the most important barrier of all. It is partly born of historical training but is more a result of managers viewing themselves as having power in the sense of 'position power' or 'resource power' (as Charles Handy has described[10]). Their attitude is, 'I am who I am' or, 'I have authority' or, 'I control the money, the physical resource', rather than, 'Expect power' – 'I speak with authority', where such managers can command respect without ordering it. For Handelsbanken, educating their managers to the disciplines of this new 'power' – and in some cases resigning themselves to losing otherwise good people who could not adapt – was a difficult but key part of the change. However, middle management attitudes are also a reflection of the uncertainties of the role, as Table 8.4 shows. Based on American research,[11] this table shows that middle managers have very different expectations of their role relative to their superiors than they have of their subordinates.

Problem 5: Top management is a barrier

Middle management, as Leo McKee observed, do want to belong, to succeed, but there is a further barrier – top management themselves. If middle management see they have little power to change their boss, they may exhibit an

Table 8.4 Master and servant: a comparison of role expectations.

	Desired traits	*Percentage of managers who mentioned traits. Multiple choices were possible*
What managers expect from subordinates:	Good task performance	78
	Loyalty and obedience	60
	Honesty	53
	Initiative	31
	Other skills	26
What managers expect from superiors:	Good communication and feedback	64
	Leadership	60
	Encouragement and support	50
	Delegation and autonomy	37
	Professional competence	21

exaggerated concern to please or anticipate his or her views. This type of reaction is particularly evident in strongly structured organizations. As one manager in Sainsburys observed, 'The [former and now retired] Chairman had to be careful what he said, or it was implemented.' Even in the most frank of organizations, there can be an exaggerated concern to please and to react positively to top management directives or expressed views.

Yet this is rarely middle management's fault; rather top management themselves are most often the barrier since, as Argyris states, 'Top management harm the process [of involvement].'[6] It is difficult, if not impossible, for middle management to provide the necessary leadership if they, in turn, find such leadership lacking from above. Yet often – distressingly often – the reaction of top management can be summarized in this 'created' dialogue:

CEO: Of course, it is beyond question that satisfied customers are our most important asset.

Middle Management: We take it, therefore, that you will be prepared to become personally involved in developing initiatives to increase the number of satisfied customers.

CEO: Oh no, I am far too busy with much more important things to do!

Although this dialogue is 'created', the sense, down to the usage of the key words, is from a real situation. If top management react in this way then no matter how important they *say* satisfied customers are, it is inevitable that middle managers will not believe them. In these circumstances, why take the risk of managing chaos? Better by far to eliminate it – and, in doing so, the customer focus too; or, to quote Argyris, 'inhibit the process of customer focus.' [6] The conflict created by top managements' ambivalent attitude toward service is shown in Mike Bruce's example from British Airways, Box 8.4.

Box 8.4   A struggle for the soul

'A struggle for the soul of BA, for an integrated, coherent identity that is not yet resolved – this is what is taking place. There is a split between two worlds. The first of these is the "real world", which is "hard", authoritarian, robotic, strict/safe, instrumental and traditional.

BA is seen in primarily operational terms as a physical system. This is the familiar world of BA's military, bureaucratic and civil service past. These people are technically trained and see themselves as the instruments of a purpose supplied by the hierarchy in which they have their place.

Then there is another rhetorical or service world, which is exemplified by the transformation in the culture of our customer-service personnel. This is "soft", people-oriented, humanist, flexible, caring, oriented-to-feeling, innovative and fun. It sees the organization as a "social system". These people are oriented to forming relationships and need freedom from hierarchical control to do this job properly.

The difficulty arises from the perception that these polarities are incompatible; that you either have to live in the "hard" world of the operational or the "softer" world of relationships. Our passengers don't see it that way. They want both safe, comfortable, punctual aircraft and to be treated as people, individuals whose cares and concerns matter.

The problem for us is how to integrate the two worlds – to move from an "either/or" to a "both/and" perspective.

This is a key challenge for the leadership of the company. They too have a dilemma, for they have to face two ways at once. Internally, they have to reconcile the functional and ideological perspectives through developing team work in addressing customer needs. Externally, they have to search for opportunities to build a global business in a tough, combative world that is intensely political. My fear is that the cultural change will not spread far beyond the cabin crew and other service personnel because the people at the top will only be able to look in one direction – at the hard-nosed struggle for power.

Source: Mike Bruce, quoted in Charles Hampden-Turner, '*Corporate Culture for Competitive Edge*', Economist Publications, 1990.

The resulting people problems are seen as an annoying distraction and not as the real issue or, at least, of equal importance to the 'hard-nosed' external issues. Middle managers, the crucial linkage in bringing plans and implementation together, can never be effective players if their own superiors do not give them the status and respect needed as a replacement for authority in order that they may command respect as leaders. To quote Argyris again, 'The challenge is to create a relationship where the superior can participate without endangering the autonomy of the subordinates.' [6] This requires recognizing that a 'hands-on' approach by top management towards cultural issues and culture maintenance is vital, and that this must be on a participative basis and must be given the time, space and status that its vital influence demands.

This view – so well demonstrated in action by Handelsbanken and Saga – is interesting to consider in the light of both Mike Bruce's comments (see box 8.4) and recent revelations at British Airways. Here was an organization which had set itself some clear principles for doing business, yet it was the guilty party at the centre of a major ethics scandal. Whatever the precise reasons, management had failed to give the time, space and status that maintaining a vision requires. More than that, the case also reflects a point about change made in Chapter 1, namely that customers seek more open relationships; that there has to be greater transparency.

In attempting to extricate themselves from the mess, BA management thought that making a clean breast of the affair would quickly dissipate criticism, but it overlooked the greater demands today for transparency. Looking into the organization, the public saw – and modern media means they can see – that the shining facade hid something less, or apparently less, impressive. Just as Judy Garland was able to pull back the curtains in the film *The Wizard of Oz* and show that the wizard was, in truth, just another frail human, so BA was exposed relentlessly to the harsh light of judgement by its own standards, and seen to be less than the image it conveyed.

The vision that a service company creates has to impact on everyone and at all times. You cannot have 'sometimes' principles that are 'for others' or 'for good times' only, and top management, in particular, have to set a clear lead not only in their behaviour but in their actual priorities. The days of the autocrat are numbered (unless he or she is a genius who can 'deliver' on their own) as the departures of Lord King at BA and Robert Horton at BP have shown, both victims of their own 'standards'.

It is necessary to realize that good visioning and good leadership can produce results which are not easy to overturn, and getting other people behind plans instead of just executing them assumes a commitment both ways. Later change can be difficult as Case 8.1 shows.

Creating a dialogue

To break down these barriers it is necessary to create a true dialogue; to give middle management the opportunity both to acquire knowledge and to use it to challenge practices and ideas – in short, to act as leaders. To requote Saga, 'an educative style' is necessary. However, Argyris quotes the American writer Whittle as saying, 'Management often dominates the conversation not because they have a dominating style (although some do) but because they have the

Case 8.1   *A cautionary tale*

Persuading people that your approach is right and getting them on your side can be a powerful tool – provided you can stay with the outcome, as this extract from a recent lecture by Judith Wilcox shows:

'We didn't run the company on aggressively Christian lines – people didn't have to be a Christian to join. But we wanted our employees – and everyone else – to know just what sort of a beast they were dealing with. If they didn't like us, fine: they didn't have to have anything to do with us. But at least they knew where we stood. And if they came to work for us, they knew where they stood, too. I'm happy to say that six years later, Channel Foods was turning over £10 million and employed 350 people. It's still growing.

It's all very well running a company on these lines if you control it, or if its moral values are written once-and-for-all with indelible ink. It's another thing altogether if you bring your religious beliefs explicitly into play when the power lies elsewhere.

My company had grown and prospered, but the time came to put it under a bigger umbrella. We found a willing buyer, eager to invest and expand, so the future looked assured. Locked in to the new company with golden handcuffs, I was very happy to carry out its programme for a couple more years.

Everything went well until I was sent to Boulogne to sort out the problems of a recent acquisition, a traditional French canning company starved of investment and staggering under restrictive labour practices, but well placed as a main port of entry to bring Canadian fish into the European market for processing. I had worked in France for 20 years. I liked the people and was happy to move in.

The message I got from head office was: if you can sort out the mess and get the unions to co-operate, fine: we want to grow in the area and see this traditional old company as an excellent base for a continental European expansion programme. Bible in hand, I arrived on Boulogne quayside and immediately got to work, building a team to develop a long-term plan. I have to say that I met my match in the factory's union leader, M. Dupont, a devout Communist and leader of the CGT for Northern France. To M. Dupont, the Revolution was as fresh as if it had happened yesterday. He believed deeply that the church, the aristocracy and power bases generally were in league to exploit the common man – and that I was all of these. Even worse, I was English and a woman. His Gallic shrug said everything the workforce needed to hear.

Our struggle – conducted, I should say, with growing respect on both sides – pitted his Red Book against my Bible: the question was, whom should the workforce trust?

continues

continued

I knew what was needed to transform this factory. I had done it before, in Cornwall, and flew the whole team over to see my gleaming factory and contented workforce. I told them that to survive, the company needed my long-term plan, which offered the only hope of new investment.

So M. Dupont reluctantly agreed to a package of redundancies and the easing of restrictive practices, and away we went. We sold some buildings, designed a new flow system, decided on a new range of products and introduced modern marketing.

I worked alongside everyone and, unheard of in a traditional French industry, the President Director General – myself – was part of the team, sharing all figures and plans with the now enthusiastic workforce. I was winning: in my God we trusted, my ethic, my corporate plan. We all make mistakes and this was a big one. You know this story has a sticky end.

Back in head office, where the "power" lay, the board put into place a new plan for the safety, prosperity and greater good of the company worldwide: a rationalization programme. The whole emphasis of the company had changed and word came through to me in Boulogne: the factory must close.

What I had missed, in my enthusiasm, was that I no longer had the power to control: only the authority to act. I was experiencing, for the first time, the place of management in a large public company.

You can imagine how I felt, announcing closure to a sullen and very silent mass meeting. This was followed by strikes, demonstrations, sit-ins, accusations of asset stripping, and the whole legal tangle to unravel. In France, you can't simply close a company because it suits you: you have to fight your case through the courts.

Frequently, M. Dupont and I faced each other across the cavern of a court room, fighting for the rights of the workforce and the larger good of secure jobs for others working far away for the same company, whose "caring" had so patently failed our workers in France.

We came to respect each other as managers, M. Dupont and I. As a veteran middle manager he recognized that our power lay in the hands of others and that our job, his and mine, as managers, was to follow our personal code yet to recognize that the corporate code could change, as often happens in takeovers that cross cultures and continents.

I had failed. M. Dupont had won, yet the employees of that French company and the local business community continued to treat me with respect. I had, in their eyes, acted according to my ethical code and not changed my spots overnight.

relevant information.'[6] Listening plays a critical role in the activity of breaking down barriers and creating a dialogue. The extent of this will be more readily seen if we go back to one of the earlier concepts in this report, the service triangle, see Figure 1.2.

Looking at this triangle from the outside, consumers find the choice of any service extremely difficult; they all seem much alike. Nor is the problem resolved by concentrating on the intrinsic merits of your service. Rather, consumers relate what they see or hear to themselves; they are self-centred, seeking solutions to their problems (what might be termed the extrinsic merits of the products and services on offer), not purchases of your products.

Thus, to develop a successful service you have to demonstrate that you are the solution to the problem, not just through the core product but through all of the elements of the service mix (as we saw in Figures 5.1, 5.3 and 5.4). If someone buys from you it is because, consciously or subconsciously, they have made the decision that you understand them or their business sufficiently to provide a solution to at least some of their problems. However, you can demonstrate such an understanding only by persuading the prospective buyers to reveal their problems and by generating a recognition that they are important to you. In other words, you have to listen (see Chapter 2).

With a major customer, or for a big contract, this listening may have to be formalized through structured meetings, such as the workshop approach, outlined in Chapter 10. But in most cases, and particularly with any business which has a mass customer base, it will flow more from the manner in which you approach the consumer, since in these situations the need for listening can be repeated – and is repeated – in the many millions of interactions which are the true 'product' of the business.

For example, for someone worried by financial problems, a letter saying, 'We are worried about your consistent late payments,' is going to be seen as another part of the problem, whereas a letter saying, 'Given the [quote situation], no doubt you are worried about this,' will instantly make that customer feel that the writer is 'listening' and is approachable. You have created a dialogue, indeed the beginning of a relationship, not through what you have said, but through how you said it. Words do not have meaning; people do.

However, to revert to the triangle, such a letter is not enough. Operatives cannot write a sympathetic letter, create a dialogue and develop a relationship if the culture in which they work says, implicitly or explicitly, that there is no room or time for concern or care; that the task is to sell or collect money regardless.

This is not to suggest that infinite flexibility and responsiveness is necessary. Some organizations will need to adopt a more systematic approach, because that is relevant to their market and their culture. But invariably, if you look at service organizations that have achieved long-term success, or at those grappling with change successfully – and within our research we have such disparate organizations as a bank (Handelsbanken) and a travel company (Saga) – you will find that implementation has created a sense of involvement through good internal communication and this has been developed through listening and not simply telling. As a result, they have created a belief that concentrating on solving customer problems is more important than simply selling products. So listening as an active skill is a critical part of implementation.

One simple way of encouraging a listening environment is to create a positive procedure for your dialogue. For example, lead people through the 'four levels of message'[12] and give them a chance to participate. These four levels are:

(1) *Awareness*: people need to know why you are planning *this* move; not just the objectives, but the role and purpose of this proposal relative to the wider objectives (say, the mission statement).

(2) *Understanding*: they need to know why you are suggesting *this* solution? How does it meet and overcome the problems you have defined above? How, at local level, does this fit with the manager's (and operatives') problems and opportunities? (This can be a fruitful basis for the 'dialogue'.)

(3) *Conviction*: you must create a feeling of personal belief in and ownership of the ideas by encouraging involvement in their preparation.

(4) *Action*: then, but only then, attempt action!

Referring back to the research, and in particular the chart in Figure 6.3, it is possible to see the importance of the virtuous link style of management in this context. Managers in these situations do not abdicate control but ensure that by their manner and evident concern to develop involvement they gain the confidence of supervisors, and in turn staff, to take responsibility for their own actions.

The recognition that this can be achieved and can be linked to long-term success is arguably the most important conclusion developed as a result of the research for this study. It is, therefore, of critical importance not only to ensure that those in touch with the customer – creating the end-product – have the knowledge they need but to go beyond that to 'planning the dialogue'.

Planning the dialogue

In this context, planning is not a matter of crossing every t and dotting every i, since that would not create dialogue so much as stifle it. Planning the dialogue means:

(1) *There is clarity about the message heard*. It is more important to be clear about what the audience need to hear, rather than simply what needs to be said. The two are not necessarily the same, in fact they are

commonly quite different. 'Our' concern will be to 'sell' our message; 'their' concern will be to assess the implications for themselves, both personally and in their work, and to assess how they will cope. Most people in traditional sales jobs have to come to terms with this and see it as part of the challenge of their work. With 'products', their role is also not an integral part of what is bought. If the change is small, it may not anyway present a severe problem. For most service businesses, however, the majority of staff are not traditional salespeople and their role is seen by the customer as integral to the 'offer'. They often don't have the experience or the immediate will to cope spontaneously with the conflicts in the message. So, they need time to make this assessment and to reconcile their concerns. Until they have done this, they simply won't 'listen'. That is why 'involvement' in our research (see figures on 'Service Management') was critical and why not one of the organizations with long-term success had a low score in this dimension.

(2) *Clear guidelines are set.* Be clear about the distinction between 'imperative points', those things which are set and determined, and 'interpretative points', those things which can be given a degree of personal interpretation. In this, it is important to bear in mind the various points that have been made about individuality. The more there is a need to increase individuality, the more there is a need to give scope for interpretation.

(3) *Feedback is sought and used.* Giving consideration to others' views and ensuring that people feel they can discuss ideas and risk taking action are critical to achieving a leadership emphasis in management. Further, feedback from those concerned with the final interpretation is feedback from those who have to 'live' the final processes of making your ideas come to success. Not only do they have vital information about the detail, which you very likely do not, but they have to be as enthusiastic and understanding as top management. In fact, they have to 'own' the idea. This may mean that ideas will have to be modified in the light of the feedback comments. This should be viewed not as an unwelcome challenge but as an opportunity to get that commitment and ownership. However difficult this may be, it is easier than allowing the process to go forward without such a check and, arguably, will give more commitment to the final outcome.

In conclusion

It is difficult, and probably impossible, to have incremental change when changing culture. Creating an environment of involvement is, at the very least, revolutionary (though not necessarily violent) if control attitudes are traditionally entrenched. Management, particularly top management, have to commit to the new culture and middle management need a new source of 'power'.

Overcoming the natural defensive barriers which change engenders needs both the affirmation and visible support of the new values. As the research shows, it is still possible for managers to exert a high degree of control, but they need to create at lower levels the feelings of involvement, interest and commitment so necessary to service.

Finally, it is important to recognize that what is needed in terms of change in management is not simply being seen – it is not 'management by walking about'. This is still only a variant of the manager deciding when they will be involved. Service management is management by being available when those who need help seek it.

References

1. von Clausewitz K. (1832). *On War*
2. Harvey-Jones J. (1988). *Making it Happen.* Collins
3. Tichy N. and Chavan R. (1989). Speed, simplicity, self-confidence: an interview with Jack Welch. In *Harvard Business Review,* September/October. © 1989 by the President and Fellows of Harvard College, all rights reserved
4. Wheatley M. (1992). *The Future of Middle Management.* British Institute of Management Report
5. National Economic Development Office. (1992). *What makes a Supervisor World Class?*
6. Argyris C. (1989). *Strategy, Change and Defensive Routines.* New York: Pitman
7. *The Service Encounter.* In the *Financial Times*, April 11, 1990.
8. Mintzberg H. (1989). *Mintzberg on Management.* The Free Press
9. von Moltke H. Writings whilst Chief of the German and Prussian General Staffs, 1858–79.
10. Handy C. (1990). *Inside Organizations.* London: BBC Books
11. © 1986 by the President and Fellows of Harvard College, all rights reserved. *Harvard Business Review*, November/December 1986.
12. Based on the work of Doyle, Dane, Bernbach Inc.

9

Service value

- Quality and price can only be judged in a context of customers' expectations and experiences.
- This gives rise to a concept of 'perceived service quality' – a quality which is subjective as well as objective.
- A key issue in this is the difference between 'threshold values', which give no distinction, merely allowing entry to a market, and 'incremental values', which confer distinction relative to competition.
- Service design – 'tending the orchard' rather than sorting the good and the bad is more important than quality or any other service improvement concept.
- Where standards and such like are necessary, they must meet certain criteria.
- Pricing is a more complex matter than one simple price/value relationship.

Quality and price in context

For most managers, the questions and possibilities surrounding service will often first take on meaning when they look at the hard facts that surround service improvement issues, such as setting quality standards or deciding on pricing. Yet, at the same time, there is probably no area of service development where so much money has been spent for so little return. We have already noted that up to four out of five service improvement initiatives fail to deliver significant results and our own research indicated a widely varying set of responses from amongst our core companies. Primarily, this is because it is in these aspects that the clash between the need for control and the need to respond to customers is the most felt – 'the dynamic tension between Managements' desire to control and set parameters and the belief that service requires greater latitude and discretion,' to requote Tim Bull, Group Development Director at Saga.

Certainly, our research shows clearly that there would appear to be no link between long-term success and the existence of such programmes, any more than whether an organization has a high or low price profile. Some companies, like Virgin Atlantic, have started to develop structured service concepts but, '...realised early on that this would simply make people [staff] conform more, when our whole philosophy was empowerment of the individual to do what seemed right at the time.' Nor is this an isolated reaction. In a report on *Making Quality Work* published last year[1], the authors said, 'Total quality programmes have, at best, led to incremental improvements in companies' performance and customer satisfaction; at worst, they have made it more difficult to increase organizations' competitiveness.'

What does appear to be at stake is a deeper question of service design, making sure that all of the elements of the service mix (see Figure 5.1) work in balance and harmony and without the role ambiguities and role conflicts which, as we have seen, can erode the delivery of the idea at that key point, the interaction. The issue, therefore, is how to make certain that those who personally manage these interactions are equipped to deal with them and have the authority to do this. Further, that others in the organization see it as their primary duty to help those in the front line in achieving this. This is more a matter of attitude and behaviour than of specific standards, for example, though these may play a part.

Expectations and experiences

This, then, is the context for quality and pricing and not only are these two aspects inextricably mixed one with another, but there is a further obvious link between them: for both, the key determinants should be the expectations and experiences of customers, and yet both are often internalized or arbitrary.

Because of their commitment to customer service, Saga were very attracted to the concepts of quality, but Tim Bull is clear that their early attempts were misguided, 'They were never capable of achieving the ends envisaged, because when we first started to think of "quality", we believed you could get an absolute view of this. We have realized since that it is useless as a concept without reference to the customers' needs. We failed to grasp sufficiently that fundamental point and as a result we structured to achieve results that were arbitrary. Also, the process became more important than the result.'

Although it may seem an obvious starting point, the high failure rate of quality programmes and such like and the poor understanding of the relationship of price to value, suggests that relating service to the consumers' expectations and experiences is not common and, as the Saga experience shows, a difficult discipline even for organizations with a customer focus.

For both quality and pricing the results of our research showed a great deal of confusion.

Quality

- Although the overwhelming majority of respondents saw quality as underpinning the success of their operation (see Table 9.1);
- And of these, a majority (though smaller) believed their company thought this too, with only staff, predominantly in retail and travel, placing the achievement of sales targets higher (see Table 9.1);
- Nevertheless, respondents could not identify what quality was, giving indiscriminate importance to a wide variety of definitions (see Table 9.2);
- And it was particularly noticeable that staff were more inclined than management to equate quality with 'avoiding making mistakes', and this was most marked in retailing.

Table 9.1   The importance of quality in achieving success.

Top factors seen as important to help company achieve success, % choosing

	'Own' opinion		Perceived company priority	
	'High quality of service'	Next most important factor*	'High quality of service'	Next most important factor**
All	55	8	37	32
Management	54	11	38	29
Supervisors	59	8	39	32
Staff	52	8	32	36
Banks	57	9	38	34
Retailers	42	8	28	41
Travel companies	53	7	32	35
Utilities	60	7	48	20

*all selected 'valuing our customers as individuals' except management ('strong leadership')
**all selected 'achieve sales targets'
Source: KIA/EIU research, 1991; Questions B2.1 and B2.2.

Table 9.2 Defining quality.

% showing as 'very important'

Quality means:	All	Mgmt.	Super.	Staff	Banks	Retail	Travel	Util.
High standards	88	82	91	91	85	92	92	85
Keeping customers happy	70	66	71	76	64	78	78	68
Encouraging more customers	75	75	75	73	77	80	84	57
Giving customers confidence	88	90	88	84	90	86	86	88
Meeting industry standards	67	58	72	73	60	62	80	70
Avoiding mistakes	55	51	55	61	61	48	55	53
Monitoring procedures	56	54	59	55	53	63	60	56
Getting personal commitment	73	74	75	67	70	78	75	70

Source: KIA/EIU research, 1991, Question C5.

Significantly, the results in successful companies were not statistically different from those in the others. It is, perhaps, inevitable that the thinking has become degraded, given the operational focus of so much of the publicity and hype surrounding quality and other such service improvement issues.

Pricing

There was a strong element of contradiction on price with substantial emphasis on low prices in dialogue but an almost total rejection of pricing as being so critical in the structured research. In fact, apart from the retailers, no respondent showed any measurable support for price as the key determinant in either their own opinion or that of the company. Even with retailers the 'own opinion' percentages were lower than the overall average of perceptions, across all 24 companies researched. Nor has the more recent research conducted in-company shown that price is other than simply one factor. (An exception is the result shown in Figure 4.4 and is explained more by an excessive display of management uncertainty than any real price-driven demand.)

Rather, what those companies who have consciously tried to develop an approach to this dilemma are saying is that there is a concept of service value in which price and quality play a part but which is, at least partially, a subjective concept. This is supported by research evidence generally. So, for example, Professor Christian Grönroos writes, 'Quality does not exist in an objective fashion. Rather it is perceived subjectively and in a personal way by every single customer... consequently, it is appropriate to talk about perceived service quality. The perceived service quality is a function of the expectations and the experiences of a given customer. If the experienced service equals the expected service, the perceived service quality will be good. On the other hand

Flight details

Flight number [ ]   Seat number [ ]   Date of departure [ ]

From: [ ]   To: [ ]

Are you travelling: Economy [ ] 1   Upper Class [ ] 2

What did you expect and how have we done?

1 **Give Virgin Atlantic a score for what you EXPECTED our service to be like and what it was ACTUALLY like on THIS flight. (1 = very poor, 5 = very good)**
Please leave BLANK the boxes next to any part of our service you have not experienced.

1 = very poor
2 = poor
3 = adequate
4 = good
5 = very good

	Expected	Actual
Check-in – speed/efficiency	[ ]	[ ]
Check-in – courtesy	[ ]	[ ]
Upper Class lounge (Upper Class passengers)	[ ]	[ ]
Clarity of cabin announcements	[ ]	[ ]
Cabin crew – helpfulness when boarding	[ ]	[ ]
Cabin crew – attentiveness during the flight	[ ]	[ ]
Cabin crew – attentiveness serving food/drinks	[ ]	[ ]
Comfort of seating	[ ]	[ ]
Legroom provided	[ ]	[ ]
Cleanliness of aircraft interior	[ ]	[ ]
Quality of entertainment system – audio	[ ]	[ ]
Quality of entertainment system – visual	[ ]	[ ]
In-flight magazine articles	[ ]	[ ]
Selection of food from which to choose	[ ]	[ ]
Quality of food selected	[ ]	[ ]
Presentation of food selected	[ ]	[ ]
Size of food portions	[ ]	[ ]
Selection of wine available	[ ]	[ ]
Quality of wine selected	[ ]	[ ]

2 **Taking everything into account, give Virgin Atlantic a score out of 100**

Figure 9.1 Virgin Atlantic research questionnaire. (*Source:* Virgin Atlantic Airways Ltd)

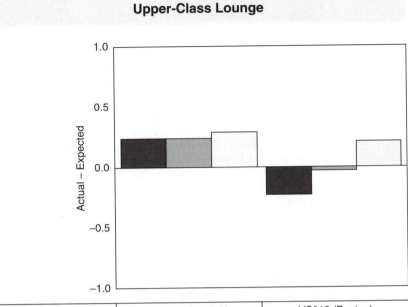

	VS011 (Gatwick)	VS012 (Boston)
▉ May 1992	0.24	−0.23
▨ June 1992	0.24	−0.03
☐ July 1992	0.29	0.21

Figure 9.2   Virgin Atlantic research results. (*Source:* Virgin Atlantic in-flight survey (May – July 1992))

if the experiences are below the expectations, the customer will probably be unsatisfied and the perceived service quality will be lower.'[2]

This potential gap between expectations and experiences is illustrated both in Case 9.1 and the research from Virgin Atlantic shown in Figures 9.1 and 9.2. Virgin Atlantic do not measure passenger reactions in abstract but in relation to their, usually high, expectations (Figure 9.1) and the positive or negative difference is then charted graphically, flight by flight. Figure 9.2 shows an extract from the results for 'Upper-Class Lounges' over a period of three months for flights to (VS011) and from (VS012) Boston. The lounge at Gatwick (VS) persistently exceeded expectations while that at Boston persistently failed until the new lounge was opened in July. Virgin Atlantic could easily have seriously deluded themselves from the results of any research based purely on 'actual' since even with the lounge at Boston these scores alone were always positive. But the experience did not match Virgin's passengers' high expectations, which was the real criterion.

Case 9.1 An epic tale

As a result of their unsatisfactory attempt to introduce a total quality concept, Saga Management felt strongly that the purpose was still right and – having now learned a great deal more about their own organization – that they should develop an approach which took more account of customers' needs.

'In our business, where so much of the work is being done to deadlines and with a direct impact on resource costs and usage, we feel it is vital to have standards,' said Tim Bull, Strategic Planning Director. 'However, our standards, whilst internal, are very much derived from a close study of customer reactions – that is experiences against expectations. So, for example, our Travel Company questionnaire seeks a response to not only each part of a holiday on these factors, but to the overall reaction – and then cross-relates them all. We then also measure "repeat buying intention" and "repeat buying actual" and include this in the equation.

The effect of our thinking today is characterized by a recent example of an hotel in Malta. All our hotels have to meet certain standards, whatever the category, and this hotel met them. But still it was the subject of a lot of complaints. Analysis of the detailed reactions of both "satisfied" and "dissatisfied" customers revealed that there were one or two specific elements involved, primarily linked to "expectations v. experiences", and most specifically its [the hotel's] position relative to the beach and some rooms being on an inner courtyard. We revised the brochure descriptions and emphasized these apparently adverse factors. I say "apparently adverse", because what our research was showing was that a substantial minority did not consider them adverse, taking everything into account. Now the numbers booking this hotel have fallen significantly but it is one of our top five for "satisfaction ratings"! A few years ago we would have simply deleted this hotel and so lost a good prospect for a significant number of our customers. Now we have both retained this opportunity and avoided disappointment for others.'

These characteristics pervade all of Saga's approach to service design. So, Saga have primarily quantitative standards (e.g. the Insurance Division produces a monthly trend graph of relationship of complaint letters to business flow) but they seek to balance these either through qualitative review, in this case it is a regular item at a Directors quality-review, or by other measures. So, for example:

- Telephone sales agents are expected to achieve targets in terms of numbers of calls answered and average duration *but* in addition – and more importantly – Saga audit conversion rates – that is, who takes up the offer;
- Saga concentrate effort and measures against the 'key points of experience'. So, for a holiday it is 'reservation, confirmation, tickets, arrival at holiday'. 'So, we know the truly important issues and can concentrate resources – such as training – accordingly';

continues

continued

- Saga constantly 'listen-in' to 'phone calls and use the results to provide individual development plans and training and feedback on problems – problems the Company may themselves have created through poor design.

'It is a very difficult process,' says Chairman, Roger De Haan, '...as it's not just numbers. But if we are to retain the responsiveness to our customers which we see as such a vital part of our "offer", we must develop an approach which allows responsiveness. For example, we still have a manual for local representatives (customer service in resorts) but it's no longer so that they have a reference if something goes wrong. Now, the manuals give guidance as to the limits of authority, encouraging matters to be dealt with on the ground, and only then reporting action and results. Our previous approach encouraged a bureaucratic attitude, so we have concentrated instead on training them to respond to the situation. Now the representative has the authority to do whatever is necessary, at the time.'

Echoing Tom Hedelius at Handelsbanken, Tim Bull says, 'It doesn't just happen. We, the Group Board, have to work very hard at it.'

Defining service value

This, in turn, leads on to having to recognize that within the concept of service value also lies a further enormous distinction in the customers' mind, between those values which the customer sees as so essential that they are simply accepted, and those that give competitive distinction. These are:

- *Threshold values*, which are the essential values, like legs and stability in a table or safety in an airline. They merely provide entry to a market;
- *Incremental values*, which are those attributes which the customer sees as providing distinction.

In determining service value, therefore, it is vital to bear in mind these differences in perceptions. So whilst both Handelsbanken and Yorkshire Bank are straightforward High Street banks – probably more simple in technical, product and image terms than most of their competitors – to their customers they are much more than that. Yorkshire Bank, for example, is perceived as, 'Overall more positively, and with a better image, than the 'Big Four' banks. Whilst seen as long established and traditional, it is also seen as forward looking and customer oriented. For personal customers, it is friendly, approachable, efficient and accurate. Overwhelmingly, customers felt that the willingness of the Bank to help with financial difficulties exceeded or at least met expectations. For small business customers, again a similar view was found and the Bank is perceived to have managers who understand their needs.'[3]

Both banks have well-above average success because they have not only the basic (threshold) ingredients that their customers need for their banking but also a distinctiveness which, in the eyes of their customers, sets them aside. This in turn stems from a deeper consistency:

- With Handelsbanken, a clear definition of the relationship and interaction with the customer as the key to long-term profitability, and so the branch as the focus of all activity;
- With Yorkshire Bank, a clear focus on the (almost non-aspirational) customer who seeks security and certainty – and, again, an emphasis on the branch.

Not surprisingly, perhaps, in our research not one respondent from either bank saw price as the key determinant of success – neither 'own view' nor personal 'perceptions of Company view'.

So the concept of service value can be seen as a much more complex concept than simply that of, say, price and quality of output. Rather, it is the whole way in which the business works – its philosophy and its processes related to the customer. Indeed, as we have seen, services are essentially a process. Value has to be related to the discontinuities within this process – the interactions and the factors that build to these – or the 'critical experiences', as Saga refer to them.

There are two features of particular importance to this which are often not taken into account with normal quality considerations:

- The shaping of customer expectations;
- Role ambiguity, as referred to in Chapter 2, and again, in relation to segmentation, in Chapter 7.

We can see these as features of both Handelsbanken and Yorkshire Bank. The understanding of, and clarity about, expectations and roles is there. Neither bank is glamorous, indeed visually they both look rather dull compared to competition, but instead their customers feel a depth of understanding and support that is not found generally in banking. For their staff, too, roles are without many of the conflicts inherent in so many staff/customer or internal staff/external staff relationships, because this simple focus with the customer is acknowledged openly and widely by the business as critical.

A further case is that of the Royal Albert Hall (Chapter 7). Here we see as a result of the changes made in 1989:

- A clarification of the expectations of the two key customer groups – promoters and event-goers;
- The build-up of the business – structure, philosophy, activity – around these expectations;
- Through this, a lessening of the role ambiguities felt by staff and management with a consequent increase in confidence and greater likelihood of meeting expectations;
- A reinforcement over time, both from good experiences and from recruitment linked to clear, customer-led outcomes.

These illustrations emphasize that the consumer is not simply someone at the end of the chain, the hopefully happy recipient of the service, but the real point of the service. David Hamid, managing director of Mastercare, the servicing subsidiary of the electrical retailers Dixons, says, 'Customers' main concern about any service business is that they won't do as they say they will. So, if we don't turn up at the time we say we will, we give them £20 of gift vouchers and we make this offer very public. But it goes deeper than that. The pay back of excellence requires that *customers perceive us* as different and better.

To make the point we have to evidence to our customers that we have really considered the way they use their electrical products and how a little thought can make the rather unpleasant need to have something repaired into a positive experience. We have even designed a little 'cable tidy' to solve the 'spaghetti' problem of long flexes, which we can give every time we call at a customer's house. It's not expensive, but it demonstrates that we really care how they feel and not just about repairing their product. It's part of a programme we call 'Finishing Touches', to make sure we show we really care.'

In other words, service value is about understanding, and demonstrating understanding. It is not simply the product we sell and its immediate utility, but about the context of the purchase and, more importantly, the problems as the customer sees them. This may very well centre around things which are not directly to do with you. So, for Mastercare, customers' concerns related to their general concerns about service. Or it may be quite unrelated, say the re-election of a mayor, a not uncommon outcome of the 'good and reliable service' provided by Lyonnaise-des-Eaux to the ultimate customers for water or street cleaning – his or her constituents.

So, service value must be defined in relation to the service received or perceived and the experience. It is about the process not simply the product, and about the overall worth, the 'perceived service quality' of Grönroos, rather than simple intrinsic worth.

Setting standards

One of the most controversial elements in the achievement of quality is that of standards, since they so clearly reflect the 'dynamic tension' referred to earlier. In fact, neither the absence of standards – 'We don't feel such "quality standards" are helpful in improving business effectiveness, because what lies behind them is so fundamental to our way of running the company,' says Arne Mårtensson of Handelsbanken – nor their presence – 'We feel that showing success with "hard" results has made it easier to go forward, as we widen the scope to "soft" factors,' says Morgan Svensson of Televerket – seems an indicator of success. The problem with standards is not that they are wrong in themselves but that they pose the danger of having the bureaucracy before, or even without, the reality. The standards become the focus, as we saw with Saga.

Sainsburys see service enhancement as one – but only one – of the benefits of an organically evolving total quality approach. 'We deliberately eschewed a top-down corporate TQ programme' says David Quarmby, 'instead we have encouraged and facilitated local – and individually quite different – total quality approaches in different parts of the organization. What is fascinating is the enthusiasm and commitment from grass roots management, from whom "ownership" starts with proud ownership of their quality programme'. Total ownership of the service objective – whether to internal or external customers – and of their own business performance is the objective, and emerging result of these initiatives.

There is the old story of the apple producer who consistently produced the best apples. Asked how one day by a pleased but inquisitive customer he replied, 'Well, there are three ways of producing good apples. Sort the good from the bad; sort the bad from the good; or tend the orchard. I tend the orchard.'

In a service, tending the orchard is creating that culture which:

- Reflects the customer – understanding, meeting and even exceeding his expectations;
- Is founded on close values, with low role ambiguity and role conflict.

The British Standard BS 5750 provides an excellent example of how the good intentions of this can go wrong. The purpose is right, as the preamble to the Standard shows (see Box 9.1), but the detail that then follows – and has to be met for accreditation under the Standard – is necessarily complex and primarily rule driven. Even introduced into a setting which has the necessary basic culture it is likely to create a diversion without careful and sympathetic handling; without such a setting it is doomed to failure.

The 'system' then has a tendency to become defensive of its own views and to work against that individuality and spontaneity, which are the vital ingredients. Standards and standardization are, necessarily, the same for everyone – and consequently the friend of those who want to withhold authority. They also concentrate on measuring output and in doing so can legitimize errors, since normally there must be an allowance for a percentage error in a Standard. Finally, they can cause you to forget that service and perceived service value are as much, if not more, about people, management and staff, and in many service situations other customers, as about 'things' which can be measured purely quantitatively.

Box 9.1   Principal concepts of quality

An organization should seek to accomplish the following three objectives with regard to quality:

(1) The organization should achieve and sustain the quality of the product or service produced so as to meet continually the purchaser's stated or implied needs.

(2) The organization should provide confidence to its own management that the intended quality is being achieved and sustained.

(3) The organization should provide confidence to the purchaser that the intended quality is being, or will be, achieved in the delivered product or service provided. When contractually required, this provision of confidence may involve agreed demonstration requirements.

Source: British Standard BS 5750, 1987.

This is because the, necessarily, unstructured environment of the interaction – and the need for the culture at this point to reflect the internal culture, as we saw in the service triangle in Figure 1.2 – calls for a high degree of authority to deal with issues as they arise. This means that there has to be a high level of tolerance for mistakes, the absence of which, our research showed, was the key factor in positioning between 'responsiveness' and 'formality' on the service structure matrix; in other words, a key contributor to role ambiguity. If standards become the focus they lead to an erosion, not support, of such authority. All of our core respondents who had experience of standards recognized this problem and it is also illustrated by the quote in Box 9.2.

We cease to tend the orchard and instead concentrate on sorting the good from the bad and vice versa, a pleasing outcome for some because as John Harvey-Jones has observed, 'In all companies there is a lot of comfort to be derived from administrative systems that purport to be "fair" but in reality remove from individual managers the responsibility.'[4]

Box 9.2   Standards erode service

'Organizations are building bureaucracies of standards – setting up commit-
tees and service guarantee claims departments. This work adds to their costs
and has the underlying assumption that they will always fail to perform to
100% and will always have to administer (whether defensively or not) claims
made against them. The whole of this effort provides the wrong focus.
Everybody involved is spending time on what's not working instead of working on how to improve things.

Furthermore, other staff begin to use 'guarantees' as ways of helping
problems to go away. I believe the rise in service guarantees reflects a serious
problem: the failure of management to trust people in the front line.'

Quote from *I Want You to Cheat*, J Seddon, Vanguard Press, 1992.

Value and cost

A further dilemma appears to be concern about costs. Yet the evidence from
our research is that the more a successful organization is strong on quality, or
value, it is low on costs, relative to its aims or customer expectations. Again,
we can take Handelsbanken as an illustration. For them, as for the others we
have studied, low cost has been an *outcome* of the pursuit of excellence, not
the purpose, because costs are directed solely at meeting customer expectations
and are not frittered away on side issues and reworking. Identifying the key
issues, for the customer in terms of his expectations and what he or she
experienced, is critical.

There is also a tendency for the costs of a pursuit of service or quality to
get out of line with the benefits to both customer and organization if this line is
pursued. The Florida Light & Power Company – birthplace of the much
applauded 'quality' work of Crosby[5], and the first non-Japanese winner of
the Deming Award for service excellence – were quoted as having had to cut
back their 85-strong quality department to 6 and 1900 'quality teams' to just a
handful because, 'The customer had been lost sight of in the system.'[6]

An illustration of the fact that quality need not cost more is provided by
SAS, who had identified from research that a key customer expectation was
'being on time' (it is to do with psychology as well as time demands). However,
this service value was traditionally seen as requiring more staff (extra costs) or
a relaxation of quality (more relaxed schedules). But by analysing why bad
timekeeping occurred, and developing a set of simple rules for dealing with the

main obstacles, tackling the root causes and not simply the manifestations, timekeeping was improved to a point where SAS were winning awards for timekeeping – without extra cost and without the hidden costs of delay.

It has become something of a fashion to talk of 'process redesign' or 'service process re-engineering' and, indeed, this is what is required. Not simply trying to do the job cheaper or better but re-examining all activities and costs, and this is a point missed in most re-engineering, against those critical discontinuities – the key experiences – and ensuring that value to the customer is increased. This is more likely to succeed than any productivity approach, with its manufacturing overtones. Indeed, the recent spate of criticisms of service organizations are worrying – as, for example, the article *The New Productivity Challenge* by the normally brilliant writer Peter Drucker[7] – for their suggestion that productivity is the answer, without really having anything to go on other than that the Luddites were wrong! These criticisms fail to show how value to the customer will be increased or to tackle the question of whether, in a service, it is the over-investment in technology which is wrong. 'Taking people out', will not of itself solve anything if, in the end, all that happens is that experiences never equate with expectations. Added value, relative to these, is the answer.

Benchmarking

Nevertheless, for many organizations setting some form of benchmark is going to be a necessary part of achieving their objectives. For others, in at least some part of their business, benchmarking may be a vital ingredient. Virgin Atlantic, for example, say, 'We can hardly run an aircraft maintenance business without some very rigorous standards.' In such situations, there are some basic rules which will help to make this more rewarding and, as Saga discovered, it is better to create a gradual approach which reflects and builds on your existing systems, rather than a bolt-on affair. In The Economist report referred to earlier[1], the authors state, 'After looking at companies which have made a sustained effort to apply Total Quality, two conclusions stand out:

- First, that rigid predetermined Total Quality programmes, particularly those imposed from outside the organization, do not work.
- Second, companies which have gone furthest in applying Total Quality, have never had a Total Quality initiative or programme – in them Total Quality has developed organically.'

If any form of benchmarking, such as a quality initiative, is to work it must meet the criteria discussed below.

1 Reflect expectations

Service received should be at least of the quality that the customer expects. This is the threshold of quality and is fundamental to any service or quality programme. Without the knowledge of these expectations you waste money, either through falling short, so wasting the expense entirely and maybe even causing a negative reaction, or overspending on a level of service or quality not needed.

'Standards' set to such expectations can be seen at four levels:

(1) Below threshold service:
    You fail to meet the expectations.
(2) Basic threshold service:
    You meet the expectations, neither more nor less.
(3) Enhanced threshold service:
    You identify that the customer would appreciate an element of service which they may not spontaneously expect, but will see as no more than a reasonable meeting of expectations once delivered.
(4) Incremental service:
    You identify that there are elements of service which you can deliver, at a sensible cost relative to revenue, and which the customer would see as exceeding expectations, so providing distinction.

To illustrate these it is simplest to take an example, say a complaint following a failure to pay a life assurance maturity on time. You could meet this by:

- Payment alone – below threshold;
- Payment with apology – basic threshold quality;
- Payment with apology plus interest – enhanced threshold quality;
- Payment with apology and interest plus gift or small sum as recognition of inconvenience – incremental quality.

Decisions about such service levels can only be taken if you have a clear view of customers and their expectations.

2 Make it simple

Where standards are desirable as benchmarks they should be simple enough for both customers and staff to understand – even if that means being less exacting – and to give latitude for authority. So Televerket's original:

'70% of repairs will be cleared on the day of receipt'

is less good than their subsequent:

'all repairs will be cleared within two days of receipt'.

In the latter, the issues are clear and unambiguous; both customers and staff know when you have succeeded or failed. In the former, for those in the 30%, the other 70% are academic!

This need for simplicity also overlaps the need to allow for 'qualitative' aspects. For example, an insurance company may stress in its standards the speed of settlement of claims but omit an acknowledgement of receipt of the claim; whereas research shows that the reassurance that a claim is being dealt with, compassionately and with understanding, is more important than speed. Even if the acknowledgement – sensitively written – costs more, it would still be worthwhile for building relationships, and in many cases the removal of the need for speed (as an overriding factor, not in its entirety) will more than compensate.

Equally, most telephone users would happily trade reliability of connection for speed of connection, yet it is more usual to see telecom organizations putting stress on speed. Speed is used so often as a measure because it appears simple, but even where it is important it will rarely produce distinction. Rather, standards need to give an opportunity for a degree of interpretation allied to simplicity of measurement, both by the customer and internally.

3   Measure

Service levels won't improve unless measured, mainly for two reasons:

(1)   They will be swamped by other, often short-term, measurable objectives, for example sales.
(2)   They will be insufficiently concrete. As we have seen, service always has a strong element of subjectivity so it is necessary to be as objective as you can. However, you cannot have a control which 'tests to destruction' every so many items, but you can be clear about what you intend to be the specific outcome in terms of expectations and experiences, and then measure that and how it changes over time.

In this it is important to recognize the crucial role of the customer as a quality controller. It is the customers' interpretation of what has been done which is critical. In this there is also an echo of listening; it is not 'what' you say but what others 'hear' that matters. The checks on customer experiences we saw with Saga and Virgin Atlantic are excellent examples of this.

4   Make it integral

Too often quality or service standards are imposed on top of other measures, for example cost measures and standards of safety or job measurement, to take but two common examples. This can leave the employee or his supervisor guessing at the real priority! When you benchmark:

- Look at your key organizational objectives. If you use something like 'the service star' (see Figure 5.1) you will have a good basis for this as it will have summarized these points.
- Look at all measures of performance used, apply them as part of an integrated plan and identify the priorities.

The clear ranking of priorities for safety and quality developed by SAS is a good example. All quality/service standards are secondary to safety standards, so no aircraft may take off without being fully safe. Of the quality/service standards, timekeeping is the priority because of both passenger reactions (SAS targets business travellers for whom time is key) and costs (late planes are expensive). So for example no aircraft may be late because the food has not been loaded. It all seems very simple but often there is no such integration or ranking.

5   Be consistent

Quality or service standards are in many respects the specification of a brand, a stamp of approval and guaranteed delivery. It must be right, every time; like a brand, it cannot have 'sometimes' elements. It's what happens at the interaction that matters, otherwise you are committing a crime parallel to that of manufacturers when they say, 'But it was alright when we shipped it!' In a service, the unpredictability makes this difficult, but segmentation (see Chapter 8) will assist this measurably, allowing benchmarks to be developed with a clearer reference to the subjectivity of both specific customers and employees.

6   Reflect the culture

There are those who believe that systems are everything, that all human error and incompetence can be eliminated by being systematic about design: total control will ensure total achievement. As we have already seen, no one approach to management is right, so this may be true in some businesses. It may also be particularly applicable in some national cultures more than in others. It has already been observed in Chapter 2, that in the USA there is a marked tendency toward structured services and the belief that systems will deliver. But such a view is difficult to substantiate in most businesses and is rarely true in European cultures.

Even in the USA this is beginning to change – or, more importantly, managers are seeing even greater potential for change in the face of societal change and staff shifts in attitude. General Electric, Levi Strauss and others have moved swiftly in recent years to adopt a stance of recognizing culture as critical to success. In our own study, two 'formal' organizations, Sainsburys and Yorkshire Bank, had strong cultural influences which, in the case of Yorkshire Bank certainly, and in the case of Sainsburys possibly, outweighed the systems in establishing what the customer experienced. For Virgin Atlantic, the culture is almost everything.

Indeed, however good the system, quality or any other such concept will only have meaning when it reflects the values and cultural aspirations of the organization. So a benchmark which sets an objective of being spontaneous is unlikely to gain much acceptance in a routine-driven organization.

Such cultural matching is likely to be one of the most important factors you have to deal with because:

- Cultural values are in essence what the customer is buying, at least in terms of *making you distinctive* among possible substitutes;
- You may need to consider changing, or at least modifying, your cultural values to meet changed market needs.

7   Make it for everyone

Finally, it is vital to achieve the commitment of top management. Bearing in mind the changes in society outlined in Chapter 1, this last point is of particular significance. Many organizations are trying to move from a more rigid, sometimes rigidly internalized, position to one which is more responsive. In this, the need for top management as a whole to be visibly and unequivocally behind one set of values which are simple and achievable is paramount. Indeed, the recent BIM study quoted earlier in the book[8] showed that it was a lack of this singlemindedness, along with a failure to measure change, which was the greatest cause of failure (or, more often, the 'slow death') of quality initiatives. For Woolworths this is seen as a key factor in their success and it has resulted in wholesale changes at Board and top management level, as they have developed a more cohesive culture based on their aims of service.

Why benchmarking fails

If benchmarking, whether as quality or some other such initiative, is to be of serious value in a service there are a number of pitfalls to avoid:

(1)   Being internally orientated;
(2)   Defining the service too narrowly;
(3)   Mismatching or failing to note change.

Internal orientation

The ideas may be good but they are not based on a true understanding of consumer expectations. Quite often this can be because they simply meet threshold expectations and are not distinctive from competition in the eyes of the consumer.

This is illustrated by the example in Table 9.3 based on a true situation. Neither Company A nor Company B does well – just above average – because they have failed to match up to consumers' expectations. In these cases, 'value' in the context of the customer is not being applied to the most important aspects of the process. However, Company A has superior overall performance on two of the three most important measures, enabling it to overcome a perceived price disadvantage.

Table 9.3 Quality analysis – an example in insurance.

Consumer's view		Consumer's rating of company performance (on scale 0–10)	
Key elements of satisfaction	Relative importance (weighting)	Insurance Co. A	Insurance Co. B
Policy: simple wording	10	7	5
wide cover	10	9	8
Known/helpful contact	20	5	3
Claims: speed of settlement	15	7	7
certainty*	25	4	3
Price	20	7	9
Total	100	39	35
Weighted score	max. 1000	605	550

*Knowing where you stand/feeling secure.

Narrow definition

This is really a variation of the above, in which the quality idea is restricted to only some elements of the service mix (see Figures 5.1, 5.3 and 5.4). Typically, consumers see their purchase as being broader than the supplier defines it and including elements which are under others' control.

A common example is that the delivery of the 'promise' against expectations is missing. For instance, an airline may not take into account sufficiently the impact of poor service at baggage collection. This can be both a time of great anxiety ('Will my baggage have been lost?') and of slight regret (it is the 'signing off' of a, hopefully, good relationship), yet it is often ignored by airlines, even at airports notorious for bad service, because, typically, it is in the hands of an airport authority or 'host' airline. However, even though the airline may maintain that this is then the responsibility of someone else, research shows clearly that, for the customer, they still 'own' the problem – and the opportunity.

Meeting expectations – or exceeding them – in this context may mean providing resources which back up or even duplicate those provided by a subcontractor if the particular aspect of delivery is a critical point in the process – and, as shown in Figure 5.6, baggage collection is critical; it is a key experience.

Mismatch

The service idea is perfect, the core product first class – but nobody has recognized a change in patterns of usage. Fax machines can be a good example of this. The increasingly widespread use of fax means that patterns of usage are now substantially different from those of even a few years ago. Furthermore, machines are often sold which are insufficiently robust for the amount of work they will be required to do. Looking at averages over a week may be misleading if there are occasional periods of intense usage or, as with most telecoms statistics, they hide pockets of persistent difference. However much the specifier – the customer – may be at fault, he will blame the supplier. It is the supplier who owns the problem.

Value in this context is dynamic. The introduction by Virgin Atlantic of their Mid Class is a case in point. (Mid Class is a business class seat for the full economy fare but without all of the business class frills.) Customer expectations – and views on price – have moved on so there is a need for a 'mezzanine' class, above standard economy. So, the type of analysis illustrated in Table 9.3 is only right at the time it was carried out. It may become quickly outdated where consumers' perceptions and usage patterns are changing in the face of rapid social or technological change.

A particular example of this, and of great importance to services, is that today people generally are much less prepared to accept bureaucratic answers, but rather want to be given both individual solutions and sensible explanations. For example, part of the problem for a service such as the railways or ferry services, at least in most countries, is that though they have upgraded their information and other services to travellers they have failed to keep pace with the changing expectations of the consumer, who increasingly has experience of information which is better still, as for example at most airports and with most airlines. These are all examples of yesterday's incremental values (values which gave distinction) becoming today's threshold values. Now they are expected, being of concern only when they are missing.

Pricing a service

Price is another facet of customer expectations and experiences in a service. But often price is overstated as value, that is as an absolute measurement of judgement. Kotler[9] advances three reasons for this emphasis on pricing:

(1) *Historical.* Ever since Adam Smith, price has been at the centre of economic theory.
(2) *Technical.* Price is quantitative, unambiguous and undimensional. It is easier to speculate what a price increase of x% will do than a similar percentage increase in, say, quality.
(3) *Social.* Price is an elegant rationale of efficiency for free market systems. In principle, a competitive system characterized by flexible prices leads to maximum effectiveness.

However, for most people price is merely an indicator of what they are buying. Because services are difficult to judge, naturally it is easy for price to figure high on the list of considerations. If two offers seem so alike then, 'Why pay more?' or, 'Maybe, I should play safe' are going to be key thoughts. Nor should pricing be seen as a purely economic factor. Whilst marketing is based on economic theory, it is not economics. There is ample evidence to suggest that the role of non-price variables is as great, and in many cases greater, than price.

Further, in most markets, indeed the overwhelming majority of markets so far as the Western world is concerned, non-price variables are gaining at the expense of price. This has, in fact, been happening for some considerable time, and as we saw from the quotation from John Maynard Keynes in Chapter 1, has been forecast as an outcome of economic progress for at least the past 60 years. As people become more used to economic power, the focus will move from basic to higher needs, a direct echo of Maslow's theory of the hierarchy of needs.[10] In such circumstances, the importance of relating both price and quality to consumer needs, as they see it from both their expectations and experiences, is clearly critical and the extremely low emphasis on price in our core respondents a reflection of their stronger customer focus.

However, where there are no other factors, price as a value judgement is becoming increasingly important. Because of the shifts in demand change, outlined in Chapter 1, the 'Discriminating Aware Customer' may often demonstrate his awareness by being smart and going for low prices. But being smart, in this context, involves more complex issues than simply price. For example, British Airways found through research that the key reason for passengers buying the cheapest ticket was the fear that someone else would make them feel foolish by having bought cheaper than them. But given enough reasons, many passengers can be persuaded to pay more – how much more depending on their circumstances and perceptions of what they wanted, or feelings reflecting their perceptions of themselves. Virgin Atlantic's Mid Class can be seen as an important pricing response in this context.

In service markets, therefore, the classical price models, of which an example is shown in Figure 9.3, are of questionable value in arriving at pricing decisions. They assume a direct relationship between supply and demand and a single market for price. Of course, there is a relationship between price and demand but it is not the direct relationship of economics. Where it does exist, it is also probable that it exists over a band of price/value relationships, which progressively degenerate at either end of that band. In other words, a small variation in price may have a direct relationship, as in the classical supply/demand model, though even then, the impact of inflation and more volatile price conditions may equally make small adjustments less sensitive. But a large change in price may break such a relationship entirely. This is illustrated in Figure 9.4. What is small and what is large must be a matter for specific judgement in a particular case.

There are few (published) comparisons of pricing and value, but recently an OECD Scientific Committee[11] looked at the question of quality and pricing in telecommunications, and it is their chart which is shown in Figure 9.4. In this extract from their report, the word quality is used in a form which makes it, effectively, synonymous with value. In commenting on this, the report says:

> 'In a deregulated market, in which there are a number of firms offering services of different quality at a range of different prices, (classical economic) principles are challenged. The commodity supplier (low price, basic quality) may still find that a reduction in price leads to an increase in demand but he would risk losing some customers who fear that the reduction equals a quality reduction. These customers may opt for the "standard supplier" who offers a guaranteed quality for a moderate price. At the top end of the scale, the "premium supplier", who offers an enhanced quality for a high price cannot afford to lower the relative price of his service for fear of being perceived as just an overpriced standard supplier. Indeed, there is little incentive for the premium supplier to extend the total size of the market but rather he must compete for an increased share of the existing market. To do this, he must enhance his differential of quality over the standard supplier and increase the range of his services so that the particular aspect of quality which is being improved is targeted to a particular sub-set of the user base.'

The point made about the premium supplier having little incentive to extend the total market is questionable, since this assumes, oddly in the context, that this will only depress price, and so ignores the demand changes higher quality may bring, though it is true to say that quality markets can become degraded through oversupply. Otherwise, this highlights the typical situation well – and emphasizes the need for segmentation noted in Chapter 7 – but, it is fair to say, the problem of pricing in such an abstract form usually only arises with a totally new service. In mass markets this will be a relatively rare but, for

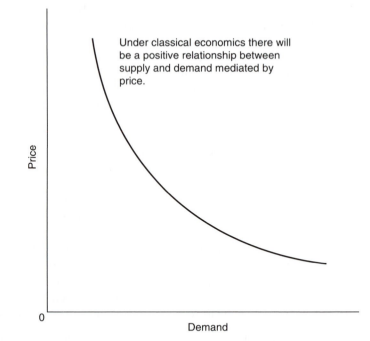

Figure 9.3   Price/demand I: classical economics. (*Source:* OECD Working Party 1990)

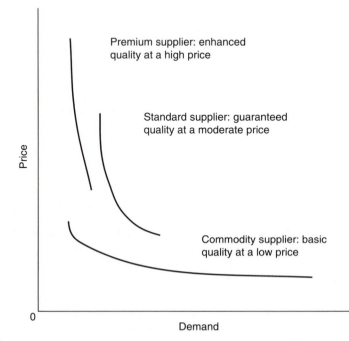

Figure 9.4   Price/demand II: price and value. (*Source:* OECD Working Party 1990)

that reason, often critical decision; in industrial markets, or markets with high values, this may be every time you quote a price. The increasing emphasis on value may well change this balance, and the need to consider breaks in pricing patterns which will cut the old relationships, as in Figure 9.4, may become more frequent, therefore. However, by definition, these will be increasingly non-economic models, and based on a deeper perception of market needs.

In conclusion

Pricing and quality are interrelated to a high degree but in a way which is linked to value. Increasingly the heightened expectations of consumers is leading to a break up of many of the simple price/demand relationships. This affects business in many different ways, because of the variety of service markets. So, you must see price more as a part of the total service mix, rather than a free-standing element on its own. In many cases this will mean price, and so profit, enhancement through improved services tapping new needs, rather than price pressure and so profit reduction.

References

1. Binney G. (1992). 'Making Quality Work', London: Economist Publications
2. Grönroos C. (1984). *Strategic Management and Marketing in the Service Sector*. University of Lund
3. Yorkshire Bank, independent research with customers, 1992.
4. Harvey-Jones J. (1989). *Making It Happen*, Collins
5. Crosby P. B. (1978). *Quality is Free: The Art of Making Quality Certain*. New York: McGraw
6. Quoted in *The Economist*. 18 April 1992
7. Drucker P. (1991). The New Productivity Challenge. In *Harvard Business Review*, November/December
8. British Institute of Management (1990). *Beyond Quality*
9. Kotler P. (1967). *Marketing Management, Analysis and Control*. Englewood Cliffs, NJ: Prentice Hall
10. Maslow A. (1954). *Motivation & Personality*. New York: Harper
11. OECD Committe (1990). *Information, Computer and Communications Policy*

10

Service implementation

- The implementation of a service strategy is integral to its preparation – the interaction with the customer is not an outcome of strategy but its very purpose.

- The mission statement, or vision, of the organization should be the guiding idea for all aspects of implementation and give it focus.

- Without this service improvement initiatives have limited value and their purpose and meaning become vague and unfocused.

- Involvement is crucial, both so that the strategy may evolve to meet changing circumstances and to ensure that those who must make it happen with the customer can play their role with conviction.

- The activity needed to achieve service orientation can be seen under three interrelated headings:
  - Changing values
  - Providing a framework for management change
  - Developing service improvement initiatives.

- Planning cannot be a question of top down or bottom up, but must be a dynamic mixture of both.

- Rewards must match the objectives and values; perceptions of others' judgement can be as critical as tangible rewards.

Implementing service strategies

The implementation of strategy in a service is integral to the preparation because of the very nature of a service:

- The final production processes only happen at the moment of purchase or consumption;
- The customer is involved in the interactions at this point, not passively but as an active participant, shaping and forming not only his or her own perceptions but sometimes those of others;
- The person who delivers the service is equally involved and perceived by the customer as integral to it and to the perceptions it generates – the whole experience;
- Culture is a key factor and culture is equally open to immediate influences during delivery.

So, von Moltke's words, quoted in Chapter 7, 'Strategy is the evolution of the original guiding idea according to changing circumstances.'[1] can be seen to be of particular significance. For von Moltke's 'guiding idea' we can read vision or mission statement, and it is this which should be the 'guide' to activity. So it follows that:

- In Saga, the Chairman, Roger De Haan, uses the mission statement to brief new hotel space buyers, 'So that we select only accommodation that reflects our aims.'
- With Virgin Atlantic, the vision of the airline constantly appears in internal literature, 'When we founded Virgin Atlantic in 1984, we had the ambition to build an airline unlike any other.' '[Today] we constantly need to challenge ourselves if we are to stay ahead of the competition. It's about doing everything better and some things differently,' writes Chairman, Richard Branson to all staff, in the booklet *Our Airline*.
- In Lyonnaise des Eaux-Dumez, 'It is the vision of our President, Jerome Monod, which guides this group,' says Managing Director, Guy de Panafieu.
- In Woolworths, Managing Director, Mair Barnes, talks of, 'Creating a vision-driven organization which is striving toward superior performance.'

So, creating vision, providing sure guidelines and giving direction are key and then, 'The strategy must go with the Army into the field in order to arrange particulars on the spot.'[2]

In developing implementation we must also ensure the following:

- That action reflects not only immediate objectives, such as sales targets, but also the overall strategic objectives, since good services need the development of relationships, and this takes time.

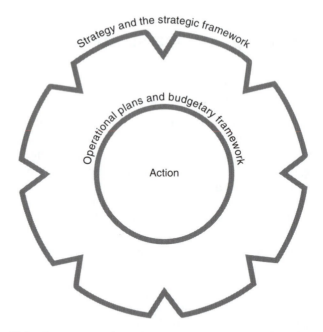

Figure 10.1   Strategy to action. (*Source:* KIA Management Consultants 1984)

- We match the monitoring and reward systems (including the informal rewards) to the needed mix and balance of short- and long-term objectives. If all of these measures of performance and progress on, say, a monthly basis, emphasize short-term sales or cost saving, long-term development will inevitably be left to one side. This is one reason why so many companies have tended to emphasize the pursuit of new customers rather than the development of existing ones; banks and insurance companies are particularly prone to this. This short-term emphasis also means there is a 'cutting-off' of action from strategy, and this is graphically illustrated in Figure 10.1. A strategy provides the prescriptive boundary within which the operational plans, such as budgets, develop. But, in turn, these operational plans can provide a further boundary, which cuts off the influence of the strategy from action. This action, the core of the business, is then conditioned by the purely short-term considerations of, for example, the budget or, as we saw in the previous chapter, systems such as standards. Typically, the incidental features of a great idea gain the day but the idea itself gets lost along the way.

Quite commonly implementation initiatives fail because activities on the bottom axis of The Service Triangle, (Figure 1.2) are treated in isolation. This happens because:

- No one recognizes the problem such an approach creates;
- Or they do, but no one wants to know or be bothered – they name the problem but don't seek a real solution;
- Or the problem is recognized but everyone feels powerless to do anything about it.

Services are particularly prone to this fuzziness in implementation because the ideas have to travel through the organization and then be finalized through a production process which is a one off, is out of immediate control and involves the customer directly. It is this fact that requires the establishment of a relationship and you simply cannot do this by concentrating solely on individual aspects.

So, there is a need for simple guidelines which clarify our objectives and values (as in the mission statements in earlier chapters) within the context of the relationship we seek to establish. The Avis, 'We Try Harder' (which incidentally started life as, 'We're Not the Biggest So We Try Harder' and was successful enough to make the first part untrue) is a powerfully simple expression of what one organization wanted from its relationships – from those millions of interactions both with the consumer and internally which made for the success of the business. The Service Mix Model (Figure 5.1) is a particularly valuable technique in this, since it allows for not only a direct relationship between the vision and the interaction but also an opportunity to hold in balance all the elements involved in achievement.

The Finnish author Lehtinen quotes an example of a successful Danish interior decorating materials company which, despite selling tangible goods, saw its distinctiveness to the customers in terms of service. In its view, 'It is of the utmost importance how the customers feel about us. When selling interior decorations, the physical quality of the goods is important [but] they have to fit with a customer's expectation. This is the reason why "interactive" quality is important. It is the ability of the salesman to advise [which is key to our success].'[3]

The organization/market relationship inherent in this has certain characteristics which must be foremost in developing expectations. For one party, the customer, the meetings at the interaction are most likely fleeting. For the other party, the employee, they may together form a whole working day, even a large and important part of life. The purpose of creating clear expectations, and so the task of any service improvement initiative, must be to make each of those fleeting moments, an experience which is:

- Memorable for the customer, not merely transient;
- At least not boring and at best exciting for the employee.

If the employee's input is not to be merely repetitive, there needs to be a focus on what is changing, and thereby stimulating, rather than on what is boring and thereby mechanistic. The focus must be on the customer's reaction to the experience – the individual's satisfaction from the transient point of the relationship – and not the product. So, for example, being a guide and pointing out the same aspects of a building or city will, inevitably, become boring – and so appear repetitious and lifeless – if the focus is solely that building or city. But change that focus to the experience, the interest being felt by those guided – the exciting revelation or new insight, the sheer pleasure – then it is never repetitious and always has fascination. The descriptions have life because they touch on the individual and his or her needs and interests.

This concentration of values on achievement is crucial to the development of good service. It involves, for example, recognizing that:

- Concern for and interest in the emotional upset and concern of an insurance claimant are as important as a cheque;
- A meal may be viewed as an important marker in the development of a social relationship or the achievement of a business relationship and not just food;
- Displaying care and concern may be as important as providing a cure for a patient;
- An airline trip may be the most exciting event in someone's life, or the key to a successful holiday.

In each case, one aspect – 'our' speciality, the cheque, the food, the cure, the 'plane trip – is relatively unchanging; the other aspect is always fresh and capable of providing interest, allied to worry, success or excitement. It is providing bridges for customers to 'our world' from 'their world' – but through our crossing to theirs and seeing what it is like.

This is of enormous importance for planning services because it can only be through adding value (see Box 10.1) and achieving a distinctiveness, even a uniqueness, that an offer is transformed from being simply a commodity. Further, such relationship building is more important than simply 'feeling good' or achieving the sale; it is about making money. As Tom Hedelius at Handelsbanken says (where 'relationships' as a base for business have been developed into an art), 'Customers make profit'. Over the long term this can be of considerable significance as a number of researches have shown. One report on this concluded, 'As a customer relationship with the Company lengthens, profits rise. And not just a little. Companies can boost profit by almost 100% by retaining just 5% more of their customers [because holding existing customers is relatively efficient].'[4]

Box 10.1   Adding value

It is rare for the function of an article, or a service, to be a complete solution. Most of the solutions you buy – whether manufactured or a service – have some element of value added: a car may be luxurious, or safe or

continues

continued

prestigious; staying at a particular hotel or banking with a particular bank may look smart. It is these often intangible or even unadmitted 'added' values which set most purchases apart from being the purchase of pure commodity. Even a commodity may be chosen from a particular source because of a recognition of the guarantee of quality that seller provides, and so then has an added value, albeit implicit.

However, over time many of these added values themselves become simply accepted, only being remarkable if they are absent. They have become, effectively, a commodity. For example, you have come to expect that a table should stand firmly and have a surface appropriate to its function; generally, you expect that an airline will be safe. These are threshold values. Such threshold values are critical to customer satisfaction, but because they have become taken for granted they are no more than the price of entry to a market for the supplier. They do not make the particular supplier stand out from competition, nor, as in the case of the airline, can they begin to create that relationship so important to services. To be distinctive, values have to be additional, or incremental. Incremental values are those values in a product or service which create difference in the eyes of consumers, meeting a need which competition fails to touch, at least as adequately.

A technical breakthrough can create such incremental value, but unless it can be protected in some way – patent law or 'secret ingredients' are the most usual – it will usually be short lived. In a service, such protection is rarely available; core products are easily copied and, anyway, incremental values are most often perceived and delivered through the individuality of the service.

It may be thought that individuality cannot be achieved in a mass product, but this is not necessarily so. Great acting in the theatre, as opposed to everyday acting, is great because the actor is able to make each member of the audience feel they have gone through an individual experience; the actor has spoken to 'me'. In business, such great performances are not always possible, especially in mass markets, but you can individualize all the same.

British Airways, for example, has found that even a minor acknowledgement of individual customer needs – say getting coffee when a passenger asks for it rather than waiting for a set time – can engender a feeling of being an individual. It has made the passenger feel that he or she was important enough to be responded to as an individual, and by someone who could 'bend the rules' – and so was also important!

To take another example, Burger King achieves individuality at the planning stage through careful matching of what it provides – all the elements of the service mix – to a clearly defined set of target audiences with shared tastes and preferences. Through this, it creates a feeling of a relationship and backs this up with thorough training and example. It is highly routinized but responsive.

In our research, Yorkshire Bank stood out as creating individuality, despite its formal culture, because it had clear values with which its customers could easily identify – seeing it as 'my bank' is a sign that the customer acknowledges responsiveness.

To add value to the basic idea in a service means, therefore, adding value through the relationship. To control this requires action under three interrelated headings:

(1)   Action to develop values which can act as an inspiration and guide to involvement in the relationship;
(2)   Action to provide a framework for change, so that it is not just exhortation;
(3)   Action to develop service improvement initiatives which reflect expectations and guide the relationship through experiences.

Woolworths' experience of tackling this is illustrated in Case 10.1.

Case 10.1   Making it happen

Two years on (1993) from our original study work, Woolworths has travelled a long way in terms of results, but more importantly for the long run, in terms of creating a cohesive culture. 'We are pleased with what we have achieved, but by no means complacent,' said Leo McKee, Director of Human Resources. 'We still have a long, long way to go but we have equally already travelled a long, long way from the old-style, hierarchical Woolworths, which was under performing in almost everyway. We are developing a values-driven organization. For us, our "brand", what we are to our customers and our "values" are two sides of the same coin. [see Figure 10.2] These values, we are developing with our people. Further, "living the values" is the most effective way for our Board to ensure that they permeate the organization, are reflected in everyday behaviour.'
What has Woolworths done?

(1)   The development of their values has been seen by the Board as a key factor in creating the Woolworths they see necessary for competing effectively.
(2)   However, these are no mere empty words:
    •   The values themselves have been developed through research and with 'focus groups' throughout the organization.
    •   These values are being used as a specific input to and guide of all activity. In particular, for each value management have defined explicit behaviours, which are the competencies needed from everyone if that value is to be delivered; see Figure 10.3.
(3)   Merchandise has been carefully selected within five product group areas where Woolworths can be competitive – providing good and consistent quality against the price expectations of the specific market.

continues

continued

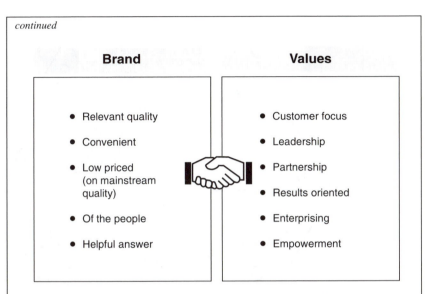

Figure 10.2   The Woolworths brand and values. (*Source:* Woolworths plc)

(4) Premises have been concentrated on sites which reflect the brand position.

(5) The organization has been stripped of layers of management, but more than that has been constructed to give real opportunities for internal promotion. Nor is this just some part of a blind attack on numbers. The new organization is a carefully thought through creation based on a clear distinction between:
- Strategic jobs, primarily the Board, who must only concern themselves with strategic issues;
- Planning, energizing, creating and controlling jobs;
- Implementation jobs.

(6) At the same time, middle management and staff have been empowered to take decisions. So, for example, an old rule of 'all refunds through one manager and one till' has been dropped. Now any member of staff – including the Saturday temporary – can give refunds.

(7) Staff numbers have been dramatically reduced but pay levels have been increased significantly above the average for the past three years. Staff now feel much more that they are recognized.

(8) Training to cope with this new responsibility has been dramatically upgraded – so in 1992, Woolworths spent £7.3 million, against £5.5 million in 1991, itself a significant increase over previous years. The company strongly believes in developing the competencies of its existing workforce.

continues

continued

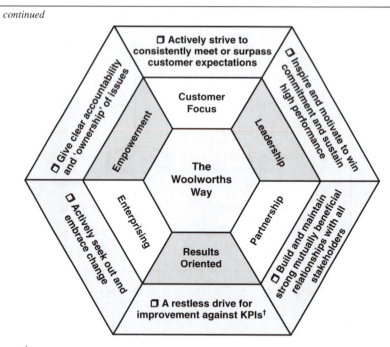

† key performance indicator

Figure 10.3   The Woolworths Way: outcomes. (*Source:* Woolworths plc)

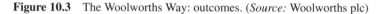

(9) Recruitment has been upgraded in terms of purposely employing higher calibre staff who both want to and can assume the new responsibility.

(10) The focus of appraisal has been shifted solely from 'what' the individual has delivered against objectives, to the 'way' and their usage of 'critical business skills' – including explicit behaviours.

(11) An integrated training programme has refocused middle management on leadership – good coaching and counselling skills, listening, delivering against statements of intent or belief, getting support by example. This training for managers to cope with this new customer-focused environment has been launched under the title 'Managing Better People Better', which emphasizes the aims of changing attitudes as well as inculcating management skills.

(12) Tasks to solve specific problems are increasingly being tackled by the formation of cross-functional project teams, rather than being assigned to an individual specialist department.

(13) The planning processes are increasingly getting built-in feedback mechanisms, to make sure they both take more account of experience and to break the old top-down mentality.

continues

continued

Leo McKee continues, 'We are trying to forge a common language, to see people as "whole human beings" whose personal ambitions – and need to give themselves self-direction – is as important to us as it is to them. For some, the changes are threatening but we are actively finding ways to tackle this, not only through our training, but through our 80/20 plan – at least 80% of management will be internal appointees, a dramatic increase from the old days.'

Managing Director, Mair Barnes sums it up, 'We are moving toward superior performance and that means that not only must we have superior merchandise in any given value range, but we must have superior people operating from superior places. For our customers, Woolworths is above all a "comfortable place to shop"; they don't feel they are being patronized or talked down to, and this is part of our "brand". So it has to be part of ourselves too and we all have to change to meet this challenge. It's not always easy to let go but this year, for example, our "Easter Spend", one of our biggest investments and traditionally a "Board decision", was made by the Trading Controller and his team – and it worked. But maybe the biggest sign of success is that we are now beginning to suffer from the attention of "headhunters", poaching our managers!'

Developing values

What is needed is to capture the potential of people to become involved in building relationships and for this it is necessary to have core values that run deep. But as the two extracts in Box 10.2 below show:

- Individuals must be inspired rather than simply respond to an initiative;
- Cosmetic changes achieve nothing;
- What is required must be within the reach of the organization
  – *it must be reflective of its culture, or what that could reasonably become.*

In the first extract, we may see a direct link to the 'spectators' in ABC in Case 4.1 in Chapter 4. In the second extract, although the bankers no doubt enjoyed the evening as much as Charles Handy, they would have had considerable difficulty in applying the style of communication and discussion elsewhere in the organization unless there was agreement by everyone (including top management) that change was necessary – had purpose in fact.

The real issue for both the development and understanding values is to get people involved in the creation of plans as well as in their execution. It is rarely possible to start with a 'green fields' situation and very often it is necessary to work with what is already there. Replacement of staff (or even of management)

Box 10.2   About values

'Zen and the Art of Motorcycle Maintenance'

While at work I was thinking about this lack of care in the digital computer manuals I was editing.... they were full of errors, ambiguities, omissions and information so completely screwed up you had to read them six times to make any sense out of them. But what struck me for the first time was the agreement of these manuals with the spectator attitude I had seen in the shop. These were spectator manuals. It was built into the format of them. Implicit in every line is the idea that, "Here is the machine, isolated in time and space from everything else in the universe. It has no relationship to you, you have no relationship to it, other than to turn certain switches, maintain voltage levels, check for error conditions" and so on. That's it. The mechanics in their attitude toward the machine were really taking no different attitude from the manual's toward the machine or from the attitude I had when I brought it in there. We were all spectators. It then occurred to me, there is no manual that deals with the real business of motorcycle maintenance, the most important aspect of all. Caring about what you're doing is considered either unimportant or taken for granted.
Source: From Robert Pirsig, *Zen and the Art of Motorcycle Maintenance*, Bodley Head, 1974.

Appearances can be deceptive

I once was asked to talk to a group of managers at the staff college of one of the large banks. It was a very formal evening. Everyone was in suits, in rows, in upright chairs. They all wore their names and titles on their lapels. After I had spoken, the session was chaired, very formally, by the head of college. I was placed for dinner at the top table between the head and his deputy. I never felt that I got close to the student managers or to their problems. I mentioned this, afterwards, to the head and said that, in my view, such formality did not encourage frank discussion or any real learning, it was all just a kind of ritual.

Next time I went everything was different. Lots of managers were in casual dress. We sat in a large circle of armchairs and sofas. Drinks were available. Supper was a buffet affair. It was all very informal and I enjoyed it immensely. I was staggered by the change. 'Is it always like this now?' I asked one of the young managers. 'Oh, no,' he said, 'just today. Look.' And he showed me a paper pinned on the notice board, headed 'Orders for the Day':

"In conformity with the wishes of our speaker tonight," it read, "dress will be informal, the session will be held in the Reading Room, not the Lecture Theatre, where drinks and supper will also be available. First names are to be used. These orders apply to this session only."

'You see,' he said, 'it's all for you.'

Outward and visible signs do not always mean what they say.
Source: From Charles Handy, *Inside Organizations*, BBC Books, 1990.

seldom changes the situation, because it is *that* sort of person who works in *that* industry. Recruitment can be a critical issue in maintaining momentum (see also Chapter 11), but, even if you are prepared to contemplate it, in reality not many organizations would be able to carry out the wholesale slaughter which accompanied British Airways' justifiably praised, but potentially destructive, change programme. Only 'sexy' industries, like airlines, can maintain any degree of cohesion with such a high level of redundancy and speed of change – such as 300 top managers all being notified of new jobs on a Thursday, told to effect hand over on the Friday and start in the new job, on a six-month tenure, on the Monday!

If people are treated as personalities, not simply as people, they are less inclined to be spectators. 'If we are returning from an incident and we see someone by the side of the road with a problem, we would simply stop and help. We don't think about the money,' said a number of the managers and staff interviewed in Falck. It may be an extreme example, though by no means exclusive to Falck in the research, but it epitomizes the essential nature of good service – you cannot buy it, you can only create the culture in which people are prepared to give it, willingly.

There can be no doubt of the power that true involvement brings. Liam Strong, until recently Marketing and Operations Director at British Airways, admits that, 'The most successful initiatives we have had are where we have captured the imagination of our staff,' and that to increase this level of success, 'we need more decentralization to give power back to the market operatives.'[5]

In this study, manager after manager testified to the differences – good and bad – that people involvement had brought. For Virgin Atlantic, such capturing of the imagination is what they are selling. 'Imagine [customers] choosing us and being able to enjoy a new exciting check-in area...,' enthuses the internal booklet *Our Airline*. The more the emphasis on involvement is as part of a genuine relationship, the more it is likely to link 'our world' and 'their world', to succeed by overcoming the inevitable problems that occur. One Finnish study showed that 93% of managers thought their staff could compensate, at least partially, for technical or other deficiencies.[6] Whilst this particular study may be a reflection of undue optimism, it nevertheless reflects a view of the importance of 'spontaneous recovery'; matters are bound to go wrong from time to time and it is more often what you do in that situation which matters, rather than the error itself.

Indeed, it is in recovery of situations that good service is most often seen. In the final analysis, staff will provide this only if they want to. At least, this is true in the European scene; money, fear or inertia may persuade people to carry out the task, but only a personal will to serve can create true service. Where there is no involvement this will be evident to the customer. Four typical examples follow.

1   Standing back from involvement

This most often occurs where staff have been too little prepared for customer involvement and feel powerless in the face of poorly structured systems or overwhelming force (strong management directives perhaps). Sometimes the two go together, with a heavily routinized system linked to a high degree of formality, which may even produce fear. Everyone has, at some time, witnessed the attitude, 'It's nothing to do with me, it's the computer/accounts/or London (or wherever) office, which produces those letters.' They are all spectators. Further, if complaints are seen as a crime, then this tendency will be even more pronounced, because as an employee you may be disciplined if you are closely involved in a troublesome situation.

'Standing back' may also be exhibited by top management, who will typically launch such an initiative and then leave it to others to execute, never querying whether or not their own behaviour reflects the values they seek in others or whether indeed the proposed course of action is compatible with such values. It is probable that the biggest single change that will be required to achieve sustained success in the future will be a change in management attitudes, but it will not happen so long as any one group or level of management sees itself as above this.

The values that can stem from a painstaking approach to this are illustrated with Handelsbanken in Case 10.2. Clarity of thinking about the customer has been linked to equally clear thinking concerning the role of management.

Case 10.2   Managing a customer focus

Handelsbanken has gone further than most – and has had a longer experience than most – in creating an organization based on a customer focus. Tom Hedelius, Chief Executive until 1991 and now Chairman, says:

'With us the customer is first; and the products are secondary to branch managers' control of the meetings with the customer. To achieve this we are totally decentralized to the branch, though it means we do have to have a good central control and steering system.

We started our change in 1970 and our then Chief Executive, Jan Wallander, who had been brought in to deal with a profitability crisis, was the man behind it. He refused to deal even with the biggest customers; it all had to go through the branch. He also instituted a profit-sharing system in which

continues

continued

everyone participates on an equal footing. If we achieve our targets – better profitability than the average of Swedish banks as a whole – then we get a proportion of this "extra" profitability credited to us, in the pension fund, in the form of shares. As a result, employees own some 10% of the bank's stock now, and those who have been with us since the beginning, like my secretary and myself, have a credit of about 600,000 kronor [about £60,000] in this way.

We still have our share of big business and it is profitable because we have a way of measuring and checking each customer. We know how much each contributes to profitability, so we can ensure we keep the best. Without doubt, this is in part responsible for our good profit record, which has improved even further since deregulation [in 1985] and has unquestionably been the factor in our having avoided the worst of the problems in the last two years.

To make it work you have to have a Chief Executive who knows the business so that people see they can get real help from a discussion – someone who can help solve problems and not just talk. It also means you have to be available at all times. My main task when I was Chief Executive was talking to people and I visited about 50 branches [out of some 500] a year. I could, and did, contact anyone direct, to query, but never override, a decision or to get information. But I rarely wrote, almost always talking on the telephone or face to face. For example, I organized all your visits myself, by telephone. [And indeed he had, and uniquely in the study they all happened at the right times with the right people!] However, I did write a personal letter to every manager, once a month, to get through any messages I felt were important.'

This might be thought to be just the Chief Executive talking, but all the ideas are set out publicly for all staff to see in a booklet entitled *Our Way* (available in English for overseas staff) and managers and staff are not only warm in their support but echo closely the terms used.

Leif Lundberg, a Senior Executive Vice President, concurs, 'We don't have any worry about our Chief Executive free ranging across the organization. We stick to our strategy and we have one point as our focus – the customer.' This unswerving focus on the customer puts a lot of pressure on the branch and another Executive Vice President, recalls his days as a branch manager, 'It was a shock when I realized I had to do it on my own. I had to get the customers. I had to make the decisions. But it was the most exciting time of my life. How do we go on keeping up momentum? We have to work hard at it. We have to sell our ideas to the branches and resell them. It can be frustrating but we have a few simple ideas and stick to them, like for every krona you spend, get two in. This is way above the industry average'. (When this was originally written (1991) this average was a 1.3 spend to 2. This is not an untypical bank average in many European countries though Abbey National in the UK claim similar figures to Handelsbanken.)

Branch managers echo this view and when pushed on, 'Is it the party line?' will admit, 'Yes, it is the way we work.' But one expressed it, 'Yes, we

continues

---

continued

are indoctrinated. But [because of the profit-sharing system] it is our Bank. We could never work anywhere else [at any other bank].'

The two ingredients that seem to support the management style most are the profit-sharing system and the rigorous attention to involving others and getting them onside. Hedelius again, 'We have had to educate managers to this. It is not uncommon for them to claim that all they get out of their discussion with their employees is centred around matters of immediate and concrete work environment. But that is exactly what we should expect. These are the questions they [the staff] can answer and which are important to them in their job and where their knowledge is superior to those above them.'

So it is possible for top management to run a large organization and yet have time for people and to make their problems seem as important as the big issues like company finance, mergers and government contracts. It involves selecting the right style for the situation and for you – and acknowledging the superior contribution those working closest to the customer can make in their areas of competence and experience.

---

2   Not allowing the customer the potential for being right or in the wrong

This is usually a more 'aggressive' form of standing back from involvement. It is most often to be seen where organizations do not allow room for mistakes, which we saw earlier was a critical factor. An example of this was a major car dealer who arranged for his staff to telephone and check that everything was satisfactory after servicing. However, the idea, good in itself, was spoilt by a negative reaction – from staff – to any criticism, because management had neither set up any back-up system for 'receiving' and dealing with complaints, nor had they provided training for handling the 'difficult' customer. So, in addition to the worry that a 'mistake' might lead to a reprimand to oneself or a colleague, there was also the fear of being criticized internally for 'creating' a complaint. There was no room or reason for the employee to place himself in these situations for the sake of a customer. As a result, the chance for real communication and deeper understanding of reactions was shut off.

3   'Going over' to the customer

This is often characterized by agreeing with the customer completely, rather than trying to explain or offering to pass the complaint upwards. This type of incident most often occurs where the staff are well prepared for, or highly motivated toward, customer involvement, but are unable to deliver because of the lack of internal flexibility, either because systems are insufficiently responsive or, often, because of management attitudes. Usually it takes the form of, 'I agree. I wish you would complain about it because it causes us a lot of problems, and they will take more notice of you.' An extreme example was quoted recently in the Service Industries Journal. It concerned the case of a well-known businessman and frequent traveller by Air France, who had checked in late for a flight at Charles de Gaulle Airport. There was, however, still time and he endeavoured to persuade the clerk to be 'responsive', and override the system, by mentioning who he was. 'Then,' said the clerk, apologetically, 'I won't check you in, because *you* are an important client who will complain and maybe the management will do something about the system!'[7] Clearly, the clerk was deeply frustrated by the system and saw the customer rather than the management as an ally in overcoming this.

4   Being inflexible at a time of crisis

Too often systems and management attitudes allow too little responsiveness when things go wrong. As the comments by Lars Nørby at Falck showed, insurance companies can be concerned with doing the 'correct' thing when what is needed is quick action which solves the problem – there and then.

Some worthy attempts by management to overcome this fail because they are mere exhortation – and are seen to be just that by middle management and staff. 'Be outrageous,' said the managing director of an appliance services company, extolling in the internal newspaper a branch manager who had settled a complaint by giving away a new refrigerator to replace a faulty one,'let's all do the same!' 'It would be nice,' said the other managers, 'but wait till he sees the expenses!'

Cosmetic change will not work. Seemingly, as everyone except top management knows, it is the reality which counts and that goes on long after the inspired speech or exhortation to 'serve our customers better'.

Providing a framework

Establishing values as an integral part of your strategy is the first step. It is then necessary to ensure that the changes in management that these values require are made a fact of life – for example, turned into 'explicit behaviours', as in Woolworths – and are not turned aside by lack of understanding, passive resistance or vested interest.

If these concerns are to be met there are two distinct, if interrelated, aspects to be considered – a method and a system. Of these, it is method which is of overwhelming importance. If simply telling people what to do is to be avoided – not because in itself it is an error necessarily, but because on its own it is an oversimplification of the role of communication – there is a need to ensure that:

- Those who have to implement the plans can get across their concerns and objections
- And in doing this, the defensive routines (see Chapter 8) are broken down.

This requires listening, not as a passive task, but as a whole way of communicating – being attentive to others' reactions and ensuring that they know they have been listened to.

Involvement by design

The best place to start implementation is at the beginning! Often, when new initiatives are launched, the final plans are treated as the starting point. As a result, much of the thinking that lies behind these plans, the sometimes agonizing but certainly valuable thought processes, is missed. The audience is rushed into the advanced stages of the plans. Given that they probably do not want to be negative, they may express a conviction, which they want to feel but which may be only skin deep, or they may indulge in negative or defensive routines, being careful not to expose themselves to the risk of failure. It is therefore necessary to start implementation by reviewing the strategy with the audience. Take them through the basis of the strategy and ensure that they understand its purpose. Then allow those who have to take ideas forward to develop confidence in handling them.

A participative workshop approach can be of great benefit in this. The purpose of such a workshop is to provide an opportunity to re-examine the thinking processes, question old values and look for possible solutions from a different perspective. Such participative workshops might be over two days, with a few people (about 12–16 is maximum). The first part would be devoted to a thorough discussion of the factors involved and is, primarily, an opportunity for drawing out contributions from and gaining the involvement of participants. The second part would then be devoted to developing action. A useful structure for the second part is the four key questions of service implementation (see Box 10.2). If participants can be encouraged to think of developments in these terms, they have gone a long way towards achieving a high level of coordination and involvement. It is also an excellent framework for constructing middle management's role since the activity required to answer these questions is precisely the sort of activity that should be at the core of their role as leaders and facilitators.

Box 10.2   The four key questions

Getting managers to become leaders and to listen to and support staff can be a difficult transition. These four questions can help to structure the approach, creating a more balanced and investigative dialogue:

(1) *What does it (the mission statement, the aim of the plans) mean to me?* The purpose of this is to get those responsible for implementation to relate personally to the ideas; to get beneath the skin and consolidate the first steps of communication (awareness and understanding); and to create a personal commitment – an acceptance of individual responsibility for making it happen.

(2) *What can I contribute?* Service implementation is, by necessity, decentralized; interactions are 'out there', and not entirely predictable. Yet often each person waits for someone else to take up the initiative — the spectator syndrome. As a result, the new plan, the new idea, the change of emphasis is lost. We have to get each individual to see how he or she can contribute and then take responsibility for this contribution – and for the support of others.

(3) *What are the barriers?* Clear and open discussion of, 'How will we do it and what will stop us?' helps to consolidate both understanding and conviction. It will also serve to highlight the real problems at working level.

(4) *What help do I need?* This completes conviction and starts action. By putting the implementers in control, it highlights individual responsibility – and starts the process of turning management and service departments into a resource to be called upon by those who carry out the work.

Most organizations that have tackled implementation successfully have found some form of approach which allows participation on a generally equal level to be of particular value. So, for example, the participative workshop approach outlined was used to develop an understanding of the research results and agreeing action with the management in Cases 3.1 and 4.1 in Chapters 3 and 4. In such situations it is important to consider what strategic choices are open and what kind of tactical implementation could result and, as is so often the case, it is necessary to contrast unpleasant truths, to weigh up the opportunities and risks, the strengths and weaknesses and set specific objectives and priorities to ensure an overall relationship, not isolated effort. Conviction must come from understanding.

Top down? Bottom up?

This perennial question is not really a question at all in a service organization. If you are to fulfil the ideas outlined, you have to tackle planning both ways: you need a strong sense of strategic direction if you are to achieve a unity of purpose and you need commitment and ownership if you are to have effective implementation.

Many organizations allow the two approaches to run in parallel, and then spend fruitless effort in endlessly reconciling the results. As the Handelsbanken example shows, you can allow individual managers to develop their own plans – within a clearly-defined structure with equally clear objectives – without having to consolidate the results to meet central expectations. Although many managers are initially sceptical about this (it smacks of 'losing control'), in practice most have found it beneficial. After all, locally developed plans can compare with the central plan in only one of three ways:

- Match exactly – in which case there is no problem;
- Exceed – again no problem, other than to be cautious about over-optimism (this is, incidentally, the usual result – most people believe they will achieve more when given the chance to take the initiative);
- Fall short – in which case management are being given a timely warning!

It is common in situations such as the third case, to go back and push each individual to a higher figure. The effect of this is usually to induce the reaction, 'If you wanted that, why not say so in the first place?' Yet, if management's figures are right, then the subordinates will exceed their target, so there really is no problem. Alternatively, if the subordinates are right, management themselves have now acquired a personal target over and above the cumulative effort, a target *they* have to achieve! After all, it was *their* opinion, not the sub-ordinates', that it could be achieved, so… . Incidentally, the Life Division of Skandia, the biggest Swedish insurance company, has done just that with great success for many years.

The most important part of planning in service implementation is to ensure that scarce resources are used to best effect against the markets selected and agreed. In order to achieve this, action plans should be designed so that:

(1) The precise usage of resources – and the scarcest of these in most service situations is time – is directed toward the agreed market objectives. So, for example, branch costs and time plans should be *directly related* to achieving specific and identified objectives for that branch.

(2) Long-term, often qualitative, objectives are given balanced treatment along with purely short-term, usually quantitative, objectives. For exam-ple, a strategic objective to move into a new market or establish better customer care or service levels may require some sub-optimization of resource usage in the short term in order to achieve better usage long term. This needs identifying, stating and controlling and it is necessary to have a mechanism for holding these long-term objectives in balance with the short term.

Since services are ultimately manufactured face to face with the consumer at the time of consumption, it is a good idea to start with the interaction, and plan back from there. So it is necessary to observe the following principles:

- Provide a clear view of the overall objectives to be fulfilled, but allow for specific plans to be built up from the roots of the business, where the 'process' happens.
- Clearly differentiate between the tasks of business or market planning (essentially a predictive task in which it is the sense and understanding of the market which matter as much as the figures) and those of budgeting (which is primarily finance based and is intended to ensure that the inputs and outputs are in balance).
- Pinpoint the critical links between activity resources and action.
- Force decisions to be made about the use of resources, especially the key scarce resource of time, and relate this to the balance between long-term and short-term objectives.
- Provide for simple but effective monitoring and reviews.

A good action plan is most effective when there are a few, simple documents which allow both those who originate the plans and those who monitor them to see all of the information necessary on a few pieces of paper. The ideal would be one side of A4, but this is often not practicable. A possible outline is shown in Box 10.3.

Box 10.3 Action planning steps

(1) Identify the local market in terms of specific sectors or segments. Textbook definitions of segments are usually less useful here than the personal terminology of the planner; for example instead of 'skilled workers', a more accurate description might be 'miners, with wages paid weekly into a branch'. This is specific, identifiable and creates a real feel for the market.

(2) Clarify what the consumers want from you, that is, the problem to which they seek a solution. This may also be seen as defining the incremental values you have – what will make you distinctive. It will also be the focus in the service mix (see Figure 5.1).

(3) Identify the service products which will be the core solutions to these needs. These may be a hard product, for example bank accounts or 'plane seats, but may also be, or include, softer elements. The definition will stem from the work you have put in on the service mix.

(4) Identify competition and decide on the best opportunities. Some segments may be less or more attractive, depending on these strengths.

(5) Develop targets, segment by segment, and work out the activity levels you need to achieve these. At this point you are beginning to match resource usage to returns.

(6) Assess the resources required and calculate the overall results. Do these fulfil company needs? Does the total activity give you the return you want? If not, you may need to make some revisions. It is possible to put such plans on a simple linear program and so work out a number of alternative scenarios at this point.

(7) Finalize and agree activity.

(8) Integrate with company-wide plans and, if required, produce budgets.

An example of an action plan is given in Table 10.1.

The key benefits of such decentralized decision making are:

- *effectiveness,* since costs are easily related at local level to specific results;
- *competitiveness,* since it helps to optimize the use of the most important resource, people, at the point of contact with the consumer;
- *better investment* than in a new core product is often the case, since local plans cannot be easily copied, whereas products rarely remain unique for long.

However, it is the way in which planning is approached which is most important. Involvement is critical, not because it is 'nice' but because of the diffuse and widespread nature of the service process. In a service, there are

Table 10.1 Example of an action plan.

Branch: Upville Date: 6 months to 31.12.81 (Extracts)

Segment	Focus/Need	Solution/Product	Market size	Current share	Target	Average value	Estimated conversion	Estimated calls for success	Total calls/time	Personnel needs/training costs	Marketing needs/costs
Large professional connections		Both				(of connection)					Head Office mailing phone check £6K
(a) Existing	(a) no surprises	Standard mortgage and survey guarantee	146 (a) 32	32	32	£65K	100%	Monthly	192	–	
(b) New	(b) we are effective		(b) 114	–	6	£60K	1:3	4 sales then each fortnight	108	Training for new approach est. £5K	
Small professional connections		Both				(of connection)					Entertainment/ sponsorship est. £10K
(a) Existing	(a) we can help build your practice	Standard mortgage and selective introductions	151 (a) 24	24	23*	£70K	100%	Monthly	138	–	
(b) New	(b) we have contacts		(b) 127	–	6	£60K	1:4	4 sales then each fortnight	132	Training for new approach est. £5K	
Houseowners +5 yrs 45 +		Both									–
(a) Existing	(a) we can help to plan the future	New savings plan	1640 (a) 95	95	90**	£3.5K	100%	No separate, counter discussion	–	–	
(b) New (to us)	(b) we can help achieve your dream		(b) 1545	–	45	£3.5K	1:10	5 minute discussion	37 ½ hrs	Training for new approach est. £5K	Leaflets etc. £2K
Houseowners New to market (and us)	We can guard against the unexpected	New savings plan	About 120	–	14	£0.2K	1:5	5 minute discussion	6 hrs	Training for new approach est. £5K	Included in above
					Total customers 216 of which new 71	Totals Loans £4.4M Savings £0.5M Commission £88K			Totals 570 call = 1 man/year 43 ½ hrs = 1 clerk	Totals Personnel £17K estimates Training £10K***	Total marketing costs £18K
											Overall costs £45K

* Note, one merger.
** Maturities; withdrawals, etc
*** Costs common to all sectors, so estimated total.
Source: KIA Management Consultants, 1981.

millions of 'moments of truth', where ideas are turned to success or failure. The best service plans are achieved at those points and thus come through dialogue and agreement, not imposition.

Rewards

A further problem is the failure to match reward systems with the ideas – and ideals – of service. David O'Brien, then managing director of Rank Xerox, summed this up. 'Our business depends upon achieving long-term relationships with customers. With many of the traditional short-term measures and targets there is a danger of incompatibility between the supplier's and the customers' objectives; eg a return on net asset base could be achieved by reducing the net asset base and cutting out facilities that should be there to improve customers' satisfaction.'[8]

This is echoed strongly in Handelsbanken where profitability is linked to customers and branches, not products. The cardinal tenet of this philosophy is doing what is best for the customer and disregarding what is, in the short term, best for the bank since as Arne Mårtensson, the Chief Executive, writes in the most recent edition of the staff booklet *Our Way:* 'If we do not offer our customers what is best for them, somebody else will, and then we may lose the customer completely'.

While some managers may believe that staff are insensitive to pressures from above, the fact is that they are very sensitive – especially to the unspoken and often subtle pressures that are applied. This was illustrated in Chapter 2 with the 'bureaucracy versus enthusiasm' concept. Those organizations that are least successful are those where the exhortations of management are out of line with the realities: where there is role ambiguity and role conflict.

What is needed is to relate rewards to the objectives (what we are to achieve) and the values (how we are to achieve them). This is 'the way we work' and should be the centre point of all review. For examples, see the 'B' questions in the research and the charts of these in Chapters 2 and 3, or the 'mission statement' examples in Chapters 3, 4 and 7. It may not be possible to link such measures to reward with money, but equally this may not be necessary. Few people work only for money, and the great majority might not see the amount as the primary factor. Rather, job satisfaction, a feeling of value and exercising responsibility all commonly score higher than money as reasons for accepting promotion.

In conclusion

In a service the implementation must be seen as integral to the strategy itself. This means that:

(1) The vision, the mission statement, must be expressed in clear and simple terms, so that it provides guidance to those involved in the translation;

(2) There must be a deep sense of belonging and ownership of this through-out the organization;

(3) Mmanagement must work seriously hard at the task of developing the business, getting individuals to assume the responsibility necessary to avoid being either spectators or cutting across each other to the detriment of the customer;

(4) There must be 'feedback loops' to provide not only information but reward.

References

1. von Moltke H. (1858-79). Writings when Chief of the German and Prussian General Staffs

2. von Clausewitz K. (1832). *On War*

3. Lehtinen J. (1986). *Quality Oriented Service Marketing*. Department of Business Economics and Business Law, University of Tampere

4. Reichheld F.E. and Earl Sasser Jnr W. (1990). Zero defections: quality comes to services. In *Harvard Business Review,* September/October. © 1990 by the President and Fellows of Harvard College, all rights reserved

5. Strong L. (1991). Presentation at the Marketing Society Annual Conference, November

6. Grönroos C. (1990). *Service Management and Marketing*. Lexington Mass: Lexington Books

7. Quoted in the *Service Industries Journal*. April 1990

8. Quoted in the *Journal of Long-Range Planning*. April 1988

11

Maintaining momentum

- Maintaining momentum is one of the most difficult tasks which management face.
- To be effective in this 'third age', it is necessary to establish a culture of continuous improvement – encouraging constructive dissatisfaction.
- In this there are ten key areas:
  - (1) Focus the business
  - (2) Make that focus external
  - (3) Get individuals to commit
  - (4) Recruit the right people
  - (5) Create dialogue not monologue
  - (6) Extend the dialogue to the customer
  - (7) Give influence
  - (8) Keep track of what is happening
  - (9) Keep top management in touch
  - (10) Be caring, be consistent.

What can we do next?

If you have done everything we have reviewed in this book so far, it is possible – though unlikely – that you will be able to sit back and enjoy the fruits of your hard work. But the probability is that you will find not only that the world has changed in terms of its needs, but that your customers – and hopefully your staff – will have become more demanding of you; many of yesterday's incremental values will have become today's threshold values. Further, some of the 'fire' may have become lost in a new bureaucracy, which has sprung up to develop and serve – but now merely to defend – the new approaches, the new values. Some, who have developed deep relationships with a stable customer base may be as lucky as the client quoted by the Swedish consultant Richard Normann, 'No, we have not changed. But our customers have! Somehow they are quite different now and that makes everything a lot more fun and you feel you get something from them, and so you also want to give.'[1]

But for most, success will have brought at least some measure, or a mix, of complacency, swelling ranks of employees and new 'staff' roles to create rules and demand information, a loss of the initial edge of excitement and moves by competitors to catch up, and maybe surpass, your initiatives. Even an organization as young and dynamic as Richard Branson's Virgin Atlantic had found this difficult, as Case 11.1 shows.

What Virgin Atlantic has done is to recognize that once the heady days of planning and then implementing the service idea are over it is all too easy to sink back into normality, even, and maybe especially, if you are successful. This 'third age' is in many respects the most difficult of all because it requires skills of stamina both in maintaining the customer's interest – often an on-going relationship – and in keeping service issues to the forefront of activity, even though big issue activities like acquisitions or capital purchase may seem not only more exciting for top management but less emotionally draining. 'We have to work seriously hard at it,' was a common refrain across our respondents.

Unfortunately, many of the issues involved in service development have become merely service improvement, often responding to fashion, with the emphasis on the quick fix rather than on a strategic aim. There are times when the quick fix is what is needed, when there needs to be action *now*! But such moves – whether they are presented as customer care or putting people first or quality service – can be, and usually are, self-defeating if they are not part of a clear and visible process toward a vision which rises above the everyday and to which everyone can subscribe, because they understand, they are convinced and they feel they 'own' what is happening. Each quick fix on its own can be justified but in the end there is no central point or purpose any more. It is like forecourt promotions in the petrol business. Each new promotion has less effect, and eventually the brand loses all sense of identity; it is simply a response, with the product sold at the lowest price.

Case 11.1   The experienced virgin

'Last year (1992) we had been going eight years and we began to realize that we had to do something more to keep up the spirit that had got us to where we were. I know it sounds a bit silly, but we became really nervous when we won so many awards, especially, the Airline of the Year Award the third year running. We knew it could breed complacency,' said Chris Moss, Marketing Director at Virgin Atlantic. 'A lot of new people had joined us in that time, many of them from backgrounds where they had been used to a lot more structure, manuals and the like. They were asking for more structure and we found ourselves wanting to respond to them but realized that this was a potential trap. We had always been taken by the Japanese concept of "kaizan", constructive and continuous improvement, and we wanted this to go on.'

Richard Branson, who founded the airline, agrees, 'We aren't interested in having just happy employees. We want employees who feel involved, prepared to express dissatisfaction when necessary. In fact, we think that the constructively dissatisfied employee is an asset we should encourage and we need an organization that allows us to do this – and encourages employees to take responsibility, since I don't believe it is enough for us to simply give it.'

For the outsider, it is not easy to understand what Virgin Atlantic has done to maintain momentum in the face of this change, since their whole philosophy is to stimulate the individual and there is something almost mystical about their approach. 'No, plan is too structured a word,' says Chris Moss, 'it's more a part of an ongoing frame of mind which encourages and allows people to do what they feel is right. We started with the Directors, getting them to write down what was special and we had something which was a thousand different answers but yet was the same. That gave us the thought of a "re-design project" but again, that is too precise. Rather, what we have done is to set up ten different projects, which have as their task to re-interpret our philosophy – of being an airline that is superior to and different from the others – in the light of both our, and of external, progress and in a way that continues to make us an airline that people like us would want to fly. They must interpret this into all the little things that make up the travelling experience.'

What have they done? The *Our Airline* booklet, referred to already, was one of the early responses, 'We weren't sure we wanted something like this, as it was easy to come across as "the thoughts of Chairman Richard,"' says Chris Moss, 'but we had to have something to capture the key points.'

It sets these out in simple form, with coloured line drawings to humorously, and memorably, bring home the important points:

- We must not be afraid to break with convention.
- We must balance continuing to be seen as the 'innovative new kids' with being a business with over a million customers a year, 'We need to grow up, but we must not end up self-important and boring like most of the other airlines.'

continues

continued

- We must be memorable, 'We are not operating a bus service. The journeys made by our customers are romantic and exciting and we should do everything we can to make them feel just that. That way they will talk about the most memorable moments long after they leave the airport.'
- Each class should reflect our originality and have its own style and character.
- We must have an obsessive attention to detail since 'we know that any journey is made up of many experiences'.
- We have a great opportunity but 'it is up to us'.

Tangibly, for the customer, there have been big improvements in seating and especially the introduction of individual TV screens, in the back of the seat, throughout the 'plane. 'We did it to give individual choice but it has had all sorts of extra spin-off advantages. People don't feel so restricted, as they can read or move around without interfering with others' enjoyment. We can serve drinks and meals more easily and we don't have the rush to the toilets when the film finishes.'

At one end, there have been big innovations, like the introduction of Mid Class (a business class seat for full economy fare) and at the other lots of small but critical initiatives such as ice creams as a snack, 'More refreshing and lifts people's spirits in the middle of a flight, with the atmosphere rather dry. No passenger ever asked for it in research, but our staff thought it up as an idea because they are involved and can see what would help.'

The new lounge at Heathrow is another innovation. 'All our research said that passengers just wanted a "straight lounge" – space, coffee, 'phones etc. But we thought that can't be right and anyway it's dull and conventional. So, we have developed a lounge with lots of things to see and do. We are even going to build a conservatory on the roof. Now we are getting an enormously enthusiastic response'. 'I wish I'd come earlier,' wrote one passenger, 'and given myself more time.'

(Interestingly, passengers using the lounge aren't asked to 'tick boxes' in research questionnaires but are asked to write their reactions. 'No we don't try to analyse these into reports. It's up to the Manager to read them and decide on what action to take or what to report back.')

'I want employees in the airline to feel that it is they who can make the difference, influence what the passenger gets,' says Richard Branson. 'I write to them all personally about every two months but often more frequently. It depends what's happening but I want them to know what is going on and why and for them to see that their ideas are what we depend on.'

Those respondents selected because of their long-term success had achieved a high degree of momentum, but the basis for this had been laid long before it was the fashion to be service orientated. With Sainsburys it was buried deep in time; with others it was the more recent development of a clear focus for the business:

- Sainsburys had lived through numerous market changes very successfully, because it had a few simple values which everyone knew and which were applied with unrelenting determination yet with innovation;
- Yorkshire Bank had established itself as something more than a local savings bank by focusing on a very clear market segment, with which the bank and its staff identified and which, in turn, identified with them;
- Saga, too, had established over more than 40 years a clear view of its market and that its responsibility – and profit – stemmed from being with its customers for the long term;
- Lyonnaise des Eaux, similarly, had built a long-term view through the long-term nature of its business, serving local authorities on, typically, 15-year, and more, contracts. In particular, this had nourished the view that it was important to get the job done quickly, and consider the problems later;
- Falck had also developed such a culture – 'Fast Help is Good Help' and, 'We don't even think about whether we should do it, we just do,' being typical quotes.

All, except Saga, were frankly hierarchical, with strong lines of authority, although Falck had developed an outstanding degree of leadership and cohesion. The other three have major challenges ahead to adapt to a market in which individual values and looser structures will be necessary, as Sainsburys have already clearly recognized. They are not alone in this. Lufthansa, Swissair and many, many others with a highly successful past based on a strong 'telling' component in management have to face up to the demands, not only of customers but also of staff and management, to be treated in a more responsive and involved way. Piecemeal changes and service improvements will simply destroy the old without a clear view of the cultural destination. The result will be chaos.

Handelsbanken was different in having largely achieved such a change, and reshaped its whole approach in just 20 years. In this, it had been well ahead of the market and, even allowing for some post-rationalizations by current management, had achieved a remarkably modern organization before most others had began to think about it, even in Sweden. Again, there was a clear set of values, which everyone understood and identified with, accompanied by an unrelenting drive from the top.

What was clearly evident about all six organizations was:

- The preparedness of top management – the very top – to become involved in and identified with the daily business;
- Their acceptance of culture (not necessarily called that) as a key part of their business – culture not as a soft value but as something real, even hard – for example Yorkshire Bank's 'good Yorkshire values'.

That these sorts of concerns are receiving widespread acceptance, even in manufacturing, is shown by the extracts from a recent article on Robert Hass, Chief Executive Officer of Levi Strauss, reproduced in Box 11.1.

Box 11.1   Strategy and values

'Levi [Levi Strauss] has always treated people fairly and cared about their welfare. The usual term is "paternalism". But it is more than paternalism, really – a genuine concern for people and a recognition that people make this business successful.

In the past, however, that tradition was viewed as something separate from how we ran the business. We always talked about the "hard stuff" and the "soft stuff". The soft stuff was the company's commitment to our workforce. And the hard stuff was what really mattered: getting pants out the door.

What we've learned is that the soft stuff and the hard stuff are becoming increasingly intertwined. A company's values – what it stands for, what its people believe in – are crucial to its competitive success. Indeed, values drive the business.

Traditionally, the business world had clear boundaries. Geographical or regional borders defined the marketplace. Distinctions between suppliers and customers, workers and managers, were well defined. Once you had a strong market position, you could go on for a long time just on inertia. You could have a traditional, hierarchical, command-and-control organization, because change happened so slowly.

People's expectations for work were also narrowly defined. They gave their loyalty and their efforts in exchange for being taken care of. They expected information and commands to come down from on high, and they did what they were told.

As a result of all the tumult of the 1980s – increased competition, corporate restructuring, the globalization of enterprises, a new generation entering the workforce – those traditional boundaries and expectations are breaking down.

There is an enormous diffusion of power. If companies are going to react quickly to changes in the marketplace, they have to put more and more accountability, authority, and information into the hands of the people who are closest to the products and the customers. That requires new business strategies and different organizational structures. But structure and strategy aren't enough.

This is where values come in. In a more volatile and dynamic business environment, the controls have to be conceptual. They can't be human any more: Bob Hass telling people what to do. It's the ideas of a business that are controlling, not some manager with authority. Values provide a common language for aligning a company's leadership and its people.

A strategy is no good if people don't fundamentally believe in it.

'Values make the company: an interview with Robert Hass', *Harvard Business Review*, September/October 1990.

Ten key areas

Given that you have gone through the critical areas of analysis and initial implementation, there are ten key areas to attend to in order to provide the momentum to go into and through this 'third age' of service change.

1   Focus the business

The dilemma facing service organizations is shown in Table 11.1, which summarizes the views on the factors for success drawn from the research carried out in 1990–91. Virtually everyone placed 'keeping customers satisfied' in the 'top 5' (columns 1 and 2), and, at this level, it is not difficult to reconcile the differences between what 'I' see as critical to success (own opinion) and what I think 'the company' sees as critical (perceived priority). Even with the narrower 'top 3', the difference can be reasonably explained by the natural perceptual differences that will always exist between such viewpoints. However, such reconciliation becomes difficult when just the 'top choice' is considered – and the sufferers appear to be the customers.

However, customers can go elsewhere or delay buying or spend their money on something else – if not now, then at some future date when there is competition. Lacking a sufficiently clear focus, too many people in the organization are unsure about the real priorities; customers suffer simply as a consequence. In the final analysis, it is the organization which is the real sufferer.

Table 11.1   Factors for success. (Base: total sample.)

Factor	Top 5 mentions				Top 3 mentions				Top mention			
	Own opinion		Perceived priority		Own opinion		Perceived priority		Own opinion		Perceived priority	
	No	%	No	%	No	%	No	%	No	%	No	%
Making high profits	1785	69	2200	85	1134	44	1835	71	491	19	979	38
Keeping costs down	2005	77	2282	88	1086	42	1837	71	155	6	472	18
Keeping customers satisfied	2525	97	2508	97	2287	88	2010	77	1463	56	899	35
Getting repeat business from old customers	1701	65	1713	66	1006	39	716	28	161	6	70	3
Getting a high volume of work	733	28	1520	59	245	9	705	27	37	1	94	4
Having a keen workforce	2238	86	1522	59	1283	49	378	15	163	6	19	1
Providing good job prospects for employees	1639	63	944	36	583	22	170	7	69	3	15	1

Source: KIA/EIU research, 1991, B1.1 and B1.2 questions.

The most important point to remember is that from the customers' point of view, it is not 'product plus service' but service which is seen as integral to what they are buying, as part of a total process. Service elements account for at least 70% of the satisfactions or dissatisfactions generated and it is the 'key points of experience' (Saga) and 'the many little experiences...that turn a happy traveller into an unhappy one' (Virgin Atlantic) which need to be the focus. This is not just a matter for marketing but one for the whole organization, since conventional functional splits are likely to hamper a translation of a vision into reality, once the early energy is expended.

Finally, be sure it's right for you. Just because it is right, for example for British Airways, does not make it right for everyone. Many of the respondents in the research felt this very strongly. For example:

- 'I'm not sure if there is another bank I know which I would organize like this one. We developed what suited us and suited our business, at that time.' (Arne Mårtensson at Handelsbanken)
- 'I don't believe we would be justified in spending the amount of money on deliberate people contact that British Airways have spent, even on a per head basis. For them, people contact is everything. For us, it is important but actual contact with customers is relatively low because of the nature of our business. The contacts we do have are as important to us as BA's are to them, but as an issue within the totality of our business they are much less.' (Nicholas Hood at Wessex Water)
- 'We are not like an airline. Every week our customers make a choice where to shop for food. That is why our quality and standards have to be so relentlessly consistent. For our customers, weekly personal experience is the most important thing. Other people's comments have an effect, but our customers sample our service regularly and form their own perceptions, by and large.' (David Quarmby at Sainsburys)

As much as anything, these statements reflect the cultures of the businesses and the characters of the people. But then, people are the raw material. If you have measured where you are and know where you are going you have a good chance of being realistic about what you can achieve.

Focus effort: be clear about the 'purpose' of the organization and make the priorities clear and simple. Summarizing in a few words or a picture is of help. Organize to support this focus. Give people a sense of social purpose, that is doing something worthwhile, what von Clausewitz would have described as 'the moral powers of an army'.[2]

2 Make that focus external

Services are relationships and a key feature of success in this is treating the customer as integral to your thinking, as an accomplice rather than simply as a sales target. So it is worrying, looking again at the results in Table 11.1, to see the

The Uni way

Figure 11.1   A market positioning. (*Source:* Uni Insurance, Oslo. 1985)

lack of importance attributed to repeat customer business. Not only is this fundamental to the building of relationships but it is also more profitable (see Chapter 1).

It is vital to keep the customer in focus at all times. 'It is only when an
organization fails to implement customer focus throughout the organization
that chaos occurs.' (Handelsbanken) Externalize all activity. For example, don't
allow teamwork development discussions or reviews of systems development
to go ahead unless they are centred around, 'How will it help the customer?'
or 'How will it help us in the marketplace?' or 'In what way does it support the
interaction?' Make action the object, not simply well-being of the group.

As our research has shown, the overwhelming majority of managers and
employees in a service business know the relevance of their job relative to the
consumer. Some may overstate this belief, but it demonstrates that they realize its
importance. However, their belief is usually obscured by a lack of focus on that
interaction or by conflicting imperatives. It is this which leads to conflict, even
chaos.

A neat way of summarizing this and putting that interaction into focus is shown in Figure 11.1.

This is really a parallel to the Cornhill case, quoted in Chapter 6. The traditional insurance situation is a faceless company with one-way communication, pushing pieces of paper onto equally faceless targets. Uni, a Norwegian insurance company, now part of the much larger Uni Storebrand, set itself a strategy of creating two-way communication between people who acknowledged each other and each others' needs in a relationship. This dialogue would be the focus – as in the service star. The purpose of all the other elements – the policies, the systems, the advertising and so on – would be to provide back up to this; 'strategically' they were all to be subordinate to achievement at the point where it mattered most – the millions of meeting points with the customer. For the 'pieces of paper' in the picture, you could easily substitute a petrol pump for a service station, or a 'plane seat for an airline, and it would make equal sense. It is the interaction which is strategically most significant for a service business.

Make the interactions between customers and the organization the basis of business.

3   Get individuals to commit

In all of the comments on people in services, the question of the individual constantly recurs. Services are largely provided by individuals to individuals; that is one of the things that distinguishes them. So, to bring about change, you must capture the individual not only *to* that change but to *make* that change.

Most people fall easily into the role of spectator, standing back and letting somebody else take the lead. Sometimes, though, it may not be lack of action but the wrong action. Robert Hass, Chief Executive Officer of Levis Strauss says: 'If people on the front line really are the keys to our success, then the manager's job is to help those people and the people they serve. That goes against the traditional assumption that the manager is in control.'[3]

So it is critical to create a culture where the individual feels he can contribute, and then to make sure he does.

In turn, this culture and the strategy need to be mutually supportive. 'We see our "brand" and our "values" as two sides of the same coin.' (Woolworths) Campbell and his colleagues wrote, 'A sense of mission comes from the link between behaviour, organization values and personal values. If managers find that the way they are being asked to behave by the organization is based on some organization values that are close to their personal values, they are likely to find work worthwhile and fulfilling.'[4]

However, even where managers are convinced of the need for clear commitment by individuals, they still don't know *what* culture they need; they don't know what type of culture they have; nor do they know what sort of management style will best achieve the change. Further, such decisions on management are made in abstract, divorced from the plans and the market.

But, as we saw in the earlier chapters, there are ways of finding such things out. Change need not be a completely hit-and-miss affair; nor need good plans be developed only to fade because the management style is either not in tune or is misdirecting the effort. The management of the three companies analysed in Cases 3.1 and 4.1 have totally different tasks on their hands:

- JHP (Case 4.1) had a dynamic, streetwise group, where energy needed to be channelled but without undue constraint. Management needed to learn to stand back;
- ABC (Case 4.1) had a spectator situation; management were already standing back too much; it needed energizing around a more exciting and worthwhile context;
- PSVR (Case 3.1) had primarily a problem at top management, but one they weren't going to recognize without research and the 'push' the knowledge brought could give.

Make individual responsibility the keynote of implementation.

4 Recruit the right people

It will be impossible to achieve any sustained service success unless the organization has the right people. Yet surprisingly few service companies have made recruitment central to their activity. Lyonnaise des Eaux is one of those exceptions. 'I see being a service places enormous reliance on staff,' says Guy de Panafieu, Group Managing Director. 'Each time a manager appoints someone, we have committed ourselves to 5 million francs. So we say, "Be sure you are right; be cautious".'

In Peter Glen's book, *It's Not My Department*, he says in a chapter headed 'Bad Service Begins with Bodies', 'Good and bad service begin right at the beginning. Bad service starts with hiring. America is plastered with Help Wanted signs, but [most of them] sound dull from the beginning. When 'Windows on the World' wanted exceptional waiters, they ran an ad in *New York* magazine that went right to the heart of the matter; it said, 'Waiters and Waitresses! If you have an interest in yourself, quit your job this afternoon and apply at 'Windows on the World'. Hordes showed up immediately with some anticipation.' He goes on to say, 'People that care are created. I don't think people are born, longing to serve humanity. They are born needing to be cared for, and unless they are interrupted, they go on feeling the world should care for them forever.'[5]

Virgin Atlantic have developed a great internal spirit by ensuring that they recruit not only technically qualified people but ones who fit into the culture of the airline. They hire people who are prepared to play their part in the team but are equally prepared to be counted, as an individual. 'We don't just want happy employees' (Richard Branson). Saga talk of, 'making sure we recruit people with the right attitude to service, then we technically train them.' During our research, the Marketing Director of Ramada Inns in Europe said, 'For us the recession has meant that we have been able to concentrate on improving the quality of our staff. This is paying off in terms of customer retention.'

The more the values of culture are important, the more you need to make sure people share your values before you hire them. Sometimes this can mean looking for someone with entirely different characteristics to those tradition-ally sought. Many restauranteurs, for example, have found that actors and actresses make the best part-time waiters. They more easily adopt a role of 'playing to the audience'. The Royal Albert Hall have recruited ex-airline staff to man the stage door, rather than security guards.

Make sure that your values are reflected in your recruitment.

5   Create dialogue not monologue

In Chapter 2 we saw the importance of listening as an active technique of real communication. Too often, presentation is confused with *real* communication. Real communication is where all those involved have a chance to adjust to, as well as understand, the message. Change is discomforting to most people. To those who have had no hand in the design, and therefore feel no element of responsibility, it can seem a threat, too. Such discomfort can be reduced by cre-ating dialogue. The outline of the cycle of communication in Box 11.2 identi-fies the circular nature of this – sending and receiving are both active processes.

Box 11.2   The cycle of communication

True communication is more than simply passing a message. It is making sure that the message has got through: that *you* have understood and acknowledged any response. In achieving this, there are two gaps in the cycle which have to be bridged:

- The thought processes of the 'listener';
- The thought processes of the 'sender'.

Unless it is clearly recognized by both listener and sender that they have heard and understood, then it is not possible to be sure there has been com-munication. A good way to achieve this is by asking questions, but asking questions is often dangerous and so they either don't get asked or are suppressed. Both sides adopt defensive routines.

continues

continued

But completion of the cycle of communication is not simply for internal communication. Customers have to know they have been heard. For example, as with Televerket, do they know action has been taken on a complaint? One of the problems is that 'telling' is equated with being active and 'listening' with being passive. That means not only that senders feel they have to justify themselves by talking, but that we all constantly underrate listening as a skill. Both listening and telling should be valued as integral to true communication.

Professor Manny Stiehl at the University of Minnesota expresses this succinctly:

'When we are listening we should learn to be as active as when we are talking. This is not the same as saying we should take turns to be 100% active or "share" the responsibility, 50/50. In either of these cases it will always be someone else's responsibility at any particular time. If we miss something, it was his or her turn "to be 100%" or "50%". Rather we should recognize it is always our responsibility, 51%! That's a mathematical impossibility, but it means "I" always have to be aware it is up to me to make myself clear, to be sure I have heard or that others have heard. I can never say, "he or she didn't make themselves clear" because it was up to me, 51%, to be sure I was clear. I can never say, "I told them clearly" if it subsequently turns out they didn't [understand], because it was up to me, 51%, to be sure they had heard.'[6]

Completing this process is completing the cycle of communication (see Figure 11.2); checking, asking questions, looking for reaction and checking this, bridges the 'communication gaps'.

Not only will a listening approach generate enthusiasm for the ideas, but it will allow new ideas to bubble up through the organization. Service relationships are complex and it is necessary to collect information in a systematic way. In fact, the segmentation profiles shown in Figures 7.2 and 7.3 were compiled from staff comments in interactive workshops, and they show how qualitative information can be quantified and compared.

As we saw with Virgin Atlantic, staff can often provide deep insights into what customers might like, sometimes more than the customer themselves, whose experience may be relatively short or spasmodic and limited in most cases only to what he or she knows from experience elsewhere. Virgin Atlantic have not just encouraged this in project teams but in daily work, 'where we are trying to move away from job descriptions, more towards "job areas", with an altogether looser framework,' says Chris Moss.

Of course, knowledge is often based on craft or profession and may well be highly formalized within the set, functional context of a specific job. It is, therefore, important to provide a way of creating a climate where this

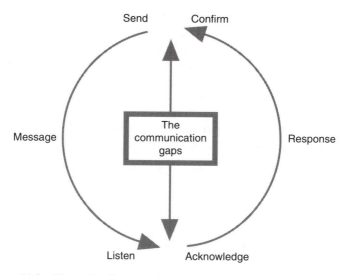

Figure 11.2   The cycle of communication. (*Source:* KIA, based on the work of
Professor Manny Stiehl, University of Minnesota, and presented at a seminar,
Gatwick 1982)

knowledge can evolve into new outcomes. The Japanese have been particularly good at this, with a strong willingness to participate in cross-functional
teams and re-examine the application of their skills. However, in the West,
there has been more stress on this in recent years, due partly to Edward de
Bono and his concept of lateral thinking, but where this has flourished – as for
example in Virgin Atlantic – it has had a similar climate to that of Japanese
success, a climate which is as much about ideals as ideas.

Some years ago, *The Daily Telegraph* reported the boss of Matsuchita
(Konosouke Matsuchita) as saying, 'We [Japan] are going to win, and the
industrial West is going to lose, because for you the essence of management is
getting ideas out of the heads of bosses into the heads of labour. For us, the core
of management is the art of mobilising and putting together the intellectual
resources of all employees in the service of the firm.'

Richard Branson is quite clear that the most important rewards and the key
to getting superior results is to involve management and staff in the question,
'What do you think should be done?' 'There is an enormous feeling of pride to
be gained from feeling "I can make a difference" and seeing that you have
influenced what the passenger is getting. Everyone becomes really committed
because they feel a real sense of it being "mine".'

The fact is that not only do we fail to get the ideas that exist 'down the
line', but we constantly underrate the capacity of staff to contribute and take
action on managements' ideas. General trends in technology exacerbate this,

rendering people helpless in the face of machine control, ignoring the human – and fallible – link in the chain. There are few more technical and dangerous environments then the deck of an aircraft carrier, yet the US Navy has responded by putting power back into ordinary people's hands. Every rating, even the most junior, can stop an aircraft taking off if they see something *they think* is wrong. Yet these ratings are probably less qualified and less educated than many staff – let alone middle management – in the typical service company. The generation of ideas and the taking of risks cannot take place in an environment where there is no reward for, or reaction to them.

Create a dialogue about what is happening and how 'we' can improve it.

6 Extend the dialogue to the customer

The example of 'Finishing Touches' (Chapter 9) exemplifies the importance of showing the customer you have listened, have treated them as an individual by letting it be known that they are a person with problems which someone else (you) understands. But it is more than that. Even if customers may not always be able to visualize what could be, they are still one of the most important sources of knowledge about how your business is performing. Some firms already use self-assessment questionnaire techniques with customers and talk to staff. But often these approaches suffer from bias. Customers who fill in questionnaires may not be typical, though that does not mean they have no value; it merely slants the result.

But even allowing this, feedback from customers is, in many ways, the only real means to quality control since with the final processes of production only taking place at the interaction, manufacturing-type controls are all but impossible. The customer experience is critical to this. Even if an individual's experience is atypical, it is still the true judge and so has a value over and above any other form of analysis and research. Of all the ways of getting at such reactions, there is no cheaper or more accurate method than analysing customer complaints, yet is rare to see this approach given recognition.

Getting complaints to the surface is a critical problem for management in a service business. So it is necessary to set up a method which brings as many complaints as possible into the system. If complaints are seen as primarily the result of failure on the part of someone, and so punishable in some way (even if that 'punishment' is merely rough comment), then they will be 'buried'. Of course, persistent failure to achieve agreed goals has to be dealt with, but very often the root cause is not the person immediately to blame but the system. The problem must be brought into the open.

The following provide two good examples of this:

- After a major incident, the Falck team in a station will get together to discuss frankly what happened and what they could have done better. They are all encouraged to share their doubts and problems; of course, it is critical that management is seen as a resource, there to help, to share the problems and admit to their own concerns;
- One insurance company instituted a centralized complaints procedure, putting it in the hands of a very senior manager, close to retirement, who could, if necessary, insist on talking to the chairman. Although he dealt with complaints sent centrally, his main tasks were to:
    - Discover the fundamental problems and catalogue complaints by these, and not by immediate causes;
    - Find ways of removing the real causes;
    - Build into the routines both an early warning system of deeper problems (for example that new computer system really was not bedded down) and a source of input to future development;
    - Encourage objectivity with complaints, particularly getting across the fact that even awkward customers can be of constructive help.

  At first, everyone was suspicious and complaints stuck at a low level. Then, as managers began to realize it wasn't a stick to beat them with and could be useful, complaints started to rise. For two years they doubled, then slowed to a 50% increase and eventually, after about four years, stabilized, then began to decrease. Of course, there was not in reality an increase in complaints; it was simply that more were available for quality control.

There is an echo here of Virgin Atlantic's 'constructively dissatisfied employee', since one major obstacle to using complaints is that the types of customer who complain are likely to be, by nature, the more difficult or argumentative (like Carole in Box 5.2). Unconstrained by hierarchy or concern for their job, they may not always be constructive, either. Most people find it difficult to deal with such emotions and suspect that the complainant is making more of it than is truly warranted, as in the other example in Box 5.2. But, far from being put off, any service organization should welcome – even be prepared to pay for – the active complainants, for it is they who are exercising a quality control role on performance. Few people complain about nothing. They may exaggerate, they may have a need to get attention, but at heart there is probably always something which is wrong. A company whose values are such that they can tolerate mistakes and question the way things are happening is one in which customers will feel free to express their views. So, the barriers to complaining need to be lowered and complaints need to be a subject of discussions not blame.

Create a dialogue with the customer. Be prepared to listen and to see listening to them as an active task. Be prepared to use what you learn.

7   Give influence

This dialogue – whether internal or external – will wither if it is not seen to be for real, as with Virgin Atlantic. So, it is necessary to ensure that it does have meaning and that there is also authority to go with it. The extract from an article in Box 11.3, *My employees are my service guarantee*, is an excellent example of bringing together dialogue in a way which creates real influence. Customers feel they have influence. Customers feel this influence because they deal with people who have influence.

The hidden problem of influence was touched on in Chapter 8 on leadership; for middle management it can be a big threat to their power and to their future. If they are not to be a negative force in the dialogue they must be relaxed about and supportive of the new approaches. This is not only important in terms of 'being negative' but it has a further, enormously important, positive aspect – it is only this level of management who can keep the momentum going by ensuring that the tasks are understood, by providing support and by ensuring feedback. But it must be recognized that this is not power in the conventional sense (see Chapter 8).

Traditionally, the status of middle management came from the power which gave them influence. Now that won't work, so you have to replace this 'influence through control' with something else. However, the leadership task has real dignity, if those who exercise it can show that they exercise 'influence through being able to bring about change'. So, get them closer to top and senior management. Make sure that they are trained so that they are able, and *feel* able, to give support to those in the front line, pass on feedback and bring about modifications or changes to plans. Take away the threats of change and give them a positive role.

Give everyone influence through the dialogue. Recognize, too, the profound impact this has on middle management and the need to see that the changes give them real status.

8   Keep track of what is happening

Perhaps the most striking aspect of the loosest organizations we researched – Handelsbanken and Virgin Atlantic – was that together with that loose structure and high level of dialogue and involvement went strong controls. As we saw in Figure 6.3, Handelsbanken exhibited that virtuous link between those at the front line feeling led – and able to make mistakes – and those at the top feeling in control. For Handelsbanken, strong centralized control systems meant that they could be relaxed about 'letting go' and keeping to their real task – strategic direction and control.

Box 11.3   My employees are my service guarantee

Timothy Firnstahl, the owner of a chain of four restaurants in and around Seattle, relates: 'My company exists for one reason only – to make other people happy. Every time a customer leaves one of our restaurants with a more optimistic view of the world, we've done our job. Every time we fail to raise a customer's spirits with good food, gratifying service, and a soothing atmosphere, we haven't done our job.

To the extent that we satisfy customers, we fulfil our company goal. This observation may seem self-evident and trivial – a useful motto, a business axiom that a lot of business-people understandably overlook in the day-to-day flood of details – but I have found it the very key to growth and profits. And after much trial and error, I have come up with a strategy for ensuring customer satisfaction that has worked wonders in our business and can, I'm convinced, work wonders in other businesses as well.

It starts with a guarantee – not that moth-eaten old promise of a cheerful refund – but a guarantee that customers will be satisfied with their whole experience of the company's products and services. It moves on to a system for giving employees complete responsibility and authority for making the guarantee stick. It ends with a process for identifying system failures – the problems in organization, training, and other internal programs that cause customer dissatisfaction.

I call the whole thing 'ultimate strategy'. That may sound pretentious. But because it redefines a company's ultimate reason for being and succeeding, and because it underlines the importance of finding the ultimate causes of every system failure, I think the name is justified.'

Timothy Firnstahl goes on to explain that the guarantee system accurately reflected 'failure costs' (like Televerket's system for pay phones, Case 5.1) by giving employees the authority to compensate customers who were dissatisfied – or had cause for dissatisfaction, without further reference. Key to this approach was that earlier 'guarantees' had not worked, 'The guarantee by itself wasn't enough. We had given employees responsibility without giving them authority. The result was they tried to bury mistakes or blame others. For our guarantee to be truly effective we had to give workers themselves the power to make good on the promise of the guarantee. Eliminate the hassle for the customer and for ourselves. No forms to fill out, no phone calls to make, no forty questions to answer, just immediate redress by the closest employee.' So, Firnstahl provided some simple guidelines – 'but don't get bogged down ... the last thing we want is nitpicking' – and told employees to go ahead. Although employees were initially wary, they got used to the idea quickly and 'liked working for a company that believed wholeheartedly in its products and services' but the most important aspect was probably the system failure costs analysis.

continues

continued

'System-failure costs are not the same as employee-failure costs. System-failure costs measure the extent of the confusion in company structure, for which management alone is to blame. By welcoming every guarantee pay-off – every system-failure expense – as an otherwise lost insight, you can make every problem pay a dividend. The trick is to reject Band-Aid solutions, to insist on finding the ultimate cause of each problem, and then to demand and expect decisive change.

In one case, our kitchens were turning out wrong orders at a rate that was costing us thousands of dollars a month in wasted food. The cooks insisted that the food servers were punching incorrect orders into the kitchen printout computer. In times past, we might have ended our search right there, accused the food servers of sloppiness, and asked everyone to be more careful. But now, adhering to the principle of system failure not people failure, we looked beyond the symptoms and found a flaw in our training. We had simply never taught food servers to double-check their orders on the computer screen, and the system offered no reward for doing so. Mistakes plummeted as soon as we started training people properly and handing out awards each month for the fewest ordering errors and posting lists of the worst offenders (no punishments, just names).

As you find and correct the ultimate causes of your system failures, you can reasonably expect your profits to improve. But you can begin to tell if you're succeeding even before you see it on the bottom line. Remember, costs will go up before they come down, so high system-failure costs and low phone-survey complaint rates probably mean you're on the right track. Conversely, low system-failure costs and a high rate of 'louses' and 'OKs' from customers almost certainly indicate that the promise is not being kept, that your expensive system failures are not getting corrected, and that your organization has yet to understand that customer satisfaction is the only reason for the company's existence.

Our own system-failure costs rose to a high of $40,000 a month two years ago and then fell to $10,000 a month. Meanwhile, sales rose 25%, profits doubled, and the cash in the bank grew two-and-a-half times.'

He finishes by saying, 'We use the same ultimate strategy to satisfy both customers and employees.'

'My employees are my service guarantee'. Timothy W Firnstahl. In *Harvard Business Review*, July/August, 1989.

Virgin Atlantic's top management have a detailed knowledge of what is happening where it matters, with the customer, but see most of this information as being for the use of the people responsible, and for them to act upon. For top management, it acts as a guide to overall performance, a sounding board, a basis for creative dialogue and an ultimate control to steer the business in the right direction. These then become self-improving systems in which the testing of ideas and exploring of potential, both within oneself as well as the business, is key – but as an exciting opportunity, not a burden.

But other more structured businesses, such as Saga, Sainsburys and Televerket reflected a high degree of awareness of the detailed performance of their business. For Woolworths, moving the organization forward to a point where 'people can make mistakes' was a critical part of continuing success.

Keep track of what is happening, at that critical point of interaction particularly. Use that information to improve rather than control daily activity.

9   Keep top management in touch

No other group has as many problems as top management in maintaining momentum. With success can come complacency, but also boredom and frustration. Once the big idea is launched and going successfully, top management will often want to stand back; delegating the task, they would call it, but in truth wanting to move on to the next big idea. Indeed, this will be a necessary part of their activity but it can quickly give the lie to those involved about the 'importance of our initiative' and the values that are attached to it.

An example of this is British Airways and the 'struggle for the soul' (see Box 8.4). Recent events would suggest that this struggle continues but that whatever the outcome there is evidence of a failure to continue to keep up the dialogue on key issues or to influence these in the way the big idea (essentially 'putting people first') had envisaged.

Maybe more importantly, management can experience frustration because they feel unable to do 'what they think best'. They want to take action and feel that they, and only they, have the knowledge, skills and vision to do so. Of course, there are emergencies that require instant reaction but not only are they relatively few but mostly they are best solved by collective agreement, not least because others do have a contribution.

As an interesting parallel, a BBC *Horizon* programme entitled *The Wrong Stuff* commented that the majority of accidents involving commercial aircraft were due to pilot error, but this was rarely a single mistake but most often an accumulation of errors or misunderstandings between the members of the 'management team', that is the flight crew. Central to this is a tendency on the part of many captains to revert to 'flying a single seat fighter, when what they need is teamwork, the full input of the crew. Their "individualism" gets in the way. What is the "right stuff" becomes the "wrong stuff".'[7]

An example of this is BP, where the Chairman, Robert Horton, left ignominiously in 1992 after the announcement of some poor results, but in this case it was the 'culture change', not the Captain, which won. Christopher Lorenz, the Business Features Editor of the *Financial Times* wrote shortly before his departure, 'Nor does it help it that the Chairman [Horton, who presided over the massive cultural change] is then quoted as wishing that he could use his "good brain" to deal with some of BP's problems himself, rather than waiting until his subordinates cope with them,' and goes on to say, 'paradoxically, Horton's newly-evident fallibility could work to everyone's advantage – provided he can temper his all-knowing air.'[8] He didn't and he was forced to leave because he simply could not carry his management team with him. Those who have seen the BBC *Horizon* film quoted above, may feel that BP narrowly avoided being crashed by a 'macho pilot', who, fortunately for the 'passengers', had an 'assertive crew'.

> *Change is difficult with success, and top management need to both keep in touch and work in a way which actively supports the changes they have brought about. In this, they may sometimes benefit from a catalyst or detached observer, who can provide an assessment of this.*

10   Be caring, be consistent

'It is only the caring companies that will survive...[as]...it is only against the background of caring that continuous change can be combined with the maintenance of the company spirit and the ability to attract the best.'[9]

Being caring is really a reflection of the points made in the previous section about continued involvement and interest. Failure in this results – as in BP where 'personal development plans' became cynically labelled as 'personal departure plans'[8] – in disillusionment and apathy. But it isn't just a passing whim or fad. Reference back to the deeper changes in society (see Box 1.1) shows that what are seeing here is firmly in line with these trends.

It is also about the very nature of a service – services are relationships, good services are good relationships. A relationship can only be a relationship if there is an element of care and concern. Since we cannot have an ambition for an external culture that is not at least empathetic to our internal culture, care and concern have to be a part of this. It is this relationship which is also our brand, and to be successful a brand has to be consistent. That is what sets it apart from a commodity. It has a clear set of properties which are what the customer relies on. To quote Leo McKee at Woolworths, 'Our brand and our culture are symbiotic, living one from the other.'

'A puppy is not for Christmas'. Developing a service approach is not a cuddly or shiny toy to be forgotten once the initial excitement has worn off but a long-term commitment to superior performance through building a sound relationship with your market.

References

1.   Normann R. (1984). *Service Management*. Chichester: John Wiley & Sons.
2.   von Clausewitz K. (1832). *On War*.
3.   Values make the company: An interview with Robert Hass. *Harvard Business Review*, September/October 1990. © 1990 by the President and Fellows of Harvard College, all rights reserved.
4.   Campbell A. et al. (1990). *A Sense of Mission*. Economist Books.
5.   Glen P. (1989). *It's Not My Department*. New York: William Morrow.
6.   Stiehl M. University of Minnesota, at a KIA seminar, Gatwick, 1982.
7.   Heimrich R. University of Texas. BBC *Horizon* programme 1986.
8.   Lorenz C. (1992). Refining the Strategy. *Financial Times,* 21 February.
9.   Harvey-Jones J. (1989). *Making It Happen*. Collins.

Appendix A
Questionnaire

Service strategies

Introduction

This questionnaire forms part of a survey being carried out across Europe by the Economist Intelligence Unit into what makes businesses working in the service sector successful.

The purpose of the questionnaire is to identify the links between the success of a company and the day-to-day working practices within the company. We are asking a few people in different departments to complete the questionnaire to make certain that the views of all types of staff are included in the survey. Your personal contribution will be invaluable in helping us.

When you have completed the questionnaire *please do not sign your name*. We would, however, appreciate an indication of the position you hold in your company at A1 below. The results of your company will be passed on to management in a summary form, together with the overall results for the industry in which you work. However, they will never see any individual responses.

Thank you for taking the time to fill in this questionnaire. We hope that you and your company will feel that the results are of interest and benefit.

Instructions for completion

Each question gives specific instructions in CAPITAL LETTERS about how to complete it. This is normally done by putting a tick in the box by the answer that comes nearest to your own opinion. Occasionally, you will be asked to write your answer in your own words in the space provided. Please ignore the numbers in the right hand margins which are for computer coding and analysis only.

When we refer to 'this company' this includes previous business names.

Example my job is:
IF YOUR ANSWER IS SUPERVISORY YOU WOULD TICK AS BELOW
Senior/Middle management   ☐
Junior management/supervisory   ☑
Other   ☐

SECTION A ABOUT YOUR WORK

A1   My job is: Senior/Middle management   ☐

                     Junior management/supervisory   ☐

                     Other   ☐

A2   I deal directly with the end customers of this business:

                     Yes   ☐

                     No   ☐

A3   I have been with this company:

                     Less than 6 months   ☐

                     6 months up to 1 year   ☐

                     1 year up to 3 years   ☐

                     3 years or more   ☐

A4   As an organization, we have undergone major changes in
        the years: TICK ALL BOXES WHICH APPLY

                     1990   ☐

                     1989   ☐

                     1988   ☐

                     1987   ☐

                     1986   ☐

                     None of these   ☐

SECTION B BACKGROUND

B1.1   Listed below are some factors which can determine the
        success of a company. Which five do you see as the most
        important for your company to be successful?
        LIST YOUR TOP 5 PRIORITIES IN ORDER OF IMPORTANCE,
        BY WRITING IN NUMBER 1 FOR YOUR FIRST PRIORITY,
        2 FOR YOUR SECOND ETC.

                     Making high profits   ☐

                     Keeping costs down   ☐

                     Keeping customers satisfied   ☐

                     Getting repeat business from old customers ☐

                     Getting a high volume of work   ☐

                     Having a keen workforce   ☐

                     Providing good job prospects for employees ☐

                     Other (WRITE IN)   ☐

        _____

B1.2   In your opinion, what are the <u>**actual**</u> priorities that your company sets in order to be successful?

LIST YOUR COMPANY'S TOP 5 PRIORITIES IN ORDER OF IMPORTANCE, BY WRITING IN NUMBER 1 FOR YOUR FIRST PRIORITY, 2 FOR YOUR SECOND ETC.

Making high profit ☐

Keeping costs down ☐

Keeping customers satisfied ☐

Getting repeat business from old customers ☐

Getting a high volume of work ☐

Having a keen workforce ☐

Providing good job prospects for employees ☐

Other (WRITE IN) ☐

_____

B2.1   Below are a number of factors which might help a company to achieve success. Which five do you think are the most important factors in achieving success in your business now?

LIST YOUR TOP 5 PRIORITIES IN ORDER OF IMPORTANCE, BY WRITING IN NUMBER 1 FOR YOUR FIRST PRIORITY, 2 FOR YOUR SECOND ETC.

To succeed in our business, I see it as important that:

Our prices are low ☐

We achieve our sales targets ☐

We are technically excellent ☐

We provide a high quality service ☐

We have strong leadership ☐

Our staff are highly motivated ☐

Our workforce is stable ☐

We work to rigorous standards ☐

We are friendly and approachable ☐

Our staff are very well trained ☐

We value our customers as individuals ☐

We guarantee a good service ☐

Other (WRITE IN) ☐

B2.2   And what do you think your company sees as the most important factors?

LIST YOUR TOP 5 PRIORITIES IN ORDER OF IMPORTANCE, BY WRITING IN NUMBER 1 FOR YOUR FIRST PRIORITY, 2 FOR YOUR SECOND ETC.

To succeed in our business, this company sees it as important that:

Our prices are low	☐
We achieve our sales targets	☐
We are technically excellent	☐
We provide a high quality service	☐
We have strong leadership	☐
Our staff are highly motivated	☐
Our workforce is stable	☐
We work to rigorous standards	☐
We are friendly and approachable	☐
Our staff are very well trained	☐
We value our customers as individuals	☐
We guarantee a good service	☐
Other (WRITE IN)	☐

_____

B2.3   Are there any other comments that you would like to make about the factors that affect success in your company? PLEASE WRITE IN

_____

_____

_____

_____

B3   Overall, do you feel that your company has been consistent in its approach to business and its methods of work...

Not at all	☐
Only this year (1990)	☐
For the last 2-3 years (since 1988)	☐
For the last 4-5 years (since 1986)	☐
For longer than the last 5 years (since before 1986)	☐ ☐

B4   Thinking about training, have you had any training in the
      last year?

                 Yes – technical   ☐

                 Yes – customer care   ☐

                 Yes – management/supervisory   ☐

                 Yes – health and safety   ☐

                 Yes – company awareness/induction training   ☐

                 Yes – other (write in)   ☐

                 No – none   ☐

IF YOU HAVE HAD ANY TRAINING IN THE LAST YEAR,
PLEASE ANSWER QB5

IF YOU HAVE NOT HAD ANY TRAINING PLEASE GO TO
SECTION C

B5   Thinking about the training you have had in the last year,
      please indicate whether or not any of the following statements
      apply to you as a result.

                 I was able to do my job better   ☐

                 I felt more frustrated by our work
                  procedures   ☐

                 I felt more involved in my job   ☐

                 I understood more clearly what we are
                  trying to achieve as a business   ☐

                 I felt more able to meet the needs
                  of our customer   ☐

                 It made no difference to the way
                  I do my job   ☐

                 Other (write in)   ☐

C1   FLEXIBILITY

Services are about responding to people – customers mainly,
but also colleagues. Some services may need to be carefully
structured, (e.g. trains need to run on time to a pre-arranged
timetable) while others may need to be highly flexible, (e.g. a
customer enquiry desk where employees have to respond to
many different queries).

Overleaf are five statements about this subject. Please indicate, by ticking the appropriate box, how far you agree or disagree with each statement, relative to your particular job.

It is important that you give your opinions about all five statements.

In the job that I do:

	Agree strongly	Agree slightly	Neither agree nor disagree	Disagree slightly	Disagree strongly
1. I often feel prevented by our procedures from making sure the customer is treated properly	☐	☐	☐	☐	☐
2. I fee I am not allowed to make mistakes	☐	☐	☐	☐	☐
3. It is more important for me to be flexible in my approach to work than to always do things in the same way	☐	☐	☐	☐	☐
4. My day to day routine is never the same	☐	☐	☐	☐	☐
5. Nothing can be done without filling in a lot of forms	☐	☐	☐	☐	☐

C2 STAFF INVOLVEMENT

Services are delivered through people, who may or may not feel involved in the business of the company.

Below are four statements about this subject. Please indicate, by ticking the appropriate box how far you agree or disagree with each statement, relative to your particular job.

It is important that you give your opinions about all four statements. In my work:

	Agree strongly	Agree slightly	Neither agree nor disagree	Disagree slightly	Disagree strongly
1. I understand how my job helps us to be successful with our customers	☐	☐	☐	☐	☐
2. Any personal problems I have at work are always taken into consideration	☐	☐	☐	☐	☐
3. There is always someone for me to discuss any problems I have with the work I do	☐	☐	☐	☐	☐
4. I am always kept well informed about events or changes happening within the company	☐	☐	☐	☐	☐

C3 CUSTOMERS

Customers are a part of the work environment for service businesses. Below are 4 pairs of statements which might apply to any company. STUDY THEM AND THEN CHOOSE ONLY 1 OF EACH PAIR.

In order to be successful/achieve our objectives:

CHOICE

1. a) It is important that we deal with as many customers as possible ☐

OR

b) We should spend as much time as is necessary with each customer ☐

----

2. a) Our work procedures should be flexible enough to satisfy all our customers ☐

OR

b) Our work procedures are standardised but meet the needs of most of our customers ☐

----

3. a) It is important to treat each customer individually ☐

OR

b) We make sure that customers know that they are all treated the same ☐

----

4. a) Customers need to fit in with the way that we work ☐

OR

b) We need to fit in with the way our customers work ☐

C4   MANAGEMENT/LEADERSHIP

These statements describe some of the ways companies are managed. Which of these apply in your job?

RANK THEM IN ORDER OF IMPORTANCE FROM 1 TO 6 (WITH 1 MOST IMPORTANT).

It is important to my success:

1. That we concentrate above all on achieving set targets (e.g. sales) ☐

2. That I consider the views of those I work with or who work for me ☐

3. That we have set procedures which we stick to at all times ☐

4. That people are told precisely what they have to do ☐

5. That my immediate manager is someone that I can use to help achieve my goals ☐

6. That people are given a chance to try out their own ideas ☐

C5   QUALITY

Below are some statements describing quality. Please indicate, by ticking the appropriate box how important you think each statement is in describing what quality means in your job.

In our business, quality means we need to:	Very important	Fairly important	Not very important	Not at all important
Always maintain high standards	☐	☐	☐	☐
Do what is necessary to keep customers happy	☐	☐	☐	☐
Encourage more customers to use our services	☐	☐	☐	☐
Give our customers confidence in what we do	☐	☐	☐	☐
Meet the standards of our industry	☐	☐	☐	☐
Avoid making mistakes	☐	☐	☐	☐
Monitor all our procedures (quality control)	☐	☐	☐	☐
Make sure that I feel committed to my work	☐	☐	☐	☐

Finally, is there anything else you would like to say that we have not covered in the questionnaire on the subject of success in business? PLEASE WRITE IN

_____

_____

_____

_____

_____

This is the end of the questionnaire. Thank you for your time. Now please return the questionnaire in the special envelope.

Appendix B
Analysis
methodology

The core of the research for this report was the examination of service culture contained in Questions C1 to C4. Of these:

- C1 and C3 referred to the structure of the organization, relative to service values, and the results have been analysed as 'service structure'.
- C2 and C4 referred to the management style of the organization, relative to service values, and the results have been analysed as 'service management'.

In all cases, the questions used had been refined down from a much larger number used in earlier research and had been shown from this experience to be key indicators.

Service structure

Service structure is charted as follows. A score for the degree of routine necessary to run a business is calculated from the customer-orientated statements at Section C3 'Customers' (C3.1b, C3.2a, C3.3a, C3.4b). This is the score for flexible/rigid scale and is plotted on the horizontal axis.

Then a score for responsiveness is derived from the statements at Section C1 'Flexibility'. This gives a measure of the responsive/formal dimension and is plotted on the vertical axis.

Service management

Service management is charted as follows. A score for involvement of management and staff is calculated from selected statements at C2 'staff involvement' and is plotted on the horizontal axis.

The score on a 'control' or 'leadership' style of management is determined from the statements at Section C4 which are of two types:

(1)   Control statements;
(2)   Leadership statements.

Two further measurements of service culture have also been made:

Service objectives

Service objectives are analysed by both the absolute 'score' given by respondents with regard to the ranking of objectives – personal beliefs and perception of reality – and the cross-relations of these. They are then illustrated by plotting the 'personal belief' scores along the base or horizontal axis and plotting the 'perceptions of reality' along the side or vertical axis.

The scores themselves are determined by taking the crude ranking of 1 to 5 in terms of order of objectives and converting these mathematically into scores out of 5.

Service values

These are determined, analysed and displayed in the same way as objectives, above.

Index